Edexcel
Economics
AS

AS

Edexcel
Economics

Peter Smith

Philip Allan Updates, an imprint of Hodder Education, an Hachette UK company, Market Place, Deddington, Oxfordshire OX15 0SE

Orders
Bookpoint Ltd, 130 Milton Park, Abingdon, Oxfordshire OX14 4SB
tel: 01235 827827
fax: 01235 400401
e-mail: education@bookpoint.co.uk

Lines are open 9.00 a.m.–5.00 p.m., Monday to Saturday, with a 24-hour message answering service. You can also order through the Philip Allan Updates website: www.philipallan.co.uk

ISBN 978-0-340-94804-0

First printed 2008
Impression number   9   8   7   6
Year   2013   2012   2011

This textbook has been written specifically to support students studying Edexcel AS Economics. The content has been neither approved nor endorsed by Edexcel and remains the sole responsibility of the author.

All website addresses included in this book are correct at the time of going to press but may subsequently change.

All photographs are reproduced by permission of Topfoto, except where otherwise specified.

Printed in Dubai

Hachette UK's policy is to use papers that are natural, renewable and recyclable products and made from wood grown in sustainable forests. The logging and manufacturing processes are expected to conform to the environmental regulations of the country of origin.

P01975

Contents

Introduction vi

Part 1   Competitive markets: how they work and why they fail

Chapter 1   Introducing economics 2

Chapter 2   The nature of demand 17

Chapter 3   The nature of supply 33

Chapter 4   Market equilibrium and price......................................42

Chapter 5   The price mechanism in action....................................59

Chapter 6   The market for labour..68

Chapter 7   Market failure and externalities..................................84

Chapter 8   Other forms of market failure 102

Chapter 9   Government intervention and government failure 117

Part 2   Managing the economy

Chapter 10   Measuring economic performance............................128

Chapter 11   Developed and developing countries 148

Chapter 12   Income, wealth and the circular flow 161

Chapter 13   Aggregate demand..169

Chapter 14   Aggregate supply and macroeconomic equilibrium...............178

Chapter 15   Economic growth..185

Chapter 16   Macroeconomic policy objectives.............................196

Chapter 17   Macroeconomic policy instruments...........................214

Chapter 18   Macroeconomic policy: priorities and conflicts 227

Index 240

Introduction

This textbook provides an introduction to economics. It has been tailored explicitly to cover the content of the Edexcel specification for AS economics. The book is divided into two parts, each covering one of the modules that make up the AS programme of study. The text provides the foundation for studying Edexcel economics, but you will no doubt wish to keep up to date by referring to additional topical sources of information about economic events. You can do this by reading the serious newspapers, visiting key sites on the internet, and by reading such magazines as *Economic Review*.

The text features the following:

➤ a statement of the intended learning outcomes for each chapter
➤ clear and concise but comprehensive explanation and analysis of economic terms and concepts
➤ definitions of key terms
➤ examples to show these concepts applied to real-world situations
➤ exercises to provide active engagement with economic analysis

A separate Teacher Guide is available that provides complete answers to all exercises, plus additional material for use in the classroom.

Assessment objectives

In common with other economics specifications, Edexcel economics entails four assessment objectives. Candidates will therefore be expected to:

➤ demonstrate knowledge and understanding of the specified content
➤ apply this knowledge and critical understanding to problems and issues arising from both familiar and unfamiliar situations
➤ analyse economic problems and issues
➤ evaluate economic arguments and evidence, making informed judgements

In the overall assessment of the A-level, the four assessment objectives count equally. However, there is a greater weighting given to the first two objectives in AS, and a greater weighting to the final two objectives in A2.

(*See the Edexcel AS/A GCE in Economics specification at* **www.edexcel.org.uk**.)

The subject

Economics is different from some other AS subjects in that relatively few students will have studied it before embarking on the AS course. The text therefore begins from the beginning, and provides a thorough foundation in the subject and its applications. By studying this book, you should develop an awareness of the economist's approach to issues and problems, and the economist's way of thinking about the world.

The study of economics also requires a familiarity with recent economic events in the UK and elsewhere, and candidates will be expected to show familiarity with 'recent historical data' — broadly defined as covering the last 7–10 years. The following websites will help you to keep up to date with recent trends and events:

➤ Recent and historical data about the UK economy can be found at the website of the Office for National Statistics (ONS) at: **www.statistics.gov.uk/**

➤ Also helpful is the site of HM Treasury at: **www.hm-treasury.gov.uk/**

➤ The Bank of England site is well worth a visit, especially the *Inflation Report* and the Minutes of the Monetary Policy Committee: **www.bankofengland.co.uk/**

➤ The Institute for Fiscal Studies offers an independent view of a range of economic topics: **www.ifs.org.uk**

For information about other countries, visit the following:

➤ **www.oecd.org/home/**

➤ **http://europa.eu.int/**

➤ **www.worldbank.org/**

➤ **www.undp.org/**

Another way of keeping up to date with economic topics and events is to read *Economic Review*, a magazine specifically written for A-level economics students which comes out four times during the academic year (also published by Philip Allan Updates).

How to study economics

There are two crucial aspects of studying economics. The first stage is to study the theory, which helps us to explain economic behaviour. However, in studying AS economics it is equally important to be able to *apply* the theories and concepts that you meet, and to see just how these relate to the real world.

If you are to become competent at this, it is vital that you get plenty of practice. In part, this means doing the exercises included in this book. However, it also means thinking about how economics helps us to explain news items and data that appear in the newspapers and on the television. Make sure that you practise as much as you can.

In economics, it is important to be able to produce examples of economic phenomena. You will find some examples in this book that help to illustrate ideas and

concepts. Do not rely solely on the examples provided here, but be aware of what is going on in the world and find your own examples. Keep a note of these ready for use in essays and exams. This will help to convince the examiners that you have understood economics. It will also help you to understand the theories.

Enjoy economics

Most important of all, I hope that you will enjoy your study of economics. I have always been fascinated by the subject and hope that you will capture something of the excitement and challenge of learning about how markets and the economy operate. I wish you every success with your studies.

Acknowledgements

I would like to express my deep gratitude to Russell Dudley-Smith, whose careful reading of the book's precursor and thoughtful and helpful comments were invaluable in improving the scope and focus of the book. I would also like to thank everyone at Philip Allan Updates, especially Penny Fisher, David Cross and Rachel Furse for their efficiency in the production of this book, and also for their support and encouragement.

Many of the data series shown in figures in this book were drawn from the National Statistics website: **www.statistics.gov.uk**. Crown copyright material is reproduced with the permission of the Controller of HMSO (PSI licence number C2007001851).

Other data were from various sources, including OECD, World Bank, United Nations Development Programme and elsewhere as specified.

While every effort has been made to trace the owners of copyright material, I would like to apologise to any copyright holders whose rights may have unwittingly been infringed.

Peter Smith

Competitive markets: how they work and why they fail

Part 1

part 1

Chapter 1

Introducing economics

Welcome to economics. Many of you opening this book will be meeting economics for the first time, and you will want to know what is in store for you as you set out to study the subject. This opening chapter sets the scene by introducing you to some key ideas and identifying the scope of economic analysis. As you learn more of the subject, you will find that economics is a way of thinking that will broaden your perspective on the world around you.

Learning outcomes

This chapter will introduce you to:
➤ the nature and scope of economic analysis
➤ the concept of opportunity cost
➤ the notion of factors of production
➤ the distinction between renewable and non-renewable resources and the idea of sustainability
➤ the role of models and assumptions in economics
➤ the production possibility frontier
➤ the concept of the division of labour
➤ how specialisation can improve productivity
➤ the role of markets and what is meant by a mixed economy
➤ the distinction between microeconomics and macroeconomics
➤ positive and normative statements

The fundamental economic problem

For any society in the world, the fundamental economic problem faced is that of **scarcity**. You might think that this is obvious for some societies in the less-developed world, where poverty and hunger are rife. But it is also true for relatively prosperous economies such as those of Switzerland, the USA or the UK.

Key term

scarcity: a situation that arises when people have unlimited wants in the face of limited resources

It is true in the sense that all societies have *finite resources*, but people have *unlimited wants*. A big claim? Not really. There is no country in the world in which all wants can be met, and this is clearly true at the global level.

Talking about *scarcity* in this sense is not the same as talking about *poverty*. Poverty might be seen as an extreme form of scarcity, in which individuals lack the basic necessities of life; whereas even relatively prosperous people face scarcity, because resources are limited.

Scarcity and choice

The key issue that arises from the existence of scarcity is that it forces people to make choices. Each individual must choose which goods and services to consume. In other words, everyone needs to prioritise the consumption of whatever commodities they need or would like to have, as they cannot satisfy all their wants. Similarly, at the national level, governments have to make choices between alternative uses of resources.

It is this need to choose that underlies the subject matter of economics. Economic analysis is all about analysing those choices made by individual people, firms or governments.

Opportunity cost

This raises one of the most important concepts in all of economic analysis — the notion of **opportunity cost**. When an individual chooses to consume one good, she does so at the cost of the item that would have been next in her list of priorities. For example, suppose you are on a strict diet, and at the end of the day you can 'afford' either one chocolate or a piece of cheese. If you choose the cheese, the opportunity cost of the cheese is the chocolate that you could have had instead.

Key *term*

opportunity cost: in decision making, the value of the next-best alternative that could have been chosen

This important notion can be applied in many different contexts, because whenever you make a decision you reject an alternative in favour of your chosen option. You have chosen to read this book — when instead you could be watching television or meeting friends.

The notion of opportunity cost is related to an important tool in economics known as **marginal analysis**. This is based on the idea that people take decisions by considering small (marginal) changes. For example, in choosing whether to read this book, you may consider if the extra benefit you will receive from doing so will exceed the additional benefit you would receive from watching television. Firms may also take decisions in this way, perhaps by checking whether the cost of producing and selling an additional unit of output will exceed the extra (marginal) return they receive from selling it. This approach will become familiar to you as you continue to study economics.

Key *term*

marginal analysis: an approach to economic decision making based on considering the additional (marginal) benefits and costs of a small change in behaviour

Exercise 1.1

Andrew has just started his AS, and has chosen to take economics, mathematics, geography and French. Although he was certain about the first three, it was a close call between French and English. What is Andrew's opportunity cost of choosing French?

As you move further into studying economics, you will encounter this notion of opportunity cost again and again. For example, firms take decisions about the sort of economic activity in which to engage. Or a market gardener has to decide whether to plant onions or potatoes; if he decides to grow onions, he has to forgo the opportunity to grow potatoes. From the government's point of view, if it decides to devote more resources to the National Health Service, then it will have fewer resources available for, say, defence.

The coordination problem

With so many different individuals and organisations (consumers, firms, governments) all taking decisions, a major question is how it all comes together. How are all these separate decisions coordinated so that the overall allocation of resources in a society is coherent? In other words, how can it be ensured that firms produce the commodities that consumers wish to consume? And how can the distribution of these products be organised? These are some of the basic questions that economics sets out to answer.

A **market economy** is one in which market forces are allowed to guide the allocation of resources within a society. Prices play a key role in this sort of system, providing signals and incentives to producers and consumers.

In contrast, a **centrally planned economy** is one in which the government undertakes the coordination role, planning and directing the allocation of resources. Such micro-management has proved costly to implement administratively. The collapse of the Soviet bloc in the 1990s largely discredited this approach, although a small number of countries (North Korea, Cuba) continue to stick with central planning.

Most economies operate a **mixed economy** system, in which market forces are complemented by some state intervention. It has been argued that any such state intervention should be *market-friendly*; in other words, when governments do intervene in the economy, they should do so in a way that helps markets to work, rather than trying to have the government replace market forces.

Another important concept that is at the heart of economic analysis is the notion that individuals respond to *incentives*. The difference in the way in which the coordination problem is handled in different forms of economy is through different

Key terms

market economy: an economy in which market forces are allowed to guide the allocation of resources

centrally planned economy: an economy in which decisions on resource allocation are guided by the state

mixed economy: an economy in which resources are allocated partly through price signals and partly on the basis of intervention by the state forms of incentives that influence decision making. In a market economy, prices and profits provide incentives, whereas these incentives are replaced by state directives in a centrally planned economy.

Factors of production

People in a society play two quite different roles. On the one hand, they are the consumers, the ultimate beneficiaries of the process of production. On the other, they are a key part of the production process in that they are instrumental in producing goods and services.

More generally, it is clear that both *human resources* and *physical resources* are required as part of the production process. These productive resources are known as the **factors of production**.

> **Key term**
>
> **factors of production:** resources used in the production process; *inputs* into production, in particular including labour, capital, land and entrepreneurship

The most obvious human resource is labour. Labour is a key input into production. Of course, there are many different types of labour, encompassing different skill levels and working in different ways. *Entrepreneurship* is another key human resource. An entrepreneur is someone who organises production and identifies projects to be undertaken, often bearing the risk of the activity. *Management* might also be classified as a key human resource. *Natural resources* are also inputs into the production process. In particular, all economic activities require some use of land, and most use some raw materials.

There are also *produced resources*, inputs that are the product of a manufacturing process. For example, machines are used in the production process; they are resources manufactured for the purpose of producing other goods. These inputs are referred to as capital, which may include things like factory buildings and transport equipment as well as plant and machinery.

The way in which these inputs are combined in order to produce output is another key part of the allocation of resources. Firms need to take decisions about the mix of inputs used in order to produce their output. Such decisions are required in whatever form of economic activity a firm is engaged.

Factors of production — labour (workers), capital (buildings) and land

Sustainability

An important distinction is between *renewable resources* such as forests, and *non-renewable resources* such as oil or coal.

In the case of renewable resources, there have been many debates in recent years about the dangers of depleting such resources at too rapid a rate to allow replacement. One example of this has been the stocks of some fish such as cod, where it has been argued that over-fishing may lead to the extinction of the species. Similar arguments have been applied to other resources such as the rainforests. This has highlighted the importance of **sustainable development**, which has been defined as 'development which meets the needs of the present without compromising the ability of future generations to meet their own needs' (Brundtland Commission, 1987). Applying this to the case of cod fishing, for example, sustainable fishing would be seen in terms of not catching so many cod that the overall population becomes unsustainable.

> **Key** *term*
>
> **sustainable development:** 'development which meets the needs of the present without compromising the ability of future generations to meet their own needs' (Brundtland Commission, 1987)

For non-renewable resources, reserves are finite — by definition — so concern has arisen over their possible exhaustion. Attention has tended to focus on oil, which is much in demand, especially given rapidly rising car ownership. This has led to a search for renewable sources of energy, which would also contribute to sustainability. One economic issue here is whether the prices of resources such as oil will rise as reserves are depleted. This could then have the effect of giving incentives to firms to develop alternative sources of energy. It could also mean that some reserves of oil that are currently uneconomic may become viable. This is one example of how prices can be seen to guide resource allocation.

Exercise 1.2

Classify each of the following as human, natural (renewable or non-renewable) or produced resources:

a timber
b services of a window cleaner
c natural gas
d solar energy
e a combine harvester
f a computer programmer who sets up a company to market his software
g a computer

By now you should be getting some idea of the subject matter of economics. The American economist Paul Samuelson (who won the Nobel Prize for Economic Sciences in 1970) identified three key questions that economics sets out to investigate:

1 *What?* What goods and services should be produced in a society from its scarce resources? In other words, how should resources be allocated among producing DVD players, potatoes, banking services and so on?

2 *How?* How should the productive resources of the economy be used to produce these various goods and services?

3 *For whom?* Having produced a range of goods and services, how should these be allocated among the population for consumption?

Exercise 1.3

With which of Samuelson's three questions (what, how, for whom) would you associate the following?

a A firm chooses to switch from producing CD players in order to increase its output of DVD recorders.

b The government reduces the highest rate of income tax.

c Faced with increased labour costs, a firm introduces labour-saving machinery.

d There is an increase in social security benefits.

e The owner of a fish-and-chip shop decides to close down and take a job in a local factory.

Summary

➤ The fundamental problem faced by any society is scarcity, because resources are finite but wants are unlimited. As a result, choices need to be made.

➤ Each choice has an opportunity cost — the value of the next-best alternative.

➤ Decisions need to be coordinated within a society, either by market forces or by state intervention, or a mixture of the two.

➤ The amount of output produced in a period depends on the inputs of factors of production.

➤ The rate at which renewable resources are used needs to be seen in the light of the notion of sustainability.

➤ Economics deals with the questions of what should be produced, how it should be produced, and for whom.

Models and assumptions

Economics sets out to tackle some complex issues concerning what is a very complex real world. This complexity is such that it is essential to simplify reality in some way; otherwise the task would be overwhelming. Economists thus work with **models**. These are simplified versions of reality that are more tractable for analysis, allowing economists to focus on some key aspects of the world.

Key *term*

model: a simplified representation of reality used to provide insight into economic decisions and events

Often this works by allowing them to focus on one thing at a time. A model almost always begins with assumptions that help economists to simplify their questions. These assumptions can then be gradually relaxed so that the effect of each one of

them can be observed. In this way economists can gradually move towards a more complicated version of reality.

To evaluate a model, it is not necessary that it be totally realistic. The model's desired objectives may help in predicting future behaviour, or in testing empirical evidence collected from the real world. If a model provides insights into how individuals take decisions, or helps to explain economic events, then it has some value, even if it seems remote from reality.

However, it is always important to examine the assumptions that are made, and to ask what happens if these assumptions do not hold.

The production possibility frontier

Economists rely heavily on diagrams to help in their analysis. In exploring the notion of opportunity cost, a helpful diagram is the **production possibility frontier** (**PPF**). This shows the maximum combinations of goods that can be produced with a given set of resources.

First consider a simple example. In an earlier exercise Andrew was studying for his AS. Suppose now that he has got behind with his homework. He has limited time available, and has five economics questions to answer and five maths exercises. An economics question takes the same time to answer as a maths exercise.

> **Key term**
>
> **production possibility frontier (PPF):** curve showing the maximum combinations of goods or services that can be produced in a given period with available resources

What are the options? Suppose he knows that in the time available he can either tackle all the maths and none of the economics, or all of the economics and none of the maths. Alternatively, he can try to keep both teachers happy by doing some of each. Figure 1.1 shows his options. He can devote all of his efforts to maths, and leave the economics for another day. He will then be at point *A* in the figure. Alternatively, he can do all the economics exercises and no maths, and be at point *B*. The line joining these two extreme points shows the intermediate possibilities. For example, at *C* he does 2 economics exercises and 3 maths problems.

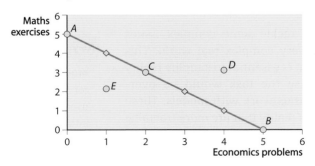

Figure 1.1
The production possibility frontier

The line shows the maximum combinations that Andrew can tackle — which is why it is called a 'frontier'. There is no way he can manage to be beyond the frontier (for example at point *D*), as he does not have the time (i.e. resources) to do so. However, he could end up *inside* the frontier, at a point such as *E*. This could happen if he gives up, and squanders his time by watching television; that would be an inefficient use of his resources – at least in terms of tackling his homework.

As Andrew moves down the line from left to right, he is spending more time on economics and less on maths. The opportunity cost of tackling an additional economics question is an additional maths exercise forgone.

Figure 1.2 shows how the *PPF* provides information about opportunity cost. Suppose we have a farmer with 10 hectares of land who is choosing between growing potatoes and onions. The *PPF* shows the combinations of the two crops that could be produced. For example, if the farmer produces 300 tonnes of onions on part of the land, then 180 tonnes of potatoes could be produced from the remaining land. In order to increase production of potatoes by 70 tonnes from 180 to 250, 50 tonnes of onions must be given up. Thus, the opportunity cost of 70 extra tonnes of potatoes is seen to be 50 tonnes of onions.

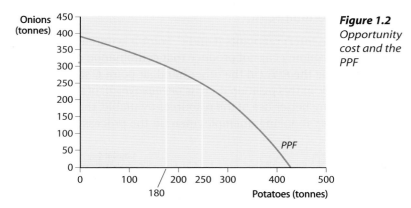

Figure 1.2
Opportunity cost and the PPF

Consumption and investment

To move from thinking about an individual to thinking about an economy as a whole, it is first necessary to simplify reality. Assume an economy that produces just two types of good: capital goods and consumer goods. Consumer goods are for present use, whereas the capital goods are to be used to increase the future capacity of the economy – in other words, for investment.

Figure 1.3 illustrates society's options in a particular period. Given the resources available, society can produce any combination of capital and consumer goods along the *PPF* line. Thus, point *A* represents one possible combination of outputs, in which

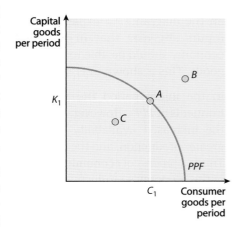

Figure 1.3 *Capital and consumer goods*

the economy produces C_1 consumer goods and K_1 capital goods. (Economists often use K to denote capital — because they normally use C to denote costs.)

As with the simpler example, if society were to move to the right along the *PPF*, it would produce more consumer goods — but at the expense of capital goods. Thus, it can be seen that the opportunity cost of producing consumer goods is in terms of forgone opportunities to produce capital goods. Notice that this time the *PPF* has been drawn as a curve instead of a straight line. This is because not all factors of production are equally suited to the production of both sorts of good. When the economy is well balanced, as at *A*, the factors can be allocated to the uses to which they are best equipped. However, as the economy moves towards complete special-isation in one of the types of goods, factors are no longer being best used, and the opportunity cost changes. For example, if nearly all of the workers are engaged in producing consumer goods, it becomes more difficult to produce still more of these, whereas those workers producing machinery find they have too few resources with which to work. In other words, the more consumer goods are being produced, the higher is their opportunity cost.

It is now possible to interpret points *B* and *C*. Point *B* is unreachable given present resources, so the economy cannot produce that combination of goods. This applies to any point outside the *PPF*. On the other hand, at point *C* society is not using its resources efficiently. In this position there is *unemployment* of some resources in the economy. By making better use of the resources available, the economy can move towards the frontier, reducing unemployment in the process.

Economic growth

Figure 1.3 focused on a single period. However, if the economy is producing capital goods, then in the following period its capacity to produce should increase, as it will have more resources available for production. How can this be shown on the diagram? An expansion in the available inputs suggests that in the next period the economy should be able to produce more of both goods. This is shown in Figure 1.4.

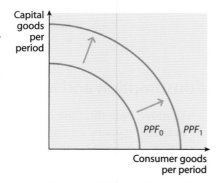

Figure 1.4 Economic growth

In the initial period the production possibility frontier is at PPF_0. However, in the following period the increased availability of resources enables greater production, and the frontier moves to PPF_1. This is a process of **economic growth**, an expansion of the economy's productive capacity through the increased availability of inputs.

Key term

economic growth: an expansion in the productive capacity of the economy

Notice that the decision to produce more capital goods today means that fewer consumer goods will be produced today. People must choose between 'more jam today' or 'more jam tomorrow'.

Total output in an economy

Remember that the *PPF* is a model: a much simplified version of reality. In a real economy there are many different goods and services produced by a wide range of different factors of production — but it is not possible to draw diagrams to show all of them.

The total output of an economy like the UK is measured by its **gross domestic product (GDP)**.

By calculating the *average* level of GDP per person in a country, it is possible to derive a measure of the average amount of resources per person — or average income per head.

> **Key term**
>
> **gross domestic product (GDP):** a measure of the economic activity carried out in an economy over a period

---

Exercise 1.4

Beverly has been cast away on a desert island, and has to survive by spending her time either fishing or climbing trees to get coconuts. The *PPF* in Figure 1.5 shows the maximum combinations of fish and coconuts that she can gather during a day. Which of the points *A* to *E* represent each of the following?

a a situation where Beverly spends all her time fishing

b an unreachable position

c a day when Beverly goes for a balanced diet — a mixture of coconuts and fish

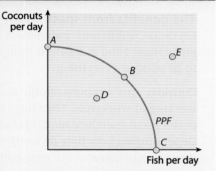

Figure 1.5 *Fish and coconuts*

d a day when Beverly does not fancy fish, and spends all day collecting coconuts

e a day when Beverly spends some of the time trying to attract the attention of a passing ship

---

Specialisation

How many workers does it take to make a pin? The eighteenth-century economist Adam Smith figured that 10 was about the right number. He argued that when a worker was producing pins on his own, carrying out all the various stages involved in the production process, the maximum number of pins that could be produced in one day was 20 — given the technology of his day, of course. This would imply that 10 workers could produce about 200 pins if they worked in the same way as the lone worker. However, if the pin production process were broken into 10 separate stages, with one worker specialising in each stage, the maximum production for a day's work would be a staggering 48,000. This is known as **division of labour**.

> **Key term**
>
> **division of labour:** a process whereby the production procedure is broken down into a sequence of stages, and workers are assigned to particular stages

The division of labour is effective because individual workers become skilled at performing specialised tasks. By focusing on a particular stage, they can become highly adept, and thus more efficient, at carrying out that task. In any case, people are not all the same, so some are better at certain activities. Furthermore, this specialisation is more efficient because workers do not spend time moving from one activity to another. Specialisation may also enable firms to operate on a larger scale of production. You will see later that this may be advantageous.

This can be seen in practice in many businesses today, where there is considerable specialisation of functions. Workers are hired for particular tasks and activities. You do not see Michael Owen pulling on the goalkeeper's jersey at half time because he fancies a change. Earlier in the chapter, it was argued that 'labour' is considered a factor of production. This idea will now be developed further by arguing that there are different types of labour, having different skills and functions. At another level, firms and even nations specialise in particular kinds of activity.

The benefits from specialisation

Everyone is different. Individuals have different natural talents and abilities that make them good at different things. Indeed, there are some lucky people who seem to be good at everything.

Consider this example. Colin and Debbie try to supplement their incomes by working at weekends. They have both been to evening classes and have attended pottery and jewellery-making classes. At weekends they make pots and bracelets. Depending on how they divide their time, they can make differing combinations of these goods; some of the possibilities are shown in Table 1.1.

Colin		Debbie	
Pots	**Bracelets**	**Pots**	**Bracelets**
12	0	18	0
9	3	12	12
6	6	6	24
3	9	3	30
0	12	0	36

Table 1.1
Colin and Debbie's production

The first point to notice is that Debbie is much better at both activities than Colin. If they each devote all their time to producing pots, Colin produces only 12 to Debbie's 18. If they each produce only bracelets, Colin produces 12 and Debbie, 36. There is another significant feature of this table. Although Debbie is better at producing both goods, the difference is much more marked in the case of bracelet production than pot production. So Debbie is relatively more proficient in bracelet production: in other words, she faces a lower opportunity cost in making bracelets. If Debbie switches from producing pots to producing bracelets, she gives up 6 pots for every 12 additional bracelets that she makes. The opportunity cost of an additional bracelet is thus 6/12 = 0.5 pots. For Colin, there is a one-to-one trade-off between the two, so his opportunity cost of a bracelet is 1 pot.

More interesting is what happens if the same calculation is made for Colin and pot making. Although Debbie is absolutely better at making pots, if Colin increases his production of pots, his opportunity cost in terms of bracelets is still 1. But for Debbie the opportunity cost of making pots in terms of bracelets is 12/6 = 2, so Colin has the lower opportunity cost.

Why does this matter? It illustrates the potential benefits to be gained from specialisation. Suppose that both Colin and Debbie divide their time between the two activities in such a way that Colin produces 6 pots and 6 bracelets, and Debbie produces 6 pots and 24 bracelets. Between them, they will have produced 12 pots and 30 bracelets. However, if they each specialise in the product in which they face the lower opportunity cost, their joint production will increase. If Colin devotes all his time to pottery, he produces 12 pots, while Debbie, focusing only on bracelets, produces 36. So between them they will have produced the same number of pots as before — but 6 extra bracelets.

One final point before leaving Colin and Debbie. Figure 1.6 shows their respective production possibility frontiers. You can check this by graphing the points in Table 1.1 and joining them up. In this case the *PPF*s are straight lines. You can see that because Debbie is better at both activities, her *PPF* lies entirely above Colin's. The differences in opportunity cost are shown by the fact that the two *PPF*s have different slopes, as the opportunity cost element is related to the slope of the *PPF* — the rate at which one good is sacrificed for more of the other.

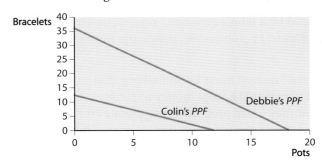

Figure 1.6 Colin and Debbie's production possibilities

Summary

➤ Adam Smith introduced the notion of division of labour, which suggests that workers can become more productive by specialising in stages of the production process.

➤ Specialisation opens up the possibility of trade.

➤ The gains from specialisation and trade result from differences in opportunity cost.

Markets

You will find that in economics the term **market** is used frequently, so it is important to be absolutely clear about what is meant by it.

A market need not be a physical location (although it could be — you might regard the local farmers' market as

Key term

market: a set of arrangements that allows transactions to take place

an example of 'a set of arrangements that allows transactions to take place'). With the growth of the internet, everyone is becoming accustomed to ways of buying and selling that do not involve direct physical contact between buyer and seller, so the notion of an abstract market should not be too alien a concept.

In relation to a particular product, a market brings together potential buyers and sellers. This will be explored in the next chapters.

Markets are important in the process of resource allocation, with prices acting as a key signal to potential buyers and sellers. If a firm finds that it cannot sell its output at the price it has chosen, this is a signal about the way that buyers perceive the product. Price is one way that firms find out about consumers and their will-ingness to pay for a particular product. This will be explored more carefully in Chapter 5.

Money and exchange

Imagine a world without money. It is lunchtime, and you fancy a banana. In your bag you have an apple. Perhaps you can find someone with a banana who fancies an apple? But the only person with a banana available fancies an ice cream. The problem with such a *barter economy* is that you need to find someone who wants what you have and who has what you want — a *double coincidence of wants*. If this problem were to be faced by a whole economic system, undertaking transactions would be so inefficient as to be impossible. Hence the importance of *money* as a *medium of exchange.*

In order to fulfil this role, money must be something that is acceptable to both buyers and sellers. Nobody would accept money in payment for goods or services if they did not trust that they could proceed to use money for further transactions. Money must thus also act as a *store of value*: it must be possible to use it for future transactions. This quality of money means that it can be used as one way of storing wealth for future purchases. Money also allows the value of goods, services and other assets to be compared — it provides a *unit of account.* In this sense, prices of goods reflect the value that society places on them, and must be expressed in money terms.

A further role for money is that it acts as a *standard of deferred payment.* For example, a firm may wish to agree a contract for the future delivery of a good, or may wish to hire a worker to be paid at the end of the month. Such contracts are typically agreed in terms of a money value.

All of these *functions of money* are important to the smooth operation of markets, and are crucial if prices are to fulfil their role in allocating resources within society. This will become apparent as you learn more about economics.

Microeconomics and macroeconomics

The discussion so far has focused sometimes on individual decisions, and sometimes on the decisions of governments, or of 'society' as a whole. Economic thinking is applied in different ways, depending on whether the focus is on the decisions taken by individual agents in the economy or on the interaction between economic variables at the level of the whole economy:

➤ **Microeconomics** deals with individual decisions taken by households or firms, or in particular markets.

➤ **Macroeconomics** examines the interactions between economic variables at the level of the aggregate economy.

In some ways the division between the two types of analysis is artificial. The same sort of economic reasoning is applied in both types, but the focus is different.

Key terms

microeconomics: the study of economic decisions taken by individual economic agents, including households and firms

macroeconomics: the study of the interrelationships between economic variables at an aggregate (economy-wide) level

Exercise 1.5

Think about the following, and see whether you think each represents a microeconomic or macroeconomic phenomenon:

a The overall level of prices in an economy.
b The price of ice cream.
c The overall rate of unemployment in the UK.
d The unemployment rate among catering workers in Aberdeen.
e The average wage paid to construction workers in Southampton.

Positive and normative statements

Economics tries to be objective in analysis. However, some of its subject matter requires careful attention in order to retain an objective distance. In this connection, it is important to be clear about the difference between **positive** and **normative** statements.

In short, a positive statement is about *facts.* In contrast, a normative statement is about *what ought to be.* Another way of looking at this is that a statement becomes normative when it involves a *value judgement.*

Key terms

positive statement: a statement about what *is,* i.e. about facts

normative statement: a statement about what *ought to be*

Suppose the government is considering raising the tax on cigarettes. It may legitimately consult economists to discover what effect a higher tobacco tax will have on the consumption of cigarettes and on government revenues. This would be a *positive* investigation, in that the economists are being asked to use economic analysis to forecast what will happen when the tax is increased.

A very different situation will arise if the government asked whether it *should* raise the tax on cigarettes. This moves the economists beyond positive analysis, because it entails a value judgement – so it is now a *normative* analysis. There are some words that betray normative statements, such as 'should' or 'ought to' – watch for these.

Most of this book is about positive economics. However, you should be aware that positive analysis is often called upon to inform normative judgements. If the aim of a policy is to stop people from smoking (which reflects a normative judgement about what *ought* to happen), then economic analysis may be used to highlight the strengths and weaknesses of those alternatives in a purely positive fashion.

Critics of economics often joke that economists always disagree with one another; for example, it has been said that if you put five economists in a room together they will come up with at least six conflicting opinions. However, although economists may arrive at different value judgements, and thus have differences when it comes to normative issues, there is much greater agreement when it comes to positive analysis. Nonetheless, value judgements do influence economic decision making and policy because different people — and political parties — may have different views about what is desirable for society, even if they agree on how policies may work.

Increasing taxes on tobacco affects consumption of cigarettes and government revenue

Summary

> The production possibility frontier shows the maximum combinations of goods or services that can be produced in a period by a given set of resources.

> At any point on the frontier, society is making full use of all resources.

> At any point inside the frontier, there is unemployment of some resources.

> Points beyond the frontier are unattainable.

> In a simple society producing two goods (consumer goods and capital goods), the choice is between consumption and investment for the future.

> As society increases its stock of capital goods, the productive capacity of the economy increases, and the production possibility frontier moves outwards: this may be termed 'economic growth'.

> Microeconomics deals with individual decisions made by consumers and producers, whereas macroeconomics analyses the interactions between economic variables in the aggregate — but both use similar ways of thinking.

> Positive statements are about what is, whereas normative statements are about what ought to be.

Chapter 2

The nature of demand

The demand and supply model is perhaps the most famous of all pieces of economic analysis; it is also one of the most useful. It has many applications that help explain the way markets work in the real world. It is thus central to understanding economics. This chapter introduces the 'demand' side of the model. Chapter 3 will introduce supply.

Learning outcomes

After studying this chapter, you should:

➤ be familiar with the notion of the demand for a good or service
➤ be aware of the relationship between the demand for a good and its price
➤ be familiar with the demand curve and the law of demand
➤ understand the distinction between a movement along the demand curve and a shift in its position
➤ be aware of the distinction between normal and inferior goods
➤ understand the other influences that affect the position of the demand curve
➤ understand the concept of elasticity measures and appreciate their importance and applications

Demand

Consider an individual consumer. Think of yourself, and a product that you consume regularly. What factors influence your **demand** for that product? Put another way, what factors influence how much of the product you choose to buy?

When thinking about the factors that influence your demand for your chosen product, common sense will probably mean that you focus on a range of different points. You may think about why you enjoy consuming the product. You may focus on how much it will cost to buy the product, and whether you can afford it. You may decide that you have consumed a product so much that you are

Key term

demand: the quantity of a good or service that consumers choose to buy at any possible price in a given period

ready for a change; or perhaps you will decide to try something advertised on television, or being bought by a friend.

Whatever the influences you come up with, they can probably be categorised under four headings that ultimately determine your demand for a good. First, the *price* of the good is an important influence on your demand for it, and will affect the quantity of it that you choose to buy. Second, the *price of other goods* may be significant. Third, your *income* will determine how much of the good you can afford to purchase. Finally, almost any other factors that you may have thought of can be listed as part of your *preferences*.

This commonsense reasoning provides the basis for the economic analysis of demand. You will find that a lot of economic analysis begins in this way, by finding a way to construct a model that is rooted in how we expect people or firms to behave.

Individual and market demand

A similar line of argument may apply if we think in terms of the demand for a particular product — say, DVDs. The market for DVDs can thus be seen as bringing together all the potential buyers (and sellers) of the product, and market demand can be analysed in terms of the factors that influence all potential buyers of that good or service. In other words, market demand can be seen as the total quantity of a good or service that all potential buyers would choose to buy at any given price. The same four factors that influence your own individual decision to buy will also influence the total market demand for a product. In addition, the number of potential buyers in the market will clearly influence the size of total demand at any price.

R. Parkes/Ontanet

Demand and the price of a good

Assume for the moment that the influences mentioned above, other than the price of the good, are held constant, so that the focus is only on the extent to which the price of a good influences the demand for it. This is a common assumption in economics, which is sometimes expressed by the Latin phrase **ceteris paribus**, meaning 'other things being equal'. Given the complexity of the real world, it is often helpful to focus on one thing at a time.

> **Key term**
>
> **ceteris paribus:** a Latin phrase meaning 'other things being equal'; it is used in economics when we focus on changes in one variable while holding other influences constant

This ceteris paribus assumption is used a lot in economics, and is a powerful tool. Focusing on one influence at a time is a way of coping with the complexities of the real world and makes the analysis of economic issues much clearer than if we try to analyse everything at once. You will see many instances of it as the course proceeds.

So how is the demand for DVDs influenced by their price? Other things being equal (ceteris paribus), you would expect the demand for DVDs to be higher when the price is low and lower when the price is high. In other words, you would expect an inverse relationship between the price and the quantity demanded. This is such a strong phenomenon that it is referred to as the **law of demand**.

If you were to compile a list that showed how many DVDs would be bought at any possible price and plot these on a diagram, this would be called the **demand curve**. Figure 2.1 shows what this might look like. As it is an inverse relationship, the demand curve slopes downwards. Notice that this need not be a straight line: its shape depends on how consumers react at different prices. According to this curve, if price were to be set at £40, the quantity demanded would be 20,000 per period. However, if the price were only £20, the demand would be higher, at 60,000.

Key terms

law of demand: a law that states that there is an inverse relationship between quantity demanded and the price of a good or service, ceteris paribus

demand curve: a graph showing how much of a good will be demanded by consumers at any given price

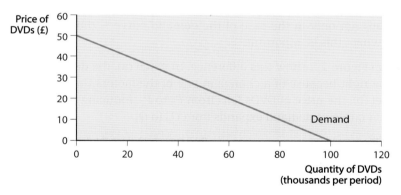

Figure 2.1
A demand curve for DVDs

Exercise 2.1

Table 2.1 shows how the demand for oojits varies with their price. Draw the demand curve.

Table 2.1 *The demand for oojits*

Price	Quantity
100	0
90	3
80	7
70	15
60	25
50	40
40	60
30	85
20	120

Extension point

An analysis of why the demand curve should be downward sloping would reveal that there are two important forces at work. At a higher price, a consumer buying a DVD has less income left over. This is referred to as the *real income effect* of a price increase. In addition, if the price of DVDs goes up, consumers may find other goods more attractive and choose to buy something else instead of DVDs. This is referred to as the *substitution effect* of a price increase.

As the price of a good changes, a movement along the demand curve can be observed as consumers adjust their buying pattern in response to the price change.

Notice that the demand curve has been drawn under the ceteris paribus assumption. In other words, it was assumed that all other influences on demand were held constant in order to focus on the relationship between demand and price. There are two important implications of this procedure.

First, the price drawn on the vertical axis of a diagram such as Figure 2.1 is the *relative* price — it is the price of DVDs under the assumption that all other prices are constant.

Second, if any of the other influences on demand change, you would expect to see a shift of the whole demand curve. It is very important to distinguish between factors that induce a movement *along* a curve, and factors that induce a shift *of* a curve. This applies not only in the case of the demand curve — there are many other instances where this is important.

The two panels of Figure 2.2 show this difference. In panel (a), the demand curve has shifted to the right because of a change in one of the factors that influences demand. In panel (b), the price of DVDs falls from P_0 to P_1, inducing a movement along the demand curve as demand expands from Q_0 to Q_1.

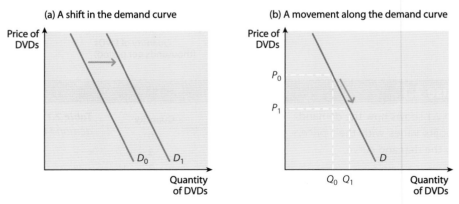

Figure 2.2 *A shift in the demand curve and a movement along it*

Snob effects

It is sometimes argued that for some goods a 'snob effect' may lead to the demand curve sloping upwards. The argument is that some people may value certain goods more highly simply because their price is high, especially if they know that other people will observe them consuming these goods; an example might be Rolex watches. In other words, people gain value from having other people notice that they are rich enough to afford to consume a particular good. There is thus a *conspicuous consumption* effect, which was first pointed out by Thorstein Veblen at the end of the nineteenth century.

However, although there may be some individual consumers who react to price in this way, there is no evidence to suggest that there are whole markets that display an upward-sloping demand curve for this reason. In other words, most consumers would react normally to the price of such goods.

Demand and consumer incomes

The second influence on demand is consumer incomes. For a **normal good**, an increase in consumer incomes will, ceteris paribus, lead to an increase in the quantity demanded at any given price. Foreign holidays are an example of a normal good because, as people's incomes rise, they will tend to demand more foreign holidays at any given price.

Rolex watches may benefit from the conspicuous consumption effect

Figure 2.3 illustrates this. D_0 here represents the initial demand curve for foreign holidays. An increase in consumers' incomes causes demand to be higher at any given price, and the demand curve shifts to the right – to D_1.

However, demand does not always respond in this way. For example, think about bus journeys. As incomes rise in a society, more people can afford to have a car, or to use taxis. This means that, as incomes rise, the demand for bus journeys may tend to fall. Such goods are known as **inferior goods**.

This time an increase in consumers' incomes in Figure 2.4 causes the demand curve to shift to the left, from its initial position at D_0, to D_1 where less is demanded at any given price.

Key terms

normal good: one where the quantity demanded increases in response to an increase in consumer incomes

inferior good: one where the quantity demanded decreases in response to an increase in consumer incomes

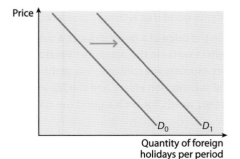

Figure 2.3 *A shift in the demand curve following an increase in consumer incomes (a normal good)*

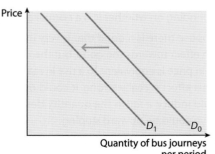

Figure 2.4 *A shift in the demand curve following an increase in consumer incomes (an inferior good)*

The relationship between quantity demanded and income can be shown more directly on a diagram. Panel (a) of Figure 2.5 shows how this would look for a normal good. It is upward sloping, showing that the quantity demanded is higher when consumer incomes are higher. In contrast, the income demand curve for an inferior good, shown in panel (b) of the diagram, slopes downwards, indicating that the quantity demanded will be lower when consumer incomes are relatively high.

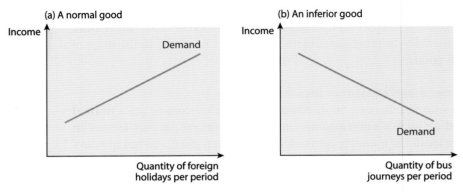

Figure 2.5 *Demand and income*

Exercise 2.2

Identify each of the following products as being either a normal good or an inferior good:

a digital camera   c potatoes   e fine wine
b magazine   d bicycle   f cheap wine

Extension point: a Giffen good

Remember that a consumer's response to a change in the price of a good is made up of a substitution effect and a real income effect (see the extension point on page 20). The substitution effect always acts in the opposite direction to the price change: in other words, an increase in the price of a good always induces a switch *away* from the good towards other goods. However, it can now be seen that the real income effect may operate in either direction, depending on whether it is a normal good or an inferior good that is being considered.

Suppose there is a good that is *very* inferior. A fall in the price of a good induces a substitution effect towards the good, but the real income effect works in the opposite direction. The fall in price is equivalent to a rise in real income, so consumers will consume less of the good. If this effect is really strong, it could overwhelm the substitution effect, and the fall in price could induce a *fall* in the quantity demanded: in other words, for such a good the demand curve could be upward sloping.

Such goods are known as *Giffen goods*, after Sir Robert Giffen, who pointed out that this could happen. However, in spite of stories about the reaction of demand to a rise in the price of potatoes during the great Irish potato famine, there have been no authenticated sightings of Giffen goods. The notion remains a theoretical curiosity.

Demand and the price of other goods

The demand for a good may respond to changes in the price of other related goods, of which there are two main types. On the one hand, two goods may be **substitutes** for each other. For example, consider two different (but similar) breakfast cereals. If there is an increase in the price of one of the cereals, consumers may switch their consumption to the other, as the two are likely to be close substitutes for each other. Not all consumers will switch, of course — some may be deeply committed to one particular brand — but some of them are certainly likely to change over.

> **Key terms**
>
> **substitutes:** two goods are said to be substitutes if the demand for one good is likely to rise if the price of the other good rises
>
> **complements:** two goods are said to be complements if an increase in the price of one good causes the demand for the other good to fall

On the other hand, there may also be goods that are **complements** — for example, products that are consumed jointly, such as breakfast cereals and milk, or cars and petrol. Here a fall in the price of one good may lead to an increase in demand for *both* products.

Whether goods are substitutes or complements determines how the demand for one good responds to a change in the price of another. Figure 2.6 shows the demand curves (per period) for two goods that are substitutes — tea and coffee.

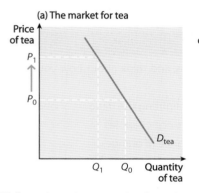
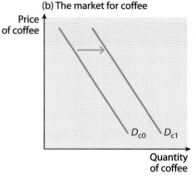

Figure 2.6
A shift in the demand curve following an increase in the price of a substitute good

If there is an increase in the price of tea from P_0 to P_1 in panel (a), more consumers will switch to coffee and the demand curve in panel (b) will shift to the right — say, from D_{c0} to D_{c1}. For complements the situation is the reverse: in Figure 2.7 an

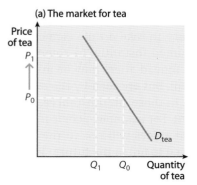
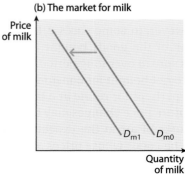

Figure 2.7
A shift in the demand curve following an increase in the price of a complementary good

increase in the price of tea from P_0 to P_1 in panel (a) causes the demand curve for milk to shift leftwards, from D_{m0} to D_{m1}.

Demand, consumer preferences and other influences

The discussion has shown how the demand for a good is influenced by the price of the good, the price of other goods, and by consumer incomes. It was stated earlier that almost everything else that determines demand for a good can be represented as 'consumer preferences'. In particular, this refers to whether you like or dislike a good. There may be many things that influence whether you like or dislike a product. In part it simply depends on your own personal inclinations – some people like dark chocolate, others prefer milk chocolate. However, firms may try to influence your preferences through advertising, and sometimes they succeed. Or you might be one of those people who get so irritated by television advertising that you compile a blacklist of products that you will never buy! Even this is an influence on your demand.

In some cases your preferences may be swayed by other people's demand – again, this may be positive or negative. Fashions may influence demand, but some people like to buck (or lead) the trend.

You may also see a movement of the demand curve if there is a sudden surge in the popularity of a good – or, indeed, a sudden collapse in demand.

Exercise 2.3

Sketch some demand curves for the following situations, and think about how you would expect the demand curve to change (if at all):

a the demand for chocolate following a campaign highlighting the dangers of obesity

b the demand for oranges following an increase in the price of apples

c the demand for oranges following a decrease in the price of oranges

d the demand for DVDs following a decrease in the price of DVD players

e the demand for VCRs following a decrease in the price of DVD recorders

f the demand for private transport following an increase in consumer incomes

g the demand for public transport following an increase in consumer incomes

The above discussion has covered most of the factors that influence the demand for a good. However, in some cases it is necessary to take a time element into account. Not all of the goods bought are consumed instantly. In some cases, consumption is spread over long periods of time. Indeed, there may be instances where goods are not bought for consumption at all, but are seen by the buyer as an investment, perhaps for resale at a later date. In these circumstances, expectations about future price changes may be relevant. For example, people may buy fine wine or works of art in the expectation that prices will rise in the future. There may also be goods whose prices are expected to fall in the future. This has been common with many high-tech products; initially a newly launched product may sell at a high price, but as production levels rise, costs may fall, and prices also. People may therefore delay purchase in the expectation of future price reductions.

Summary

➤ A market is a set of arrangements that enables transactions to take place.
➤ The market demand for a good depends on the price of the good, the price of other goods, consumers' incomes and preferences, and the number of potential consumers.
➤ The demand curve shows the relationship between demand for a product and its price, ceteris paribus.
➤ The demand curve is downward sloping, as the relationship between demand and price is an inverse one.
➤ A change in price induces a movement along the demand curve, whereas a change in the other determinants of demand induces a shift in the demand curve.
➤ When the demand for a good rises as consumer incomes rise, that good is referred to as a normal good; when demand falls as income rises, the good is referred to as an inferior good.
➤ A good or service may be related to other goods by being either a substitute or a complement.
➤ For some products, demand may be related to expected future prices.

Elasticity: the sensitivity of demand

Both the demand for and the supply of a good or service can be expected to depend on its price as well as other factors. It is often interesting to know just how sensitive demand and/or supply will be to a change in either price or one of the other determinants — for example, in predicting how market equilibrium will change in response to a change in the market environment. The sensitivity of demand to a change in one of its determining factors can be measured by its **elasticity**.

> **Key terms**
>
> **elasticity:** a measure of the sensitivity of one variable to changes in another variable
>
> **price elasticity of demand (PED):** a measure of the sensitivity of quantity demanded to a change in the price of a good or service. It is measured as:
>
>
> $$\frac{\text{\% change in quantity demanded}}{\text{\% change in price}}$$

The price elasticity of demand

The most common elasticity measure is the **price elasticity of demand (PED)**. This measures the sensitivity of the quantity demanded of a good or service to a change in its price.

The elasticity is defined as the percentage change in quantity demanded divided by the percentage change in the price.

When the demand is highly price sensitive, the percentage change in quantity demanded following a price change will be large relative to the percentage change in price. In this case, *PED* will take on a value that is numerically greater than 1.

For example, suppose that a 2% change in price leads to a 5% change in quantity demanded; the elasticity is then −5 divided by 2 = −2.5. When the elasticity is numerically greater than 1, demand is referred to as being *price elastic.*

There are two important things to notice about this. First, because the demand curve is downward sloping, the elasticity will always be negative. This is because the changes in price and quantity are always in the opposite direction. Second, you should try to calculate the elasticity only for a relatively small change in price, as it becomes unreliable for very large changes.

When demand is not very sensitive to price, the percentage change in quantity demanded will be smaller than the original percentage change in price, and the elasticity will then be numerically less than 1. For example, if a 2% change in price leads to a 1% change in quantity demanded, then the value of the elasticity will be −1 divided by 2 = −0.5. In this case, demand is referred to as being *price inelastic.*

Calculating the price elasticity of demand

Define the percentage change in price as $100 \times \Delta P/P$ (where the Δ means 'change in' and P stands for price). Similarly, the percentage change in quantity demanded is $100 \times \Delta Q/Q$. Then the formula for the elasticity is:

$$PED = \frac{100 \times \Delta Q/Q}{100 \times \Delta P/P}$$

If you look at this expression, you will see that it can be simplified. First, the 100s top and bottom cancel out:

$$PED = \frac{\Delta Q/Q}{\Delta P/P}$$

This can be written as:

$$PED = \frac{\Delta Q}{\Delta P} \times \frac{P}{Q}$$

An example

Figure 2.8 shows a demand curve for pencils. When the price of a pencil is 40p, the quantity demanded will be 20. If the price falls to 35p, the quantity demanded will rise to 30. The percentage change in quantity is $100 \times 10/20 = 50$ and the percentage change in price is $100 \times -5/40 = -12.5$. Thus, the elasticity can be calculated as $(50/-12.5) = -4$. At this price, demand is highly price elastic.

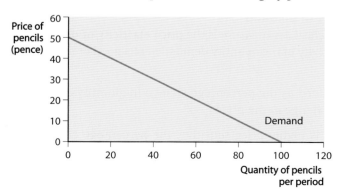

Price of pencils (pence)

Quantity of pencils per period

Demand

Figure 2.8
A demand curve for pencils

At a lower price, the result is quite different. Suppose that price is initially 10p, at which price the quantity demanded is 80. If the price falls to 9p, demand increases to 82. The percentage change in quantity is now $100 \times 2/80 = 2.5$, and the percentage change in price is $100 \times -1/10 = -10$, so the elasticity is calculated as $2.5/-10 = -0.25$, and demand is now price inelastic.

This phenomenon is true for any straight-line demand curve: in other words, demand is price elastic at higher prices and inelastic at lower prices. At the halfway point the elasticity is exactly -1, which is referred to as *unit elasticity*.

Why should this happen? The key is to remember that elasticity is defined in terms of the percentage changes in price and quantity. Thus, when price is relatively high, a 1p change in price is a small percentage change, and the percentage change in quantity is relatively large — because when price is relatively high, the initial quantity is relatively low. The reverse is the case when price is relatively low. Figure 2.9 shows how the elasticity of demand varies along a straight-line demand curve.

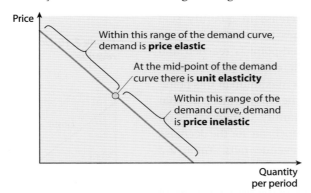

Figure 2.9
The PED of demand varies along a straight line

Extension material

An alternative way of looking at this is to notice that, because the demand curve is drawn as a straight line, the ratio of the change in quantity to the change in price $(\Delta Q/\Delta P)$ is always the same. (In fact, this is the slope of the demand curve.) However, the ratio of the level of quantity to price varies along the demand curve. When price is relatively high, quantity is relatively low, so P/Q is high and elasticity is high. Conversely, when price is low, quantity is high and P/Q is low.

The price elasticity of demand and total revenue

One reason why firms may have an interest in the price elasticity of demand is that, if they are considering changing their prices, they will be eager to know the extent to which demand will be affected. For example, they may want to know how a change in price will affect their total revenue. As it happens, there is a consistent relationship between the price elasticity of demand and total revenue.

Total revenue is given by price multiplied by quantity. In Figure 2.10, if price is at P_0, quantity demanded is at Q_0 and total revenue is given by the area of the rectangle OP_0AQ_0. If price falls to P_1 the quantity demanded rises to Q_1, and you can

see that total revenue has increased, as it is now given by the area OP_1BQ_1. This is larger than at price P_0, because in moving from P_0 to P_1 the area P_1P_0AC is lost, but the area Q_0CBQ_1 is gained, and the latter is the larger. As you move down the demand curve, total revenue at first increases like this, but then decreases — try sketching this for yourself to check that it is so.

For the case of a straight-line demand curve the relationship is illustrated in Figure 2.11. Remember that demand is price elastic when price is relatively high. This is the range of the demand curve in which total revenue rises as price falls. This makes sense, as in this range the quantity demanded is sensitive to a change in price and increases by more (in percentage terms) than the price falls. This implies that, as you move to the right in this segment, total revenue rises. The increase in quantity sold more than compensates for the fall in price. However, when the mid-point is reached and demand becomes unit elastic, total revenue stops rising — it is at its maximum at this point. The remaining part of the curve is inelastic: that is, the increase in quantity demanded is no longer sufficient to compensate for the decrease in price, and total revenue falls. Table 2.2 summarises the situation.

Thus, if a firm is aware of the price elasticity of demand for its product, it can anticipate consumer response to its price changes, which may be a powerful strategic tool.

One very important point must be made here. If the price elasticity of demand varies along a straight-line demand curve, such a curve cannot be referred to as either elastic or inelastic. To do so is to confuse the elasticity with the *slope* of the demand curve. It is not only the steepness of the demand curve that determines the elasticity, but also the point on the curve at which the elasticity is measured.

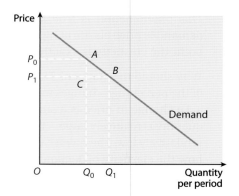

Figure 2.10 *Demand and total revenue*

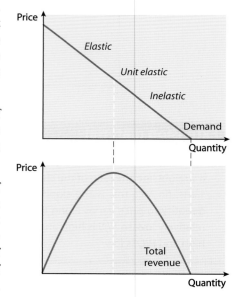

Figure 2.11 *Elasticity and total revenue*

	Price elasticity of demand	For a price increase, total revenue...	For a price decrease, total revenue...
Table 2.2 *Total revenue, elasticity and a price change*	Elastic	falls	rises
	Unit elastic	does not change	does not change
	Inelastic	rises	falls

Two extreme cases of the *PED* should also be mentioned. Demand may sometimes be totally insensitive to price, so that the same quantity will be demanded whatever price is set for it. In such a situation, demand is said to be *perfectly inelastic*. The demand curve in this case is vertical — as in D_i in Figure 2.12. In this situation, the numerical value of the price elasticity is zero, as quantity demanded does not change in response to a change in the price of the good.

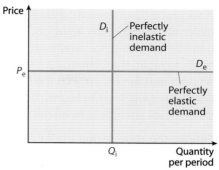

Figure 2.12 *Perfectly elastic and inelastic demand*

The other extreme is shown on the same figure, where D_e is a horizontal demand curve and demand is *perfectly elastic*. The numerical value of the elasticity here is infinity. Consumers demand an unlimited quantity of the good at price P_e. No firm has any incentive to lower price below this level, but if price were to rise above P_e, demand would fall to zero.

An example

A study by the Institute for Fiscal Studies for the UK found that the price elasticity of demand for wine was –1.69. This means that demand for wine is elastic. If the price of wine were to increase by 10% (ceteris paribus), there would be a fall of 16.9% in the quantity of wine demanded.

Influences on the price elasticity of demand

A number of important influences on the price elasticity of demand can now be identified. The most important is the availability of substitutes for the good or service under consideration. For example, think about the demand for cauliflower. Cauliflower and broccoli are often seen as being very similar, so if the price of cauliflower is high one week, people might quite readily switch to broccoli. The demand for cauliflower can be said to be price sensitive (elastic), as consumers can readily substitute an alternative product. On the other hand, if the price of all vegetables rises, demand will not change very much, as there are no substitutes for vegetables in the diet. Thus, goods that have close substitutes available will tend to exhibit elastic demand, whereas the demand for goods for which there are no substitutes will tend to be more inelastic.

Associated with this is the question of whether an individual regards a good or service as a necessity or as a luxury item. If a good is a necessity, then demand for it will tend to be inelastic, whereas if a good is regarded as a luxury, consumers will tend to be more price-sensitive. This is closely related to the question of substitutes, as by labelling a good as a necessity one is essentially saying that there are no substitutes for it.

Hemera Technologies

Demand for wine is price elastic

A second influence on the *PED* is the relative share of the good or service in overall expenditure. You may tend not to notice small changes in the price of an inexpensive item that is a small part of overall expenditure, such as salt or sugar. This tends to mean that demand for that good is relatively inelastic. On the other hand, an item that figures large in the household budget will be seen very differently, and consumers will tend to be much more sensitive to price when a significant proportion of their income is involved.

Finally, the time period under consideration may be important. Consumers may respond more strongly to a price change in the long run than to one in the short run. An increase in the price of petrol may have limited effects in the short run; however, in the long run, consumers may buy smaller cars or switch to diesel. Thus, the elasticity of demand tends to be more elastic in the long run than in the short run. Habit or commitment to a certain pattern of consumption may dictate the short-run pattern of consumption, but people do eventually adjust to price changes.

Summary

➤ The price elasticity of demand (*PED*) measures the sensitivity of the quantity of a good demanded to a change in its price.

➤ As there is an inverse relationship between quantity demanded and price, the price elasticity of demand is always negative.

➤ Where consumers are sensitive to a change in price, the percentage change in quantity demanded will exceed the percentage change in price. The elasticity of demand then takes on a value that is numerically greater than 1, and demand is said to be elastic.

➤ Where consumers are not very sensitive to a change in price, the percentage change in quantity demanded will be smaller than the percentage change in price. Elasticity of demand then takes on a value that is numerically smaller than 1, and demand is said to be inelastic.

➤ When demand is elastic, a fall (rise) in price leads to a rise (fall) in total revenue.

➤ When demand is inelastic, a fall (rise) in price leads to a fall (rise) in total revenue.

➤ The size of the price elasticity of demand is influenced by the availability of substitutes for a good, the relative share of expenditure on the good in the consumer's budget and the time that consumers have to adjust.

Exercise 2.4

Examine Table 2.3, which shows the demand for a particular red wine at different prices.

a Draw the demand curve.

b Calculate the price elasticity of demand when the initial price is £8.

c Calculate the price elasticity of demand when the initial price is £6.

d Calculate the price elasticity of demand when the initial price is £4.

Price (£)	Quantity demanded (bottles per week)
10	20
8	40
6	60
4	80
2	100

Table 2.3
Demand for Château Econ

The income elasticity of demand

Elasticity is a measure of the sensitivity of a variable to changes in another variable. In the same way as the price elasticity of demand is determined, an elasticity measure can be calculated for any other influence on demand or supply. **Income elasticity of demand (YED)** is therefore defined as:

$$YED = \frac{\% \text{ change in quantity demanded}}{\% \text{ change in consumer income}}$$

Unlike the price elasticity of demand, the income elasticity of demand may be either positive or negative. Remember the distinction between normal and inferior goods? For normal goods the quantity demanded will increase as consumer income rises, whereas for inferior goods the quantity demanded will tend to fall as income rises. Thus, for normal goods the *YED* will be positive, whereas for inferior goods it will be negative.

Suppose you discover that the *YED* for wine is 0.7. How do you interpret this number? If consumer incomes were to increase by 10%, the demand for wine would increase by 10 × 0.7 = 7%. This example of a normal good may be helpful information for wine merchants, if they know that consumer incomes are rising over time.

On the other hand, if the *YED* for coach travel is −0.3, that means that a 10% increase in consumer incomes will lead to a 3% fall in the demand for coach travel — perhaps because more people are travelling by car. In this instance, coach travel would be regarded as an inferior good.

In some cases the *YED* may be very strongly positive. For example, suppose that the *YED* for digital cameras is +2. This implies that the quantity demanded of such cameras will increase by 20% for every 10% increase in incomes. An increase in income is encouraging people to devote more of their incomes to this product, which increases its share in total expenditure. Such goods are referred to as **luxury goods**.

Cross-price elasticity of demand

Another useful measure is the **cross-price elasticity of demand (XED)**. This is helpful in revealing the interrelationships between goods. Again, this measure may be either positive or negative, depending on the relationship between the goods. It is defined as:

$$XED = \frac{\% \text{ change in quantity demanded of good X}}{\% \text{ change in price of good X}}$$

If the *XED* is seen to be positive, it means that an increase in the price of good Y leads to an increase in the quantity demanded of good X. For example, an increase in the price of apples may lead to an increase in the demand for pears. Here apples and pears

are regarded as substitutes for each other; if one becomes relatively more expensive, consumers will switch to the other. A high value for the *XED* indicates that two goods are very close substitutes. This information may be useful in helping a firm to identify its close competitors.

On the other hand, if an increase in the price of one good leads to a fall in the quantity demanded of another good, this suggests that they are likely to be complements. The *XED* in this case will be negative. An example of such a relationship would be that between coffee and sugar, which tend to be consumed together.

Examples

A study by the Institute for Fiscal Studies using data for the UK found that the cross-price elasticity of demand for wine with respect to a change in the price of beer was –0.60, whereas the cross-price elasticity with respect to the price of spirits was +0.77. The negative cross-price elasticity with beer suggests that wine and beer are complements: a 10% increase in the price of beer would lead to a 6% fall in the quantity demanded of wine. In contrast, the cross-price elasticity of demand for wine with respect to the price of spirits is positive, suggesting that wine and spirits are substitutes. An increase in the price of spirits leads to an increase in the quantity demanded of wine.

Summary

➤ The income elasticity of demand (*YED*) measures the sensitivity of quantity demanded to a change in consumer incomes. It serves to distinguish between normal, luxury and inferior goods.

➤ The cross-price elasticity of demand (*XED*) measures the sensitivity of the quantity demanded of one good or service to a change in the price of some other good or service. It can serve to distinguish between substitutes and complements.

Chapter 3

The nature of supply

The previous chapter introduced you to the demand curve. The other key component of the demand and supply model is, of course, supply. For any market transaction, there are two parties, buyers and sellers. The question this chapter considers is what determines the quantity that sellers wish to supply to the market.

Learning outcomes

After studying this chapter, you should:
- ➤ be familiar with the notion of the supply of a good or service
- ➤ be aware of the relationship between the supply of a good and its price in a competitive market
- ➤ understand what is meant by the supply curve and the factors that influence its shape and position
- ➤ be able to distinguish between shifts of the supply curve and movements along it
- ➤ be aware of the effect of taxes and subsidies on the supply curve
- ➤ understand what is meant by the price elasticity of supply

Supply

In discussing demand, the focus of attention was on consumers, and on their willingness to pay for goods and services. In thinking about supply, attention switches to firms, as it is firms that take decisions about how much output to supply to the market. It is important at the outset to be clear about what is meant by a 'firm'. A **firm** exists to organise production: it brings together various factors of production, and organises the production process in order to produce output.

> **Key** term
>
> **firm:** an organisation that brings together factors of production in order to produce output

There are various forms that the organisation of a firm can take. A firm could be a *sole proprietor*: probably a small business, such as a newsagent, where the owner of the firm also runs the firm. A firm could be in the form of a *partnership* — for

example, a dental practice in which profits (and debts) are shared between the partners in the business. Larger firms may be organised as private or public *joint stock companies*, owned by shareholders. The difference between private and public joint stock companies is that the shares of a public joint stock company are traded on the stock exchange, whereas this is not the case with a private company.

In order to analyse how firms decide how much of a product to supply, it is necessary to make an assumption about what it is that firms are trying to achieve. Assume that they aim to maximise their profits, where 'profits' are defined as the difference between a firm's total revenue and its total costs.

As discussed in Chapter 2, the demand curve shows a relationship between quantity demanded and the price of a good or service. A similar relationship between the quantity supplied by firms and the price of a good can be identified in relation to the behaviour of firms in a **competitive market** — that is, a market in which individual firms cannot influence the price of the good or service that they are selling, because of competition from other firms.

Key terms

competitive market: a market in which individual firms cannot influence the price of the good or service they are selling, because of competition from other firms

supply curve: a graph showing the quantity supplied at any given price

In such a market it may well be supposed that firms will be prepared to supply more goods at a high price than at a lower one (ceteris paribus), as this will increase their profits. The **supply curve** illustrates how much the firms in a market will supply at any given price, as shown in Figure 3.1. As firms are expected to supply more goods at a high price than at a lower price, the supply curve will be upward sloping, reflecting this positive relationship between quantity and price.

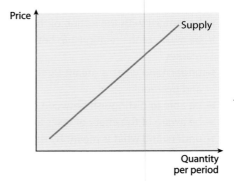

Figure 3.1 *A supply curve*

A movement along the supply curve

A change in the price of a good will induce firms to change their supply decision. For example, consider Figure 3.2. Suppose that initially the price of the good is at P_0. Firms will choose to supply the quantity Q_0 of the good. If the price then falls to P_1, firms will find it less profitable to supply the good, and will reduce their supply, causing a movement along the supply curve to a new quantity at Q_1.

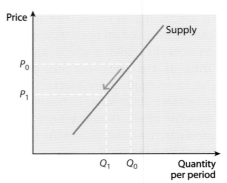

Figure 3.2 *A movement along the supply curve*

Exercise 3.1

The following table shows how the supply of oojits varies with their price. Draw the supply curve.

Price	Quantity
100	98
90	95
80	91
70	86
60	80
50	70
40	60
30	50
20	35
10	18

Table 3.1 The supply of oojits

Notice that the focus of the supply curve is on the relationship between quantity supplied and the price of a good in a given period, ceteris paribus — that is, holding other things constant. As with the demand curve, there are other factors affecting the quantity supplied. These other influences on supply will determine the position of the supply curve: if any of them changes, the supply curve can be expected to shift.

What influences supply?

We can identify five important influences on the quantity that firms will be prepared to supply to the market at any given price:

➤ production costs
➤ the technology of production
➤ taxes and subsidies
➤ the price of related goods
➤ firms' expectations about future prices

Costs and technology

If firms are aiming to maximise profits, an important influence on their supply decision will be the costs of production that they face. Chapter 1 explained that in order to produce output, firms need to use inputs of the factors of production — labour, capital, land etc. If the cost of those inputs increases, firms will in general be expected to supply less output at any given price. The effect of this is shown in Figure 3.3, where an increase in production costs induces firms to supply less output at each price. The curve shifts from its initial position at S_0

Improved technology means firms can produce more cost-effectively

to a new position at S_1. For example, suppose the original price was £10 per unit; before the increase in costs, firms would have been prepared to supply 100 units of the product to the market. An increase in costs of £6 per unit that shifted the supply curve from S_0 to S_1 would mean that, at the same price, firms would now supply only 50 units of the good. Notice that the vertical distance between S_0 and S_1 is the amount of the change in cost per unit.

In contrast, if a new technology of production is introduced, which means that firms can produce more cost-effectively, this could have the opposite effect, shifting the supply curve to the right. This is shown in Figure 3.4, where improved technology induces firms to supply more output at any given price, and the supply curve shifts from its initial position at S_0 to a new position at S_1. Thus, if firms in the initial situation were supplying 50 units with the price at £10 per unit, then a fall in costs of £6 per unit would induce firms to increase supply to 100 units (if the price remained at £10).

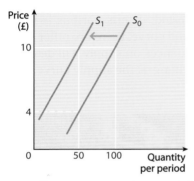

Figure 3.3 The supply curve shifts to the left if production costs increase

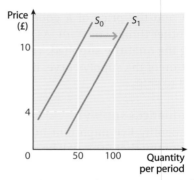

Figure 3.4 The supply curve shifts to the right if production costs fall

Taxes and subsidies

Suppose the government imposes a sales tax such as VAT on a good or service. The price paid by consumers will be higher than the revenue received by firms, as the tax has to be paid to the government. This means that firms will (ceteris paribus) be prepared to supply less output at any given market price. Again, the supply curve shifts to the left. This is shown in panel (a) of Figure 3.5, which assumes a fixed per unit tax. Such a tax is known as a specific tax, and will be discussed in more detail in Chapter 5. The supply curve shifts, as firms supply less at any given market price. On the other hand, if the government pays firms a subsidy to produce a particular good, this will reduce their costs, and induce them to supply more output at any given price. The supply curve will then shift to the right, as shown in panel (b).

Prices of other goods

It was shown earlier that from the consumers' perspective, two goods may be substitutes for each other, such that if the price of one good increases, consumers may be induced to switch their consumption to substitute goods. Similarly, there may be substitution on the supply side. A firm may face a situation in which there

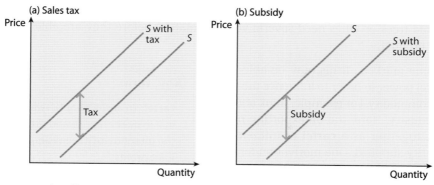

Figure 3.5 *The effects of taxes and subsidies on supply*

are alternative uses to which its factors of production may be put: in other words, it may be able to choose between producing a range of different products. A rise in the price of a good raises its profitability, and therefore may encourage a firm to switch production from other goods. This may happen even if there are high switching costs, provided the increase in price is sufficiently large. For example, a change in relative prices of potatoes and organic swedes might encourage a farmer to stop planting potatoes and grow organic swedes instead.

In other circumstances, a firm may produce a range of goods jointly. Perhaps one good is a by-product of the production process of another. An increase in the price of one of the goods may mean that the firm will produce more of both goods. This notion of joint supply is similar to the situation on the demand side where consumers regard two goods as complements.

Expected prices

Because production takes time, firms often take decisions about how much to supply on the basis of expected future prices. Indeed, if their product is one that can be stored, there may be times when a firm will decide to allow stocks of a product to build up in anticipation of a higher price in the future, perhaps by holding back some of its production from current sales. In some economic activities, expectations about future prices are crucial in taking supply decisions because of the length of time needed in order to increase output. For

Wine producers have to take supply decisions based on expected future prices

example, a firm producing palm oil, rubber or wine needs to be aware that newly planted trees or vines need several years to mature before they are able to yield their product.

In some markets, firms may be able to use market power in order to influence the supply of a commodity. For example, think about the oil industry. Here, the oil-exporting nations work together as a **cartel** to influence the quantity supplied. One motivation for this is to influence price and hence the profits of the members of the cartel.

> **Key term**
>
> **cartel:** an agreement between firms in a market on price and output with the intention of maximising their joint profits

Movements along and shifts of the supply curve: a reminder

As with the demand curve, it is important to remember that there is a distinction between movements *along* the supply curve, and *shifts* *of* the supply curve. If there is a change in the market price, this induces a movement along the supply curve. After all, the supply curve is designed to reveal how firms will react to a change in the price of the good. For example, in Figure 3.6, if the price is initially at P_0 firms will be prepared to supply the quantity Q_0, but if the price then increases to P_1 this will induce a movement along the supply curve as firms increase supply to Q_1.

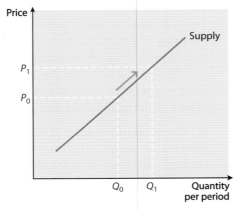

Figure 3.6 *A movement along a supply curve in response to a price change*

In contrast, as seen in the previous section, a change in any of the other influences on supply will induce a shift of the whole supply curve, as this affects the firms' willingness to supply at any given price.

Exercise 3.2

For each of the following, decide whether the demand curve or the supply curve will move, and in which direction:

a Consumers are convinced by arguments about the benefits of organic vegetables.

b A new process is developed that reduces the amount of inputs that firms need in order to produce bicycles.

c There is a severe frost in Brazil that affects the coffee crop.

d The government increases the rate of value added tax.

e Real incomes rise.

f The price of tea falls: what happens in the market for coffee?

g The price of sugar falls: what happens in the market for coffee?

Summary

➤ Other things being equal, firms in a competitive market can be expected to supply more output at a higher price.

➤ The supply curve traces out this positive relationship between price and quantity supplied.

➤ Changes in the costs of production, technology, taxes and subsidies or the prices of related goods may induce shifts of the supply curve, with firms being prepared to sell more (or less) output at any given price.

➤ Expectations about future prices may affect current supply decisions.

Price elasticity of supply

In the previous chapter, the concept of elasticity was introduced as a way of measuring the sensitivity of quantity demanded to any of the components that affect demand. As elasticity is a measure of sensitivity, its use need not be confined to influences on demand, but can also be turned to evaluating the sensitivity of quantity *supplied* to a change in its determinants — price in particular.

It has been argued that the supply curve is likely to be upward sloping, so the price elasticity of supply can be expected to be positive. In other words, an increase in the market price will induce firms to supply more output to the market. The **price elasticity of supply (PES)** is defined as:

> **Key term**
>
> **price elasticity of supply (PES):** a measure of the sensitivity of quantity supplied of a good or service to a change in the price of that good or service

$$PES = \frac{\% \text{ change in the quantity supplied}}{\% \text{ change in price}}$$

An example

Suppose that the price of a good increases from £10 to £12, and that in response, firms increase the quantity supplied from 2,000 units to 2,200 units. What is the price elasticity of supply? First, calculate the percentage changes in price and quantity. Price has changed by $100 \times 2/10 = 20\%$; the quantity supplied has changed by $100 \times 200/2,000 = 10\%$. The price elasticity of supply is therefore $10/20 = 0.5$.

The interpretation of the elasticity is straightforward. If the *PES* is 0.8, an increase in price of 10% will encourage firms to supply 8% more. As with the *PED*, if the elasticity is greater than 1, supply is referred to as being elastic, whereas if the value is between 0 and 1, supply is considered inelastic. *Unit elasticity* occurs when the *PES* is exactly 1, so that a 10% increase in price induces a 10% increase in quantity supplied.

The value of the elasticity will depend on how willing and able firms are to increase their supply. This may depend partly on the technology of the industry, and whether firms have spare capacity that allows them to increase production readily. It may also depend on whether the firm expects the change in price to be permanent or temporary.

The short run and the long run

It is important to realise that it may be more feasible for firms to change their supply decision in the long run than in the short run. For example, if firms are operating close to the capacity of their existing plant and machinery, they may be unable to respond to an increase in price, at least in the short run. So here again, supply can be expected to be more elastic in the long run than in the short run. Figure 3.7 illustrates this. In the short run, firms may be able to respond to an increase in price only in a limited way, and so supply may be relatively inelastic, as shown by S_s in the figure. However, firms can become more flexible in the long run by installing new machinery or building new factories, so supply can then become more elastic, moving to S_l. When analysing the theory of the firm, economists define the short run and the long run in this way, seeing the short run as a period in which the firm is not able to vary its inputs of all factors of production, and the long run as the period in which this becomes possible. In particular, it is often supposed that capital inputs are relatively difficult to vary in the short run, whereas firms may be more able to vary the amount of labour input.

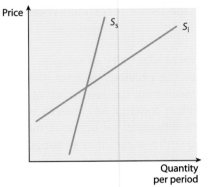

Figure 3.7 *Short- and long-run supply*

Two special cases

There are two limiting cases of supply elasticity. For some reason, supply may be fixed such that, no matter how much price increases, firms will not be able to supply any more. For example, it could be that a certain amount of fish is available in a market, and however high the price goes, no more can be obtained. Equally, if the fishermen know that the fish they do not sell today cannot be stored for another day, they have an incentive to sell however low the price goes. In these cases, supply is perfectly inelastic. At the other extreme is perfectly elastic supply, where firms would be prepared to supply any amount of the good at the going price.

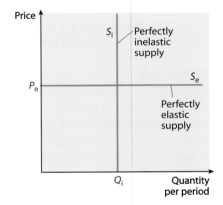

Figure 3.8 *Perfectly elastic and inelastic supply*

These two possibilities are shown in Figure 3.8. Here S_i represents a perfectly inelastic supply curve: firms will supply Q_i whatever the price, perhaps because that is the amount available for sale. Supply here is vertical. At the opposite extreme, if supply is perfectly elastic then firms are prepared to supply any amount at the price P_e, and the supply curve is given by the horizontal line S_e.

Exercise 3.3

Imagine the following scenario. You are considering a pricing strategy for a bus company. The economy is heading into recession, and the company is running at a loss. Your local rail service provider has announced an increase in rail fares. How (if at all) do you use the following information concerning the elasticity of bus travel with respect to various variables to inform your decision on price? Do you raise or lower price?

➤ price elasticity of demand   −1.58
➤ income elasticity of demand   −2.43
➤ cross-price elasticity of demand with respect to rail fares   +2.21
➤ your price elasticity of supply   +1.15

Summary

➤ The price elasticity of supply (*PES*) measures the sensitivity of the quantity supplied to a change in the price of a good or service. The price elasticity of supply can be expected to be greater in the long run than in the short run, as firms have more flexibility to adjust their production decisions in the long run.

Chapter 4

Market equilibrium and price

The previous chapters introduced the notions of demand and supply, and it is now time to bring these two curves together in order to meet the key concept of market equilibrium. The model can then be further developed to see how it provides insights into how markets operate. Indeed, it is time to take a wider view of the process of resource allocation within society. An important question is whether markets can be relied on to guide this process, or whether there are times when markets will fail. This chapter begins to address this by examining how prices can act as market signals to guide resource allocation. In this discussion, some new tools will be needed in order to identify what constitutes an efficient allocation of resources.

Learning outcomes

After studying this chapter, you should:
➤ understand the notion of equilibrium and its relevance in the demand and supply model
➤ be aware of what is meant by comparative static analysis
➤ have an overview of how the price mechanism works to allocate resources
➤ understand the meaning and significance of consumer surplus
➤ be able to see how prices provide incentives to producers
➤ understand the meaning and significance of producer surplus
➤ have an overview of how the price mechanism works to allocate resources
➤ understand the meaning and significance of consumer surplus
➤ be able to see how prices provide incentives to producers
➤ understand the meaning and significance of producer surplus
➤ be aware of the effects of the entry and exit of firms into and out of a market
➤ understand the concepts of productive and allocative efficiency
➤ be familiar with the way in which resources are allocated in a free market economy

Market equilibrium

Chapters 2 and 3 have described the components of the demand and supply model. It only remains to bring them together, for this is how the power of the model can be appreciated. Figure 4.1 shows the demand for and supply of butter.

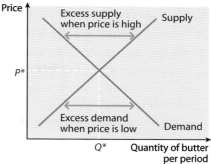

Figure 4.1 *Bringing demand and supply together*

Suppose that the price were to be set at a relatively high price (above P^*). At such a price, firms wish to supply lots of butter to the market. However, consumers are not very keen on butter at such a high price, so demand is not strong. Firms now have a problem: they find that their stocks of butter are building up. What has happened is that the price has been set at a level that exceeds the value that most consumers place on butter, so they will not buy it. There is *excess supply*. The only thing that the firms can do is to reduce the price in order to clear their stocks.

Suppose they now set their price relatively low (below P^*). Now it is the consumers who have a problem, because they would like to buy more butter at the low price than firms are prepared to supply. There is *excess demand*. Some consumers may offer to pay more than the going price in order to obtain their butter supplies, and firms realise that they can raise the price.

How will it all end? When the price settles at P^* in Figure 4.1, there is a balance in the market between the quantity that consumers wish to demand and the quantity that firms wish to supply, namely Q^*. This is the **market equilibrium**. In a free market the price can be expected to converge on this equilibrium level, through movements along both demand and supply curves.

Key term

market equilibrium: a situation that occurs in a market when the price is such that the quantity that consumers wish to buy is exactly balanced by the quantity that firms wish to supply

Exercise 4.1

Identify the equilibrium market price if demand and supply are as in Figure 4.2.

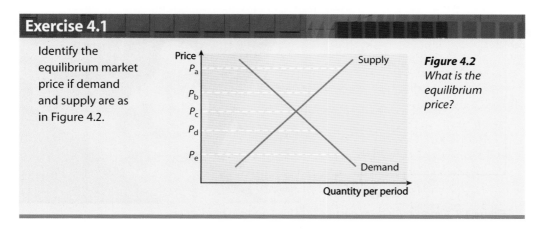

*Figure 4.2
What is the equilibrium price?*

Summary

> Bringing demand and supply together, you can identify the market equilibrium.

> The equilibrium price is the unique point at which the quantity demanded by consumers is just balanced by the quantity that firms wish to supply.

> In a free market, natural forces can be expected to encourage prices to adjust to the equilibrium level.

Comparative statics

In order to make good use of the demand and supply model, it is necessary to introduce another of the economist's key tools — comparative static analysis. You have seen the way in which a market moves towards equilibrium between demand and supply through price adjustments and movements along the demand and supply curves. This is called static analysis, in the sense that a ceteris paribus assumption is imposed by holding constant the factors that influence demand and supply, and focusing on the way in which the market reaches equilibrium.

In the next stage, one of these background factors is changed, and the effect of this change on the market equilibrium is then analysed. In other words, beginning with a market in equilibrium, one of the factors affecting either demand or supply is altered, and the new market equilibrium is then studied. In this way, two static equilibrium positions — before and after — will be compared. This approach is known as **comparative static analysis**.

> **Key term**
>
> **comparative static analysis:** examines the effect on equilibrium of a change in the external conditions affecting a market

A market for dried pasta

Begin with a simple market for dried pasta, a basic staple foodstuff obtainable in any supermarket. Figure 4.3 shows the market in equilibrium. D_0 represents the demand curve in this initial situation, and S_0 is the supply curve. The market is in equilibrium with the price at P_0, and the quantity being traded is Q_0. It is equilibrium in the sense that pasta producers are supplying just the amount of pasta that

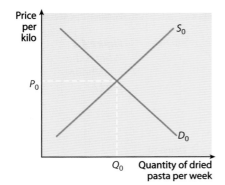

Figure 4.3 A market for dried pasta

Dried pasta in production

James King-Holmes/Pasta Co./Spl

consumers wish to buy at that price. This is the 'before' position. Some experiments will now be carried out with this market by disturbing the equilibrium.

A change in consumer preferences

Suppose that a study is published highlighting the health benefits of eating pasta, backed up with an advertising campaign. The effect of this is likely to be an increase in the demand for pasta at any given price. In other words, this change in consumer preferences will shift the demand curve to the right, as shown in Figure 4.4.

The market now adjusts to a new equilibrium, with a new price P_1, and a new quantity traded at Q_1. In this case, both price and quantity have increased as a result of the change in preferences. There has been a movement along the supply curve.

A change in the price of a substitute

A second possibility is that there is a fall in the price of fresh pasta. This is likely to be a close substitute for dried pasta, so the probable result is that some former consumers of dried pasta will switch their allegiance to the fresh variety. This time the demand curve for dried pasta shifts in the opposite direction, as can be seen in Figure 4.5. Here the starting point is the original position, with market equilibrium at price P_0 and a quantity traded Q_0. After the shift in the demand curve from D_0 to D_2, the market settles again with a price of P_2 and a quantity traded of Q_2. Both price and quantity traded are now lower than in the original position.

An improvement in pasta technology

Next, suppose that a new pasta-making machine is produced, enabling dried pasta makers to produce at a lower cost than before. This advancement reduces firms' costs, and consequently they are prepared to supply more dried pasta at any given price. The starting point is the same initial position, but now it is the supply curve that shifts — to the right. This is shown in Figure 4.6.

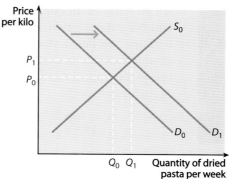

Figure 4.4 *A change in consumer preferences for dried pasta*

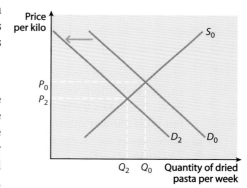

Figure 4.5 *A change in the price of a substitute for dried pasta*

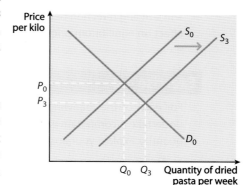

Figure 4.6 *New pasta-making technology*

Again, comparative static analysis can be undertaken. The new market equilibrium is at price P_3, which is lower than the original equilibrium, but the quantity traded is higher at Q_3.

An increase in labour costs

Finally, suppose that pasta producers face an increase in their labour costs. Perhaps the Pasta Workers' Union has negotiated higher wages, or the pasta producers have become subject to stricter health and safety legislation, which raises their production costs. Figure 4.7 starts as usual with equilibrium at price P_0 and quantity Q_0.

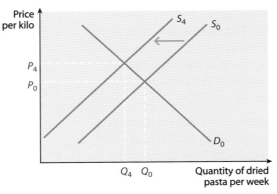

Figure 4.7
An increase in labour costs

The increase in production costs means that pasta producers are prepared to supply less dried pasta at any given price, so the supply curve shifts to the left — to S_4. This takes the market to a new equilibrium at a higher price than before (P_4), but with a lower quantity traded (Q_4).

Summary

➤ Comparative static analysis enables you to analyse the way in which markets respond to external shocks, by comparing market equilibrium before and after a shock.

➤ All you need to do is to figure out whether the shock affects demand or supply, and in which direction.

➤ The size and direction of the shifts of the demand and supply curves determine the overall effect on equilibrium price and quantity traded.

Exercise 4.2

For each of the following market situations, sketch a demand and supply diagram, and undertake a comparative static analysis to see what happens to the equilibrium price and quantity. Explain your answers.

a An increase in consumer incomes affects the demand for bus travel.

b New regulations on environmental pollution force a firm making paint to increase outlay on reducing its emission of toxic fumes.

c A firm of accountants brings in new, faster computers, which have the effect of reducing the firm's costs.

d An outbreak of bird flu causes consumers of chicken to buy burgers instead. (What is the effect on both markets?)

Exercise 4.3 Profits and superships

In August 2001, *The Financial Times* reported that ship-owners were facing serious problems. Shipping rates (the prices that ship-owners charge for carrying freight) had fallen drastically in the second quarter of 2001. For example, on the Europe–Asia route, rates fell by 8% eastbound and 6% westbound, causing the ship-owners' profits to be squeezed. Below are some relevant facts and issues:

a New 'superships', having been ordered a few years earlier, were coming into service with enhanced capacity for transporting freight.

b A worldwide economic slowdown was taking place; Japan was in lengthy recession and the US economy was also slowing, affecting the growth of world trade.

c Fuel prices were falling.

d The structure of the industry is fragmented, with ship-owners watching each other's orders for new ships.

e New ships take a long time to build.

f Shipping lines face high fixed costs with slender margins.

Assume that this is a competitive market. (This will allow you to draw supply and demand curves for the market.) There is some evidence for this, as shipping lines face 'slender margins' (see f). This suggests that the firms face competition from each other, and are unable to use market power to increase profit margins.

How would you expect the demand and supply curves to move in response to the first three factors mentioned (i.e. a, b and c)? Sketch a diagram for yourself.

Why should the shipping lines undertake a large-scale expansion at a time of falling or stagnant demand?

In 2001 shipping rates fell drastically

Prices and resource allocation

The coordination problem

As Chapter 1 indicated, all societies face the fundamental economic problem of scarcity. Because there are unlimited wants but finite resources, it is necessary to take decisions on which goods and services should be produced, how they should be produced and for whom they should be produced. For an economy the size of the UK, there is thus an immense coordination problem. Another way of looking at this is to ask how consumers can express their preferences between alternative goods so that producers can produce the best mix of goods and services.

Some alternative possibilities for handling this problem will now be considered. In a **free market economy**, market forces

> **Key term**
>
> **free market economy:** one in which resource allocation is guided by market forces without intervention by the state

are allowed to allocate resources. At the other extreme, in a centrally planned economy the state plans and directs resources into a range of uses. In between there is the mixed economy. In order to evaluate these alternatives, it is necessary to explore how each of them operates.

In a free market economy, prices play the key role; this is sometimes referred to as the laissez-faire approach to resource allocation.

Prices and preferences

How can consumers signal their preferences to producers? Demand and supply analysis provides the clue. Figure 4.8 shows the demand and supply for laptop computers. These have become popular goods in recent years. That is to say, over time there has been a rightward shift in the demand curve — in the figure, from D_0 to D_1. This simply means that consumers are placing a higher value on these goods; they are prepared to demand more at any given price. The result, as you know from comparative static analysis, is that the market will move to a new equilibrium, with price rising from P_0 to P_1 and quantity traded from Q_0 to Q_1: there is a movement along the supply curve.

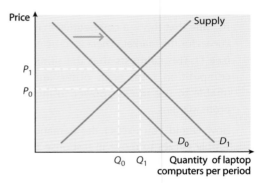

Figure 4.8 *The market for laptop computers*

The shift in the demand curve is an expression of consumers' preferences; it embodies the fact that they value laptop computers more highly now than before. The price that consumers are willing to pay represents their valuation of laptop computers.

Consumer demand for laptops has risen over the last few years

Consumer surplus

Think a little more carefully about what the demand curve represents. Figure 4.9 again shows the demand curve for laptop computers. Suppose that the price is set at P^* and quantity demanded is thus Q^*. P^* can be seen as the value that the last customer places on a laptop. In other words, if the price were even slightly above P^*, there would be one consumer who would choose not to buy: this individual will be referred to as the *marginal consumer*.

To that marginal consumer, P^* represents the marginal benefit derived from consuming this good — it is the price that just reflects the consumer's benefit from a laptop, as it is the price that just induces her to buy. Thinking of the society as a whole (which is made up of all the consumers within it), P^* can be regarded as the **marginal social benefit (MSB)** derived from consuming this good. The same argument could be made about any point along the demand curve, so the demand curve can be interpreted as the marginal benefit to be derived from consuming laptop computers.

In most markets, all consumers face the same prices for goods and services. This leads to an important concept in economic analysis. P^* may represent the value of laptops to the *marginal* consumer, but what about all the other consumers who are also buying laptops at P^*? They would all be willing to pay a higher price for a laptop. Indeed, consumer A in Figure 4.9 would pay a very high price indeed, and thus values a laptop much more highly than P^*. When consumer A pays P^* for a laptop, he gets a great deal, as he values the good so much more highly — as represented by the vertical green line on Figure 4.9. Consumer B also gains a surplus above her willingness to pay (the blue line).

If all these surplus values are added up, they sum to the total surplus that society gains from consuming laptops. This is known as the **consumer surplus**, represented by the shaded triangle in Figure 4.10. It can be interpreted as the welfare that society gains from consuming the good, over and above the price that has to be paid for it.

Key terms

marginal social benefit (MSB): the additional benefit that society gains from consuming an extra unit of a good

consumer surplus: the value that consumers gain from consuming a good or service over and above the price paid

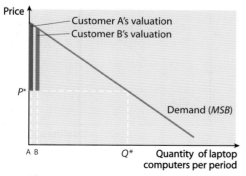

Figure 4.9 *Price as a marginal benefit*

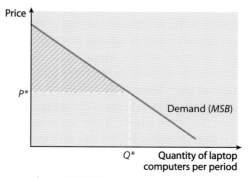

Figure 4.10 *Consumer surplus*

Prices as signals and incentives

From the producers' perspective, the question is how they receive signals from consumers about their changing preferences. Price is the key. Figure 4.8 showed how an increase in demand for laptop computers leads to an increase in the equilibrium market price. The shift in the demand curve leads to an increase in the equilibrium price, which encourages producers to supply more computers — there is a movement *along* the supply curve. This is really saying that producers find it profitable to expand their output of laptop computers at that higher price. The price level is thus a signal to producers about consumer preferences.

Notice that the price signal works equally well when there is a *decrease* in the demand for a good or service. Figure 4.11, for example, shows the market for video recordings. With the advent of DVDs, there has been a large fall in the demand for video recordings, so the demand for them has shifted to the left — consumers are demanding fewer videos at any price. Thus, the demand curve shifts from D_0 to D_1. Producers of video recordings are beginning to find that they cannot sell as many videos at the original price as before, so they have to reduce their price to avoid an increase in their unsold stocks. They have less incentive to produce videos, and will supply less. There is a movement *along* the supply curve to a lower equilibrium price at P_1, and a lower quantity traded at Q_1. You may like to think of this as a movement along the firm's production possibility frontier for DVDs and videos.

Thus, you can see how existing producers in a market receive signals from consumers in the form of changes in the equilibrium price, and respond to these signals by adjusting their output levels.

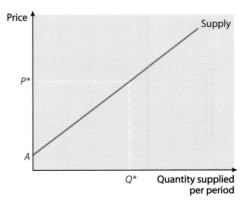

Figure 4.11 *The market for video recordings*

Producer surplus

Parallel to the notion of consumer surplus is the concept of **producer surplus**. Think about the nature of the supply curve: it reveals how much output firms are prepared to supply at any given price in a competitive market. Figure 4.12 depicts a supply curve. Assume the price is at P^*, and that all units are sold at that price. P^* represents the value to firms of the marginal unit sold. In other words, if the price had been set slightly below P^*, the last unit would not have been supplied, as firms would not have found this profitable.

Figure 4.12 *A supply curve*

Notice that the threshold at which a firm will decide it is not profitable to supply is the point at which the price received by the firm reaches the cost to the firm of producing the last unit of the good. Thus, in a competitive market the supply curve reflects **marginal cost**.

The supply curve shows that, in the range of prices between point A and P^*, firms would have been willing to supply positive amounts of this good or service. So at P^*, they would gain a surplus value on all units of the good supplied below Q^*. The total area is shown in Figure 4.13 — it is the area above the supply curve and below P^*, shown as the shaded triangle.

One way of defining this producer surplus is as the surplus earned by firms over and above the minimum that would have kept them in the market. It is the *raison d'être* of firms.

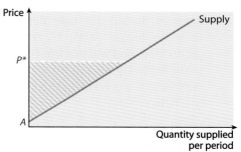

Figure 4.13 Producer surplus

Entry and exit of firms

The discussion so far has focused on the reactions of existing firms in a market to changes in consumer preferences. However, this is only part of the picture. Think back to Figure 4.8, where there was an increase in demand for laptop computers following a change in consumer preferences. The equilibrium price rose, and existing firms expanded the quantity supplied in response. Those firms are now earning a higher producer surplus than before. Other firms not currently in the market will be attracted by these surpluses, perceiving this to be a profitable market in which to operate.

If there are no barriers to entry, more firms will join the market. This in turn will tend to shift the supply curve to the right, as there will then be more firms prepared to supply. As a result, the equilibrium market price will tend to drift down again, until the market reaches a position in which there is no further incentive for new firms to enter the market. This will occur when the rate of return for firms in the laptop market is no better than in other markets.

Figure 4.14 illustrates this situation. The original increase in demand leads, as before,

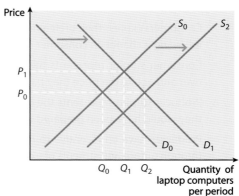

Figure 4.14 The market for laptop computers revisited

to a new equilibrium with a higher price P_1. As new firms join the market in quest of producer surplus, the supply curve shifts to the right to S_2, pushing the price back down to P_0, but with the quantity traded now up at Q_2.

If the original movement in demand is in the opposite direction, as it was for video recordings in Figure 4.11, a similar long-run adjustment takes place. As the market price falls, some firms in the market may decide that they no longer wish to remain in production, and will exit from the market altogether. This will shift the supply curve to the left in Figure 4.15 (to S_2) until only firms that continue to find it profitable will remain in the market. In the final position price is back to P_0, and quantity traded has fallen to Q_2.

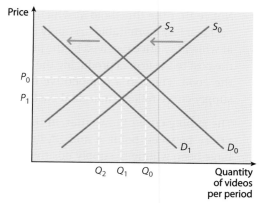

Figure 4.15 *The market for video recordings*

Exercise 4.4

a Sketch a demand and supply diagram and mark on it the areas that represent consumer and producer surplus when the market is in equilibrium.

b Using a demand and supply diagram, explain the process that provides incentives for firms to adjust to a decrease in the demand for fountain pens in a competitive market.

c Think about how you could use demand and supply analysis to explain recent movements in the world price of oil.

Summary

➤ If market forces are to allocate resources effectively, consumers need to be able to express their preferences for goods and services in such a way that producers can respond.

➤ Consumers express their preferences through prices, as prices will adjust to equilibrium levels following a change in consumer demand.

➤ Consumer surplus represents the benefit that consumers gain from consuming a product over and above the price they pay for that product.

➤ Producer surplus represents the benefit gained by firms over and above the price at which they would have been prepared to supply a product.

➤ Producers have an incentive to respond to changes in prices. In the short run this occurs through output adjustments of existing firms (movements along the supply curve), but in the long run firms will enter the market (or exit from it) until there are no further incentives for entry or exit.

Aspects of efficiency

In tackling the fundamental economic problem of scarcity, a society needs to find a way of using its limited resources as effectively as possible. In normal parlance it might be natural to refer to this as a quest for *efficiency*. From an economist's point of view there are two key aspects of efficiency, both of which are important in evaluating whether markets in an economy are working effectively.

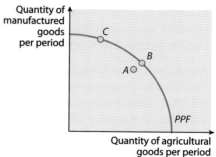

Figure 4.16 *Productive efficiency*

Chapter 1 introduced one of these aspects in relation to the production possibility frontier (*PPF*). Figure 4.16 shows a country's production possibility frontier. One of the choices to be made in allocating resources in this country is between producing agricultural or manufactured goods.

In Chapter 1 it was seen that at a production point such as *A* the economy would not be using its resources fully, since by moving to a point *on* the *PPF* it would be possible to produce more of both types of good. For example, if production took place at point *B*, then more of both agricultural and manufactured goods could be produced, so that society would be better off than at *A*.

A similar claim could be made for any point along the *PPF*: it is more efficient to be at a point *on* the frontier than at some points *within* it. However, if you compare point *B* with point *C*, you will notice that the economy produces more manufactured goods at *C* than at *B* — but only at the expense of producing fewer agricultural goods.

This draws attention to the trade-off between the production of the two sorts of goods. It is difficult to judge whether society is better off at *B* or at *C* without knowing more about the preferences of consumers.

This discussion highlights the two aspects of efficiency. On the one hand, there is the question of whether society is operating on the *PPF*, and thus using its resources effectively. On the other hand, there is the question of whether society is producing the balance of goods that consumers wish to consume. These two aspects of efficiency are known as **productive efficiency** and **allocative efficiency**, and are discussed in more detail below.

Key terms

productive efficiency: attained when a firm operates at minimum average total cost, choosing an appropriate combination of inputs (cost efficiency) and producing the maximum output possible from those inputs (technical efficiency)

allocative efficiency: achieved when society is producing an appropriate bundle of goods relative to consumer preferences

In terms of Figure 4.16, both *B* and *C* are on the *PPF*, so both are productively efficient points, but it is not possible to judge which of the two is better without knowing consumers' preferences.

An efficient point for a society would be one in which no redistribution of resources could make any individual better off without making some other individual worse off. This is known as the *Pareto criterion*, after the nineteenth-century economist Vilfredo Pareto, who first introduced the concept.

Notice, however, that *any* point along the *PPF* is a **Pareto optimum**: with a different distribution of income among individuals in a society, a different overall equilibrium will be reached.

Efficiency in a market

Aspects of efficiency can be explored further by considering an individual market. First, however, it is necessary to identify the conditions under which productive and allocative efficiency can be attained.

Productive efficiency

The production process entails combining a range of inputs of factors of production in order to produce output. Firms may find that there are benefits from large-scale production, so that efficiency may improve as firms expand production.

One way of measuring productive efficiency is in terms of the **average total cost** of production. This is simply the total cost of production divided by the quantity of output produced. Productive efficiency can then be defined in terms of the minimum average cost at which output can be produced, noting that average cost is likely to vary at different scales of output. **Economies of scale** occur when an increase in the scale of production leads to production at lower long-run average cost.

> ### Key terms
>
> **Pareto optimum:** an allocation of resources is said to be a Pareto optimum if no reallocation of resources can make an individual better off without making some other individual worse off
>
> **average total cost:** total cost divided by the quantity produced
>
> **economies of scale:** occur for a firm when an increase in the scale of production leads to production at lower long-run average cost
>
> **technical efficiency:** attaining the maximum possible output from a given set of inputs
>
> **cost efficiency:** the appropriate combination of inputs of factors of production, given the relative prices of those factors

There are two aspects to productive efficiency. One entails making the best possible use of the inputs of factors of production: in other words, it is about producing as much output as possible from a given set of inputs. This is sometimes known as **technical efficiency**. However, there is also the question of whether the *best* set of inputs has been chosen. For example, there may be techniques of production that use mainly capital and not much labour, and alternative techniques that are more labour intensive. The firm's choice between these techniques will depend crucially on the relative prices of capital and labour. This is sometimes known as **cost efficiency**.

To attain productive efficiency, both technical efficiency and cost efficiency need to be achieved. In other words, productive efficiency is attained when a firm chooses the appropriate combination of inputs (cost efficiency) and produces the maximum output possible from those inputs (technical efficiency).

It is worth noting that the choice of technique of production may depend crucially upon the level of output that the firm wishes to produce. The balance of factors of production may well change according to the scale of activity. If the firm is producing very small amounts of output, it may well choose a different combination of capital and labour than if it were planning mass production on a large scale.

Thus, the firm's decision process is a three-stage procedure. First, the firm needs to decide how much output it wants to produce. Second, it has to choose an appropriate combination of factors of production, given that intended scale of production. Third, it needs to produce as much output as possible, given those inputs. Once the intended scale of output has been decided, the firm has to minimise its costs of production. These decisions are part of the response to the question of *how* output should be produced. Remember also the concept of *marginal cost*, which refers to the cost faced by a firm in changing the output level by a small amount. This becomes an important part of the discussion.

Allocative efficiency

Allocative efficiency is about whether an economy allocates its resources in such a way as to produce a balance of goods and services that matches consumer preferences. In a complex modern economy, it is clearly difficult to identify such an ideal result. How can an appropriate balance of goods and services be identified?

Take the market for an individual product, such as the market for laptop computers that was considered earlier in the chapter. It was then argued that in the long run, the market could be expected to arrive at an equilibrium price and quantity at which there was no incentive for firms either to enter the market or to exit from it. Figure 4.17 will remind you of the market situation.

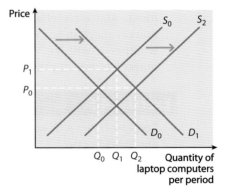

Figure 4.17 *The market for laptop computers revisited again*

The sequence of events in the diagram shows that, from an initial equilibrium with price at P_0 and quantity traded at Q_0, there was an increase in demand, with the demand curve shifting to D_1. In response, existing firms expanded their supply, moving up the supply curve. However, the lure of the producer surplus (abnormal profits) that was being made by these firms then attracted more firms into the market, such that the supply curve shifted to S_2, a process that brought the price back down to the original level of P_0.

Now think about that price from the point of view of a firm. P_0 is at a level where there is no further incentive to attract new firms, but no firm wishes to leave the market. In other words, no surplus is being made on that marginal unit, and the

marginal firm is just breaking even on it. The price in this context would seem to be just covering the marginal cost of production.

However, it was also argued that from the consumers' point of view any point along the demand curve could be regarded as the marginal benefit received from consuming a good or service.

Where is all this leading? Putting together the arguments, it would seem that market forces can carry a market to a position in which, from the firms' point of view, the price is equal to marginal cost, and from the consumers' point of view, the price is equal to marginal benefit.

This is an important result. Suppose that the marginal benefit from consuming a good were higher than the marginal cost to society of producing it. It could then be argued that society would be better off producing more of the good because, by increasing production, more could be added to benefits than to costs. Equally, if the marginal cost were above the marginal benefit from consuming a good, society would be producing too much of the good and would benefit from producing less. The best possible position is thus where marginal benefit is equal to marginal cost — in other words, where *price is set equal to marginal cost.*

If all markets in an economy operated in this way, resources would be used so effectively that no reallocation of resources could generate an overall improvement. Allocative efficiency would be attained. The key question is whether the market mechanism will work sufficiently well to ensure that this happens — or whether it will fail. In other words, are there conditions that could arise in a market, in which price would not be set at marginal cost?

Exercise 4.5

Consider Figure 4.18, which shows a production possibility frontier (*PPF*) for an economy that produces consumer goods and investment goods.

Identify each of the following (Hint: in some cases more than one answer is possible):

a a point of productive inefficiency
b a point that is Pareto-superior to B
c a point of productive efficiency
d a point of allocative efficiency
e an unattainable point (Hint: think about what would need to happen for society to reach such a point)

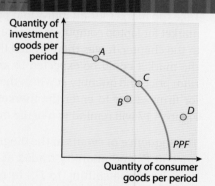

Figure 4.18 *A production possibility frontier*

The working of a market economy

The previous section showed that the price mechanism allows a society to allocate its resources effectively if firms respond to changes in prices. Consumers express changes in their preferences by their decisions to buy (or not to buy) at the going price, which leads to a change in the equilibrium price. Firms thus respond to changes in consumer demand, given the incentive of profitability, which is related to price. In the short run, existing firms adjust their output levels along the supply curve. In the long run, firms enter into markets (or exit from them) in response to the relative profitability of the various economic activities that take place in the economy. But how does this work out in practice in a 'real-life' economy?

One way of viewing this system is through the notion of opportunity cost, introduced in Chapter 1. For example, in choosing to be active in the market for video recordings, a firm faces an opportunity cost. If it uses its resources to produce video recordings, it is *not* using those resources to produce DVDs. There may come a point at which the cost of producing video recordings becomes too high, if the profitability of DVDs is so much higher than that for video recordings, because of changes in the pattern of consumer demand. When the firm finds that it is not covering its opportunity costs, it will transfer production from the video market to the DVD market.

This sort of system of resource allocation is often referred to as **capitalism**. The key characteristic of capitalism is that individuals own the means of production, and can pursue whatever activities they choose — subject, of course, to the legal framework within which they operate.

The government's role in a free capitalist economy is relatively limited, but nonetheless important. A basic framework of *property rights* is essential, together with a basic legal framework. However, the state does not intervene in the production process directly. Secure property rights are significant, as this assures the incentives for the owners of capital.

> **Key terms**
>
> **capitalism:** a system of production in which there is private ownership of productive resources, and individuals are free to pursue their objectives with minimal interference from government
>
> **invisible hand:** term used by Adam Smith to describe the way in which resources are allocated in a market economy

Within such a system, consumers try to maximise the satisfaction they gain from consuming a range of products, and firms seek to maximise their profits by responding to consumer demand through the medium of price signals.

As has been shown, this is a potentially effective way of allocating resources. In the eighteenth century Adam Smith discussed this mechanism, arguing that when consumers and firms respond to incentives in this way resources are allocated effectively through the operation of an **invisible hand**, which guides firms to produce the goods and services that consumers wish to consume. Although individuals pursue their self-interest, the market mechanism ensures that their actions will bring about a good result for society overall. A solution to the coordination problem is thus found through the free operation of markets. Such market adjustments provide a solution to Samuelson's three fundamental economic questions of what? how? and for whom?

However, Adam Smith also sounded a word of warning. He felt that there were too many factors that interfered with the free market system, such as over-protectionism and restrictions on trade. At the same time, he was not utterly convinced that a free market economy would be wholly effective, noting also that firms might at times collude to prevent the free operation of the market mechanism:

> People of the same trade seldom meet together, even for merriment and diversion, but the conversation ends in a conspiracy against the public, or in some contrivance to raise prices... (Adam Smith, *The Wealth of Nations*, Vol. I)

So there may be situations in which consumer interests need to be protected, if there is some sort of market failure that prevents the best outcome from being achieved. This will be explored in Chapters 7 and 8.

Summary

- A society needs to find a way of using its limited resources as efficiently as possible.
- Productive efficiency occurs when firms have chosen appropriate combinations of factors of production and produce the maximum output possible from those inputs.
- Allocative efficiency occurs when firms produce an appropriate bundle of goods and services, given consumer preferences.
- An allocation of resources is said to be a Pareto optimum if no reallocation of resources can make an individual better off without making some other individual worse off.
- An individual market exhibits aspects of allocative efficiency when the marginal benefit received by society from consuming a good or service matches the marginal cost of producing it — that is, when price is equal to marginal cost.
- Free markets do not always lead to the best possible allocation of resources: there may be market failure.

Chapter 5

The price mechanism in action

In the previous chapters, you have seen how the demand and supply model can be used in order to analyse market situations. It is now time to begin to apply this model in a variety of circumstances to see how it provides insights about how different markets operate. You will encounter demand and supply in a wide variety of contexts, and begin to glimpse some of the ways in which the model can help to explain how the economic world works. You will also see how government intervention in the form of indirect taxation and subsidies can affect markets.

Learning outcomes

After studying this chapter, you should be able to:
- ➤ apply demand and supply analysis in a variety of different market situations
- ➤ analyse the effect of taxes and subsidies in a market, using demand and supply analysis
- ➤ evaluate the extent to which a sales tax is borne by buyers and sellers
- ➤ use demand and supply analysis to interpret economic events in the real world

All the examples of demand and supply discussed so far were consumer goods of some sort — DVDs, butter, pencils and so on. However, it would be wrong to think that demand and supply analysis is of relevance only in that sort of market. So this chapter broadens the horizons, looking beyond consumer goods markets to markets for housing, labour and exchange rates.

Agricultural markets

The markets for agricultural produce have some interesting characteristics that can be analysed with the demand and supply model. One particular characteristic of many such markets is that the supply side of the market can be strongly affected by weather and climate, sometimes in random or unpredictable ways.

The supply side of a market can be strongly affected by weather and climate

This can create conditions in which it is difficult to forecast market outcomes in advance. In particular, this means that prices can vary quite widely from year to year, making conditions in agricultural markets difficult to predict. For some commodities attempts can be made to stabilise prices by storing surplus produce in good years to sell in bad years. This is discussed in Chapter 8.

Exercise 5.1

In April 2003 South East Asia was suffering from an outbreak of the SARS virus which had spread around the region. On 20 April one of the main wholesale fruit and vegetable markets in Singapore, at Pasir Panjang, had to be closed when workers were found to have been infected. Sketch a demand and supply diagram to predict how the retail market for vegetables was affected.

Commodity markets

Another category of market that is of particular interest is the one for commodities. This encompasses markets for various types of raw material used in the production process of many manufacturing industries. Prices in these markets too can be volatile, but this time the volatility arises from the demand side of the market.

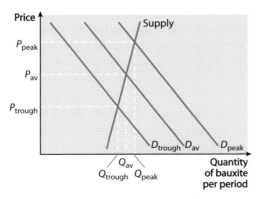

Figure 5.1
The market for bauxite

Figure 5.1 shows the market for bauxite, a commodity used as a raw material in the production of aluminium. Many countries experience fluctuations in the overall level of economic activity over time. There are periods of boom and periods of recession. The demand for aluminium (and hence for bauxite) tends to vary with these cycles of activity. D_{av} here represents the average position of the demand curve for bauxite. At the peak of the cycle demand is high and the price rises to

P_{peak}, but at the trough of the cycle prices fall to P_{trough}. The quantity traded does not vary very much. This is because the figure has been drawn showing supply to be relatively inelastic, so the main burden of adjustment to market equilibrium takes place through the price level.

Such markets are sometimes complicated by the existence of *futures markets*, in which commodities can be bought in the present period for delivery at a future date at prices agreed now. This adds a speculative element to the demand.

Exercise 5.2

The Financial Times in March 1998 reported that the Jamaican bauxite industry was experiencing a combination of record output and falling revenues. It seems that capacity in the industry was rising, and improved labour relations were increasing productivity. However, there was considerable uncertainty in the market, with weak demand for aluminium, following the Asian financial crisis. On the basis of this information, sketch a demand and supply diagram to show the market situation. From your diagram, would you expect price to increase or decrease? How about quantity?

A commodity market that has been much discussed in recent years has been the market for oil. This is seen as being especially significant for the global economy because oil is so important for the functioning of other markets, especially transport. The price of oil over time has followed something of an erratic path, as you can see in Figure 5.2. The Organisation of Petroleum Exporting Countries (OPEC) has played an influential role in the way that prices have evolved over time, but other factors have also been important. OPEC is an organisation that operates as a producer **cartel**. A cartel is an agreement between firms in a market on price and output with the intention of maximising their joint profits. Although such agreements are illegal in countries such as the UK or the USA, OPEC is an agreement between nation producers, so is less easy to regulate. Cartel agreements can interfere with the free working of the price mechanism.

> **Key term**
>
> **cartel:** an agreement between firms in a market on price and output with the intention of maximising their joint profits

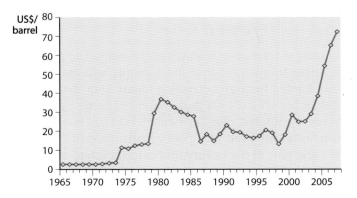

Figure 5.2
The price of oil, 1965–2007

Although this may not be a freely operating competitive market, demand and supply analysis can still help in the interpretation of how this market has evolved over time. Before the first so-called 'oil-price crisis' of 1973/74, the price of oil had been stable over a long period. Two events occurred in the early 1970s that affected the supply side of the oil market. One was the Yom Kippur War (1973) that interrupted the supply of oil from the Middle East. The second was a decision by OPEC to restrict supply. With demand being relatively inelastic, the disruption to supply resulted in a substantial increase in the price of oil.

Demand was inelastic in the short run because consumers had become accustomed to relatively low prices, and could not adjust demand quickly. For example, in the UK many houses were heated through oil-fired central heating. In addition, cars of the day were relatively fuel-inefficient. As time went by, new houses were no longer built with oil-fired heating, and cars became more efficient in their use of petrol. In other words, demand was less inelastic in the longer term.

You can see, therefore, that the first major oil price increase was supply-driven. This was also the case for the second crisis, which took place in 1979/80, when OPEC again decided to reduce supply. Looking at Figure 5.2, the sudden fall in oil prices in the mid-1980s was also the result of an oil price shock, when Saudi Arabia increased its supply of oil, leading to a fall in the price of oil.

The price rises of oil in the early 2000s arose in a rather different way. There were again some supply-side influences, such as the Iraq War. However, there were also effects on the demand side, in particular with the rapid economic growth that was taking place in China. You may find it helpful to sketch some demand and supply diagrams to analyse the effects of these changes in the oil market for yourself.

The housing market

Everyone needs somewhere to live, and housing makes up a large part of the household budget. This makes the housing market particularly important in any economy. Here too, demand and supply can be used to explain how the market operates.

The housing market is not in fact a single market, as there are different segments that may operate in quite different ways. There is the owner–occupier market and the private and public rental sectors. Of course these segments interact in some ways, but they may be influenced by different factors.

The owner–occupier housing market often features in the news. The purchase of a house is the largest single transaction that most people will make in their lifetimes, and is normally funded through borrowing (apart from the occasional lottery win!) The demand for houses to buy is thus influenced partly by the cost of borrowing — in other words, the interest rate. Later chapters of this book will cover the way in which interest rates are used as a policy instrument to stabilise the overall economy. In the early part of the twenty-first century interest rates have been relatively low by historical standards, and this has encouraged borrowing, which has fed into the demand for houses, pushing the demand curve to the right.

At the same time, the supply of houses has been expanding only slowly — at least in some regions. Building takes time, of course, but also there have been environmental concerns, and the resulting regulation has limited the growth of the housing stock by restricting the amount of new stock to be built.

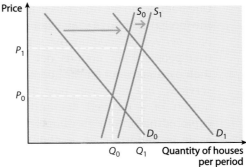

Figure 5.3 *The market for houses for owner occupation*

Figure 5.3 sketches how this might be seen in terms of demand and supply. Demand increases rapidly, but supply expands relatively slowly. The result is an increase in the equilibrium price, from P_0 to P_1, with only a modest expansion of supply, from Q_0 to Q_1. The late 1990s and the early part of this century did indeed see a rapid increase in house prices, and there has been much speculation that they were rising too rapidly to be sustainable. The importance of housing in everyone's lives makes this an important issue.

Demand and supply may help to explain why house prices have been rising. However, there are other factors to be considered before arriving at a complete explanation of the market.

The foreign exchange market

When you take your holidays in Spain you need to buy euros. Equally, when German tourists come to visit London they need to buy pounds. If there is buying going on, then there must be a market — remember from Chapter 1 that a market is a set of arrangements that enable transactions to be undertaken. So here is another sort of market to be considered. The exchange rate is the price at which two currencies exchange, and it can be analysed using demand and supply.

Consider the market for pounds, and focus on the exchange rate between pounds and euros, as shown in Figure 5.4. Think first of all about what gives rise to a demand for pounds. It is not just German tourists who need pounds to spend on holiday: anyone holding euros who wants to buy British goods needs pounds in order to pay for them. So the demand for pounds comes from people in the euro area who want to buy British goods or services — or assets. When the exchange rate for the pound in euros is high, potential buyers of British goods get relatively few pounds per euro so the demand will be relatively low, whereas if the euro per pound rate is relatively low, they get more for their money. Hence the demand curve is expected to be downward sloping.

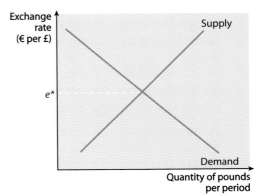

Figure 5.4 *The market for pounds sterling*

One point to notice from this is that the foreign exchange is an example of a *derived demand*, in the sense that people want pounds not for their own sake, but for the goods or services that they can buy. This notion of a derived demand is explored more fully in Chapter 6, as it is important in explaining the demand for labour. One way of viewing the exchange rate is as a means by which to learn about the

Ingram

Currencies are traded on the foreign exchange market

international competitiveness of British exports. When the exchange rate is high British goods are less competitive in Europe, ceteris paribus. Notice the ceteris paribus assumption there. This is important, because the exchange rate is not the only determinant of the competitiveness of British goods: they also depend on the relative price levels in the UK and Europe.

How about the supply of pounds? Pounds are supplied by UK residents wanting euros to buy goods or services from Europe. From this angle, when the euro/pound rate is high UK residents get more euros for their pounds, and therefore will tend to supply more pounds.

If the exchange market is in equilibrium, the exchange rate will tend to e^*, where the demand for pounds is matched by the supply.

The stock market

Another important financial market is the stock market. Firms that want to raise funds for investing in new machinery or other projects can do so by issuing 'stocks', which are then sold on the stock market. People wanting a good return on their savings may then purchase stocks and shares in the hope of receiving good dividends (sharing in the profits of the firm), or capital gains as the value of the firm (hopefully) rises with success.

Although this may sound as if it is a quite different sort of market, it too can be analysed by using demand and supply analysis. The demand for stocks comes from savers looking for a return, so the strength of demand will depend on their expectations of the future success of the firm, and future movements in the price of the stock, which will affect the capital gain. The supply will depend on firms' expectations of the future demand for the product, which will determine whether or not they are keen to invest in new capital goods.

The interaction of demand and supply will thus determine the price of the stock in the market. However, notice how important expectations are on both sides of the market. This suggests that there will be substantial uncertainty surrounding market conditions. One result of this is that there could be some instability in the positions of both demand and supply, especially where people react strongly to news about the markets. If people suddenly come to believe that stock prices are about to tumble, perhaps because of gloomy forecasts about the economy, then demand is likely to fall as savers move their funds to alternative financial assets. Demand and supply analysis then predicts that prices will fall — all because people expect this to happen. In other words, the stock market could be characterised by self-fulfilling expectations.

The labour market

Within the economy, firms demand labour and employees supply labour — so why not use demand and supply to analyse the market? This can indeed be done. Chapter 6 is devoted to examining some interesting and important features of the labour market.

Indirect taxes and subsidies

One final application of the demand and supply model is to analyse the effect on a market of the imposition of **indirect taxes** and subsidies.

In the UK, value added tax (VAT) is the most prominent example of an indirect tax, although other levies, such as excise duties on alcohol and tobacco, are also indirect taxes. An indirect tax is paid by the seller, so affects the supply curve for a product.

Key term

indirect tax: a tax levied on expenditure on goods or services (as opposed to a direct tax, which is a tax charged directly to an individual based on a component of income)

Figure 5.5 illustrates the case of a fixed rate, or specific tax — a tax that is set at a constant amount per pack of cigarettes. Without the tax, the market equilibrium is at the intersection of demand and supply, with price P_0, and quantity traded Q_0. The effect of the tax is to reduce the quantity that firms are prepared to supply at any given price; to put it another way, for any given quantity of cigarettes, firms need to receive the amount of the tax over and above the price at which they would have been prepared to supply that quantity. The effect is thus to move the supply curve upwards by the amount of the tax, as shown in the figure. A new equilibrium is reached with a higher price at P_1 and a lower quantity traded at Q_1.

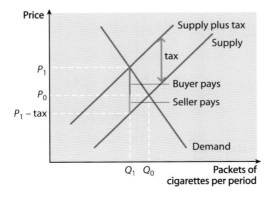

Figure 5.5 The effects of an indirect tax on cigarettes

An important question is: who bears the burden of the tax? If you look at the diagram, you will see that the price difference between the with- and without-tax situations (i.e. $P_1 - P_0$) is less than the amount of the tax, which is the vertical distance between the with and without supply curves. So, although the seller may be responsible for the mechanics of paying the tax, part of the tax is effectively passed on to the buyer in the form of the higher price. So the **incidence of the tax** falls partly upon the seller, but in Figure 5.5 most of the tax is borne by the buyer.

The price elasticity of demand determines the incidence of the tax. If demand were perfectly inelastic, sellers would be able to pass the whole burden of the tax on to buyers through an increase in price equal to the value of the tax, knowing that this would not affect demand. However, if demand were perfectly elastic sellers would not be able to raise the price at all, so they would have to bear the entire burden of the tax.

If the tax is not a constant amount, but a percentage of the price (known as an *ad valorem* tax), the supply curve is still affected; but now it steepens, as shown in Figure 5.6.

In some situations the government may wish to encourage production of a particular good or service, perhaps because it views the good as having strategic significance to the country. One way it can do this is by giving **subsidies**.

Such subsidies have been especially common in agriculture, which is often seen as being of strategic significance. In the early years of this century the USA has come under pressure to reduce the subsidies that it grants to cotton producers. Analytically, a subsidy can be regarded as a sort of negative indirect tax that shifts the supply curve down, as shown in Figure 5.7. Without the subsidy, market equilibrium is at price P_0 and quantity traded Q_0. With the subsidy in place, the equilibrium price falls to P_1 and the quantity traded increases to Q_1.

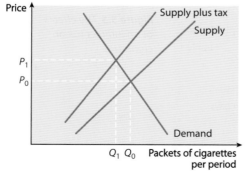

Figure 5.6 *The effects of an* ad valorem *tax on cigarettes*

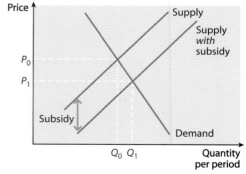

Figure 5.7 *The effects of a subsidy*

Again, notice that, because the price falls by less than the amount of the subsidy, the benefits of the subsidy are shared between buyers and sellers, depending on the elasticity of demand. If the aim of the subsidy is to increase production, it is only partially successful — the degree of success also depends on the elasticity of demand.

Summary

> In agricultural markets supply can fluctuate between seasons because of weather conditions. This causes volatility in prices.

> In commodity markets demand may fluctuate across the business cycle, again causing volatility in prices.

> The oil market has been highly influential because of the importance of oil as a source of energy.

> The housing market can be analysed using demand and supply analysis. The level of demand may be influenced by government policy on interest rates.

> Demand and supply enable you to examine how the foreign exchange rate is determined.

> The stock market is another market to which demand and supply analysis can be applied.

> An indirect tax levied on a good or service will be seen as a shift in the supply curve. The incidence of the tax (whether the burden is borne by buyers or sellers) is determined by the elasticity of demand.

Chapter 6

The market for labour

An important market in any economy is the market for labour, and no doubt you will one day be part of that market, if you are not already. Labour is a crucial factor of production for firms, so the demand for labour comes from firms wanting to hire workers. People need to work in order to earn income, which is done through the medium of supplying labour. In this chapter, you will see the way in which the demand for labour from firms and the supply of labour by workers come together in the labour market. The chapter also discusses the nature of equilibrium in the labour market, and some reasons why it might not always be possible to reach equilibrium.

Learning outcomes

After studying this chapter, you should be able to:
- ➤ understand the factors which influence the demand and supply of labour
- ➤ appreciate that the demand for labour is a derived demand
- ➤ be aware of the importance of the migration of people in influencing the supply of labour
- ➤ use demand and supply analysis to examine the effects of government policies that affect the labour market
- ➤ be familiar with the effect that trade unions have on the operation of the labour market

The demand for labour

What do firms do and why do they demand labour? In Chapter 3, a firm was defined as 'an organisation that brings together factors of production in order to produce output'. The aim of a firm, therefore, is to produce output to sell in order to generate revenue and make profits. Labour is one of the key factors of production used by firms as part of this process.

This means that firms do not demand labour for its own sake, but for the sake of the revenue that is obtained from selling the output that labour produces. The demand for labour is thus an example of a **derived demand**, and understanding this is crucial for an analysis of the labour market.

In analysing the demand for a good or a service, an important tool was the demand curve, which showed the relationship between the quantity demanded of a good and its price. In order to analyse the market for labour, a similar tool is required to show the relationship between the quantity of labour that a firm will demand and its price. Of course, in order to be able to draw such a curve, it is important to be able to identify what the 'price' of labour is. A moment's thought will suggest that this can be represented by the wage rate — the price that a firm must pay in order to obtain a certain amount of labour.

If the price of labour is relatively low, then firms will tend to demand more of it than when the price is high, because the profit that will be made from selling the output produced will be higher. Figure 6.1 shows a demand curve for labour. It is downward sloping.

Key term

derived demand: demand for a good or service not for its own sake, but for what it produces — for example, labour is demanded for the output that it produces

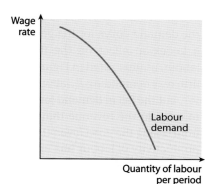

Figure 6.1 The demand for labour

The demand curve for labour shows the relationship between the quantity of labour demanded by firms and the wage rate. However, the wage rate is not the only factor that affects the demand for labour, and just as with a demand curve for a good, there are other factors that will influence the *position* of the demand curve for labour.

Factors affecting the position of the demand for labour curve

There are a number of factors that determine the *position* of a firm's labour demand curve. Remember that the demand for labour is a derived demand, so firms demand labour for the sake of the output that labour produces. This suggests that the amount of output that labour is able to produce will be an important factor. If labour becomes more productive for some reason, then this will lead to an increase in the demand for labour. For example, if a new technological advance raises the productivity of labour, it will also affect the position of the labour demand curve. In Figure 6.2, you can see how the demand for labour would shift if there were an increase in the productivity of labour as a result of new technology. Initially, demand is at D_{L0}, but the increased technology pushes the curve

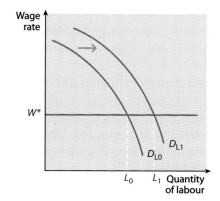

Figure 6.2 The effect of improved technology

to D_{L1}. If the wage remains at W^*, the quantity of labour hired by the firm increases from L_0 to L_1. Similarly, in the long run, if a firm expands the size of its capital stock, this will also affect the demand for labour.

It can also be seen that because the demand for labour is a derived demand, a change in the revenue that the firm receives from selling the output that labour produces will affect the demand for labour. For example, suppose that in a competitive market, the equilibrium price of a good falls — perhaps as a result of a shift in the demand curve for the good. This will have a knock-on effect on the firm's demand for labour, as illustrated in Figure 6.3. Initially, the firm was demanding L_0 labour at the wage rate W^*, but the fall in demand for the product leads to a fall in the revenue that the firm receives from selling the good (even though the physical

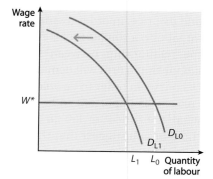

Figure 6.3 *The effect of a fall in the demand for a firm's product on the demand for labour*

productivity of labour has not changed), so the labour demand curve shifts from D_{L0} to D_{L1}. Only L_1 labour is now demanded at the wage rate W^*. It is important to understand that this arises because the demand for labour is a derived demand that is intimately bound up with the demand for the firm's product.

There are a number of possible reasons that could underlie a change in the price of a firm's product — it could reflect changes in the price of other goods, changes in consumer incomes or changes in consumer preferences. All of these indirectly affect the demand for labour.

Summary

> The demand for labour is a derived demand, as the firm wants labour not for its own sake, but for the output that it produces.

> The firm has a downward-sloping demand curve for labour.

> The position of the firm's labour demand curve depends on such factors as technology and efficiency, but also on the price of the firm's product.

Elasticity of the demand for labour

In addition to the factors affecting the *position* of the demand for labour curve, it is also important to examine its *shape*. In particular, what factors affect the firm's elasticity of demand for labour with respect to changes in the wage rate? In other words, how sensitive is a firm's demand for labour to a change in the wage rate (the cost of labour)?

Chapter 2 examined the influences on the price elasticity of demand, and identified the most important as being the availability of substitutes, the relative size of expenditure on a good in the overall budget and the time period over which the

elasticity is measured. In looking at the elasticity of demand for labour, similar influences can be seen to be at work.

One significant effect on the elasticity of demand for labour is the extent to which other factors of production such as capital can be substituted for labour in the production process. If capital or some other factor can be readily substituted for labour, then an increase in the wage rate (ceteris paribus) will induce the firm to reduce its demand for labour by relatively more than if there were no substitute for labour. The extent to which labour and capital are substitutable varies between economic activities, depending on the technology of production, as there may be some sectors in which it is relatively easy for labour and capital to be substituted, and others in which it is quite difficult.

Second, the share of labour costs in the firm's total costs is important in determining the elasticity of demand for labour. In many service activities labour is a highly significant share of total costs, so firms tend to be sensitive to changes in the cost of labour. However, in some capital-intensive manufacturing activity labour may comprise a much smaller share of total production costs.

Third, capital will tend to be inflexible in the short run. Therefore, if a firm faces an increase in wages it may have little flexibility in substituting towards capital in the short run, so the demand for labour may be relatively inelastic. However, in the longer term the firm will be able to adjust the factors of production towards a different overall balance. Therefore, the elasticity of demand for labour is likely to be higher in the long run than in the short run.

In many service activities labour is a highly significant share of total costs

These three influences closely parallel the analysis of what affects the price elasticity of demand. However, as the demand for labour is a derived demand, there is an additional influence that must be taken into account: the price elasticity of demand for the product. The more price-elastic is demand for the product, the more sensitive will the firm be to a change in the wage rate, as high elasticity of demand for the product limits the extent to which an increase in wage costs can be passed on to consumers in the form of higher prices.

In order to derive an industry demand curve for labour, it is necessary to add up the quantities of labour that firms in that industry would want to demand at any given wage rate, given the price of the product. As individual firms' demand curves are downward sloping, the industry demand curve will also slope downwards. In other words, more labour will be demanded at a lower wage rate, as shown in Figure 6.4.

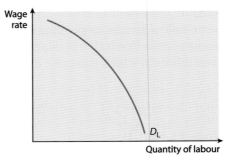

Figure 6.4 *An industry demand for labour curve*

Summary

> The elasticity of demand for labour depends on the degree to which capital may be substituted for labour in the production process.

> The share of labour in a firm's total costs will also affect the elasticity of demand for labour.

> Labour demand will tend to be more elastic in the long run than in the short run, as the firm needs time to adjust its production process following a change in market conditions.

> As the demand for labour is a derived demand, the elasticity of labour demand will also depend on the price elasticity of demand for the firm's product.

Exercise 6.1

Using diagrams, explain how each of the following will affect a firm's demand for labour:

a a fall in the selling price of the firm's product
b adoption of improved working practices, which improve labour productivity
c an increase in the wage (in a situation where the firm must accept the wage as market determined)
d an increase in the demand for the firm's product

Labour supply

On the supply side of the labour market, it is important to consider the factors that will influence the quantity of labour that workers wish to supply. Again, it may be supposed that this will depend partly on the wage rate. It is useful to think of the supply of labour first in terms of an individual worker, and then in terms of an industry.

Individual labour supply

For an individual worker, the wage rate may be seen as the return for providing labour hours. At a higher wage rate, the worker receives more income and may therefore be induced to supply more hours of labour. In this case, the individual supply of labour curve is expected to be upward sloping, as the example in Figure 6.5.

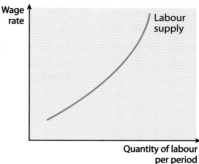

Figure 6.5 *An individual's supply of labour*

Extension material

Consider an individual worker who is deciding how many hours of labour to supply. As with other economic decisions, you need to be aware that every choice comes with an opportunity cost. If a worker chooses to take more leisure time, he/she is choosing to forgo income-earning opportunities. In other words, the wage rate can be seen as the opportunity cost of leisure. It is the income that the worker has to sacrifice in order to enjoy leisure time.

Now think about the likely effects of an increase in the wage rate. Such an increase raises the opportunity cost of leisure. This in turn has two effects. First, as leisure time is now more costly, there will be a substitution effect against leisure. In other words, workers will be motivated to work longer hours.

However, as the higher wage brings the worker a higher level of real income, a second effect comes into play, encouraging the consumption of more goods and services — including leisure, if it is assumed that leisure is a normal good.

Notice that these two effects work against each other. The substitution effect encourages workers to offer more labour at a higher wage because of the effect of the change in the opportunity cost of leisure. However, the real income effect encourages the worker to demand more leisure as a result of the increase in income. The net effect could go either way.

It might be argued that at relatively low wages the substitution effect will tend to be the stronger. However, as the wage continues to rise, the income effect may gradually become stronger, so that at some wage level the worker will choose to supply less labour and will demand more leisure. The individual labour supply curve will then be backward bending, as shown in Figure 6.6, where an increase in the wage rate above W* induces the individual to supply fewer hours of work in order to enjoy more leisure time.

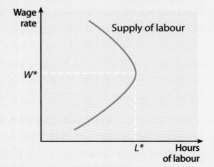

Figure 6.6 *A backward-bending individual labour supply curve*

Industry labour supply

At industry level, the labour supply curve can again be expected to be upward sloping, as in Figure 6.7. The reason for this is that more people will tend to offer themselves for work when the wage is relatively high. People will join the market at a higher wage rate, either from outside of the workforce altogether or from other industries where wages have not risen. In this way, wages act as a signal to workers about which industries are offering the best returns to work. This is another example of the way in which the price mechanism operates to allocate resources within a society.

Figure 6.7 *An industry labour supply curve*

A number of factors may influence the position of the labour supply curve. An increase in the rate of unemployment benefits payable could mean that for some industries the number of people prepared to offer themselves for work may fall, resulting in a leftward shift of the labour supply curve. An increase in the rate of immigration to a country could shift the industry supply curve of labour to the right.

Summary

> For an individual worker, a higher wage rate may induce a higher supply of labour hours.

> At the industry level, the labour supply curve is likely to be upward sloping, as more people will come into the industry at a higher wage rate.

> A number of factors may influence the position of the industry labour supply curve, such as the rate of unemployment benefit or the rate of immigration into the country.

Labour market equilibrium

Bringing demand and supply curves together for an industry shows how the equilibrium wage is determined. Figure 6.8 shows a downward-sloping demand curve (D_L) and an upward-sloping labour supply curve (S_L). Equilibrium is found at the intersection of demand and supply. If the wage is lower than W^* employers will not be able to fill all their vacancies, and will have to offer a higher wage to attract more workers. If the wage is higher than W^* there will be an excess supply of labour, and the wage will drift down until W^* is reached and equilibrium obtains.

Comparative static analysis can be used to examine the effects of changes in market conditions. For instance, a change in the factors that determine the position of the labour demand curve will induce a shift of labour demand and an adjustment in the equilibrium wage. Suppose there is an increase in the demand for the firm's product. This will lead to a rightward shift in the demand for labour, say from D_{L0} to D_{L1} in Figure 6.9. This in turn will lead to a new market equilibrium, with the wage rising from W_0 to W_1.

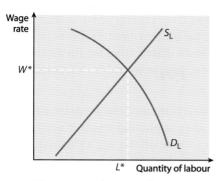

Figure 6.8 *Labour market equilibrium*

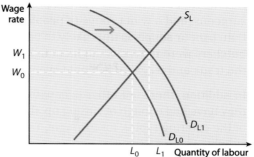

Figure 6.9 *An increase in the demand for labour*

This may not be the final equilibrium position, however. If the higher wages in this market now encourage workers to switch from other industries in which wages have not risen, this will lead to a longer-term shift to the right of the labour supply curve. In a free market, the shift will continue until wage differentials are no longer sufficient to encourage workers to transfer.

Exercise 6.2

Using diagrams, explain how the market equilibrium would change for an industry if:

a there is an increase in the rate of immigration into a country
b changes in working practices are introduced that improve labour productivity

Explaining wage differentials

A common topic of debate concerns why there should be such large differences in pay between people in different occupations. For example, why should footballers in the top teams get paid so much? Demand and supply in the labour market can provide part of the answer.

Surgeons and butchers: the importance of supply

Consider an example of differential earnings — say, surgeons and butchers. First think about the surgeons. Surgeons are in relatively inelastic supply, at least in the short run. The education required to become a surgeon is long and demanding, and is certainly essential for entry into the occupation. Furthermore, not everyone is cut out to become a surgeon, as this is a field that requires certain innate abilities and talents. This implies that the supply of surgeons is limited, and does not vary a great deal with the wage rate.

The situation may be reinforced by the fact that, once an individual has trained as a surgeon, there may be few alternative occupations to which, if disgruntled, he/she could transfer. There is a natural limit to how many surgeons there are, *and* upon their willingness to exit from the market.

How about butchers? The training programme for butchers is less arduous than for surgeons, and a wider range of people is suitable for employment in this occupation. Labour supply is thus likely to be relatively more elastic than for surgeons. If butchers were to receive high enough wages, more people would be attracted to the trade and wage rates would eventually fall.

In addition, there are other occupations into which butchers can transfer when they have had enough of cutting up all that meat; they might look to other sections of the catering sector, for example. This reinforces the relatively high elasticity of supply.

The importance of demand

Is this the whole of the story? The discussion so far has centred entirely on the supply side of the market. But demand is also important.

Indeed, it is the position of the demand curve when interacting with supply that determines the equilibrium wage rate in a labour market. It may well be that the supply of workers skilled in underwater basket weaving is strictly limited; but if there is no demand for underwater basket weavers then there is no scope for that skill to earn high wages. In the above example, it is the relatively strong demand for surgeons relative to their limited supply that leads to a relatively high equilibrium wage in the market.

Summary

> Labour market equilibrium is found at the intersection of labour demand and labour supply.
> This determines the equilibrium wage rate for an industry.
> Comparative static analysis can be used to analyse the effects of changes in market conditions.
> Changes in relative wages between sectors may induce movement of workers between industries.
> The state and position of labour demand and supply helps to explain why there should be wage differentials between occupations.

The effects of migration

An important influence on the position of the labour supply curve for an industry is the number of people who are available and prepared to take jobs. With the closer integration of the countries in the European Union, and the expansion of the membership to include countries in Eastern Europe and the Baltic states, there has been a significant increase in the amount of migration of people between countries. An important aspect of inward migration is the effect on labour supply. By adding to labour supply, migration enables an expansion in the productive capacity of the economy, thus enabling economic growth to take place. For a country like the UK, where population had been stable and ageing, this addition to labour supply may be especially valuable. The reasons behind such migration are

apparent, given the differences in average income levels between countries. The countries of origin may face costs from this process, in terms of a brain drain, especially if it tends to be the young and educated workers that are more likely to migrate. To some extent, these negative effects may be reduced if the migrant workers send part of their income to their families back home.

Effects of government intervention

Unemployment benefits

An important influence on labour supply, particularly for low-income workers, is the level of unemployment benefit. If unemployment benefit is provided at too high a level, it may inhibit labour force participation, in that some workers may opt to live on unemployment benefit rather than take up low-skilled (and low-paid) employment. In such a situation a reduction in unemployment benefit may induce an increase in labour supply.

However, such a policy needs to be balanced against the need to provide protection for those who are unable to find employment. It is also important that unemployment benefit is not reduced to such a level that workers are unwilling to leave their jobs to search for better ones, as this may inhibit the flexibility of the labour market.

Incentive effects

Similarly, there are dangers in making the taxation system too progressive. Most people accept that income tax should be progressive — i.e. that those on relatively high incomes should pay a higher rate of tax at than those on low incomes — as a way of redistributing income within society and preventing inequality from becoming extreme. However, there may come a point at which marginal tax rates are so high that a large proportion of additional income is taxed away, reducing incentives for individuals to supply additional effort or labour. Again, however, it is important to balance these incentive effects against the distortion caused by having too much inequality in society.

Minimum wage

In its manifesto published before the 1997 election, the Labour Party committed itself to the establishment of the National **Minimum Wage** (NMW). This would be the first time that such a measure had been used in the UK on a nationwide basis, although minimum wages had sometimes been set in particular industries.

After the election, a Low Pay Commission was set up to oversee the implementation of the policy, which came into force in April 1999. Initially the NMW was set at £3.60 per hour for those aged 22 and over and £3 for those aged 18–21. From 1 October 2008 the rates were adjusted to £5.73 for those aged 22 and over and £4.77 for those aged 18–21. A minimum wage of £3.53 per hour was in operation for 16- and 17-year-olds. These rates are revised each year.

Key term

minimum wage: government-set minimum wage rate below which firms are not allowed to pay

The objectives of the minimum wage policy are threefold. First, it is intended to protect workers against exploitation by the small minority of bad employers. Second, it aims to improve incentives to work by ensuring that 'work pays', thereby tackling the problem of voluntary unemployment. Third, it aims to alleviate poverty by raising the living standards of the poorest groups in society.

The policy has been a contentious one, with critics claiming that it meets none of these objectives. It has been argued that the minority of bad employers can still find ways of exploiting their workers, for example by paying them on a piecework rate so that there is no set wage per hour. Another criticism is that the policy is too indiscriminate to tackle poverty, and that a more sharply focused policy is needed for this purpose; for example, many of the workers receiving the NMW may not in fact belong to poor households, but may be women working part-time whose partners are also in employment. But perhaps most contentious of all is the argument that, far from providing a supply-side solution to some unemployment, a national minimum wage is causing an increase in unemployment because of its effects on the demand for labour.

First, consider a firm operating in a competitive market. A small firm in a market may not be able to influence the wage rate, so it must pay the going rate in the overall market of which it is a part. In Figure 6.10 the firm's demand curve is represented by D_L; labour supply is horizontal with the equilibrium wage at W^*. It thus uses labour up to l^*.

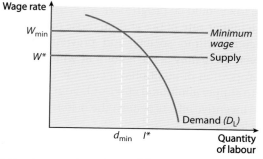

Figure 6.10
The effect of a minimum wage on a firm in a perfectly competitive labour market

If the government now steps in and imposes a minimum wage, so that the firm cannot set a wage below W_{min}, it will reduce its labour usage to d_{min}, since it will not be profitable to employ labour beyond this point.

This effect will be similar for all the other firms in the market, and the results of this can be seen in Figure 6.11. Now the demand curve is the combined demand of all the firms in the market, and the supply curve of labour is shown as upward sloping, as it is the market supply curve. In free market equilibrium the combined demand of firms in the market is L^*, and W^* emerges as the equilibrium wage rate.

When the government sets the minimum wage at W_{min}, all firms react by reducing their demand for labour at the higher wage. Their combined demand is now D_{min}, but the supply of labour is S_{min}. The difference between these $(S_{min} - D_{min})$ is unemployment. Furthermore, it is involuntary unemployment — these workers would like to work at the going wage rate, but cannot find a job.

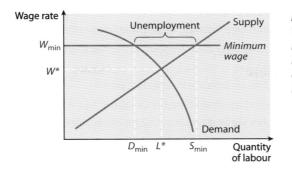

Figure 6.11
The effect of a minimum wage in a perfectly competitive labour market

Notice that there are two effects at work. Some workers who were formerly employed have lost their jobs — there are $L^* - D_{min}$ of these. In addition, however, the incentive to work is now improved (this was part of the policy objective, remember?), so there are now an additional $S_{min} - L^*$ workers wanting to take employment at the going wage rate. Thus, unemployment has increased for two reasons.

It is not always the case that the introduction of a minimum wage leads to an increase in unemployment. For example, in the market depicted in Figure 6.12 the minimum wage has been set below the equilibrium level, so will have no effect on firms in the market, who will continue to pay W^* and employ L^* workers. At the time of the introduction of the NMW, MacDonald's argued that it was in fact already paying a wage above the minimum rate set.

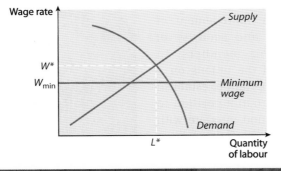

Figure 6.12
A non-binding minimum wage in a perfectly competitive labour market

Exercise 6.3

Sketch some diagrams to explore how the elasticity of demand for and the supply of labour influence the impact on market equilibrium of the imposition of a minimum wage.

Summary

➤ Migration may have beneficial effects on the receiving country, as the increase in labour supply may enable economic growth to take place.

➤ The incentive effects of government measures such as unemployment benefits and income tax can affect labour supply. For example, if unemployment benefits are set too high this may discourage labour force participation. An over-progressive income taxation structure can also have damaging incentive effects.

> Governments have intervened in labour markets to protect low-paid workers, but policies need to be implemented with care because of possible unintended side-effects.

> The Labour Government under Tony Blair introduced the National Minimum Wage in 1999.

> In a competitive labour market, a minimum wage that raises the wage rate above its equilibrium value may lead to an increase in unemployment.

> This is partly because firms reduce their demand for labour, but it also reflects an increased supply of labour as the higher wage is an incentive for more workers to enter the market.

> A minimum wage that is set below the equilibrium wage will not be binding.

Trade unions

Trade unions are associations of workers that negotiate with employers on pay and working conditions. Guilds of craftsmen existed in Europe in the Middle Ages, but the formation of workers' trade unions did not become legal in the UK until 1824. In the period following the Second World War about 40% of the labour force in the UK were members of a trade union. This percentage increased during the 1970s, peaking at about 50%, but since 1980 there has been a steady decline to below 30%.

Key term

trade union: an organisation of workers that negotiates with employers on behalf of its workers

Trade unions have three major objectives: wage bargaining, the improvement of working conditions, and security of employment for their members. In exploring the effect of the unions on a labour market, it is important to establish whether the unions are in a position to exploit market power and interfere with the proper functioning of the labour market, and also whether they are a necessary balance to the power of employers and thus necessary to protect workers from being exploited.

Union membership peaked at around 50% of the UK labour force in the 1970s, but has since declined to below 30%

There are two ways in which a trade union may seek to affect labour market equilibrium. On the one hand, it may limit the supply of workers into an occupation or industry. On the other hand, it may negotiate successfully for higher wages for its members. It turns out that these two possible strategies have similar effects on market equilibrium.

Restricting labour supply

Figure 6.13 shows the situation facing a firm The average going wage in the economy is given by W^*, so if the firm can obtain workers at that wage it is prepared to employ up to L_0 labour.

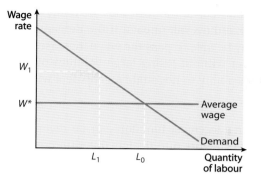

Figure 6.13
A trade union restricts the supply of labour

However, if the firm faces a trade union that is limiting the amount of labour available to just L_1, then the union will be able to push the wage up to W_1. This might happen where there is a *closed shop*, in other words where a firm can employ only those workers who are members of the union. A closed shop allows the union to control how many workers are registered members, and therefore eligible to work in the occupation.

In this situation the union is effectively trading off higher wages for its members against a lower level of employment. The union members who are in work are better off — but those who would have been prepared to work at the lower wage of W^* either are unemployed or have to look elsewhere for jobs. If they are unemployed, this imposes a cost on society. If they are working in a second-choice occupation or industry this may also impose a social cost, in the sense that they may not be working to their full potential.

The extent of the trade-off depends crucially on the elasticity of demand for labour, as you can see in Figure 6.14. When the demand for labour is relatively more elastic, as shown by D_{L0}, the wage paid by the firm increases to W_0, whereas with the relatively more inelastic demand for labour D_{L1} the wage increases by much more, to W_1.

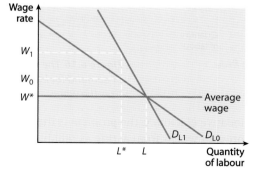

Figure 6.14
The importance of the elasticity of demand for labour

This makes good intuitive sense. The elasticity of demand for labour is likely to be low in situations where a firm cannot readily substitute capital for labour, where labour forms a small share of total costs, and where the price elasticity of demand for the firm's product is relatively inelastic. If the firm cannot readily substitute capital for labour, the union has a relatively strong bargaining position. If labour

costs are a small part of total costs, the firm may be ready to concede a wage increase, as it will have limited overall impact. If the demand for the product is price-inelastic, the firm may be able to pass the wage increase on in the form of a higher price for the product without losing large volumes of sales. Thus, these factors improve the union's ability to negotiate a good deal with the employer.

Negotiating wages

Alternatively, a trade union's foremost function can be regarded as negotiating higher wages for its members. Figure 6.15 depicts this situation. In the absence of union negotiation, the equilibrium for the firm is where demand and supply intersect, so the firm hires L_e labour at a wage of W_e.

If the trade union negotiates a wage of W^*, such that the firm cannot hire any labour below that level, this alters the labour supply curve, as shown by the kinked red line. The firm now employs only L^* labour at this wage. So, again, the effect is that the union negotiations result in a trade-off between the amount of labour hired and the wage rate. When the wage is at W^*, unemployment is shown on Figure 6.15 as $N^* - L^*$.

The elasticity of demand for labour again affects the outcome, as shown in Figure 6.16. This time, with the relatively more inelastic demand curve D_{L1}, the effect on the quantity of labour employed (to L^{**}) is much less than when demand is relatively more elastic (to L^*).

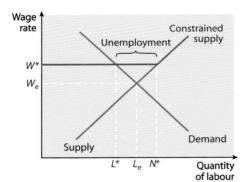

Figure 6.15 A trade union fixes the wage

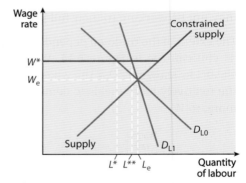

Figure 6.16 The effect of the elasticity of demand for labour when the union fixes the wage

From the point of view of allocative efficiency, the problem is that trade union intervention in the market may prevent wages from acting as reliable signals to workers and firms, and therefore may lead to a suboptimal allocation of resources.

Job security

One possible effect of trade union involvement in a firm is that workers will have more job security; in other words, they may become less likely to lose their jobs with the union there to protect their interests.

part 1

From the firm's point of view, there may be a positive side to this. If workers feel secure in their jobs, they may be more productive, or more prepared to accept changes in working practices that enable an improvement in productivity.

For this reason, it can be argued that in some situations the presence of a trade union may be beneficial in terms of a firm's efficiency. Indeed, the union may sometimes take over functions that would otherwise be part of the responsibility of the firm's human resource department.

Labour market flexibility

One of the most telling criticisms of trade unions has been that they have affected the degree of flexibility of the labour market. The most obvious manifestation of this is that their actions limit the entry of workers into a market.

This may happen in any firm, where existing workers have better access to information about how the firm is operating, or about forthcoming job vacancies, and so can make sure that their own positions against newcomers can be safeguarded. This is sometimes known as the *insider–outsider* phenomenon. Its effect is strengthened and institutionalised by the presence of a trade union, or by professional bodies such as the Royal College of Surgeons.

This and other barriers to entry erected by a trade union can limit the effectiveness and flexibility of labour markets by making it more difficult for firms to adapt to changing market conditions. Where labour markets are flexible, this can contribute to good resource allocation in a society, as this allows workers to transfer from contracting activities into expanding sectors. This in turn helps to ensure that firms are able to produce in a way that matches the pattern of consumer demand.

Summary

- Trade unions exist to negotiate for their members on pay, working conditions and job security.
- If trade unions restrict labour supply, or negotiate wages that are above the market equilibrium, the net effect is a trade-off between wages and employment.
- Those who remain in work receive higher pay, but at the expense of other workers who have either become unemployed or work in second-choice occupations or industries.
- However, by improving job security, unions may make workers more prepared to accept changes in working practices that lead to productivity gains.
- Barriers to the entry and exit of workers may reduce firms' flexibility to adapt to changing market conditions.

Chapter 7

Market failure and externalities

If markets are to be effective in guiding the allocation of resources in society, a precondition is that market prices are able to reflect the full costs and benefits associated with market transactions. However, there are many situations in which this is not so, and there are costs or benefits that are external to the workings of the market mechanism. This chapter examines circumstances in which this may happen, and provides a justification for government intervention to improve the workings of the market.

Learning outcomes

After studying this chapter, you should:

➤ recognise situations in which the free market mechanism may fail to take account of costs or benefits that are associated with market transactions
➤ be familiar with situations in which there may be a divergence between private and social costs or benefits, such that price is not set equal to marginal cost
➤ be able to use diagrams to analyse positive and negative externalities in either production or consumption
➤ appreciate reasons why government may need to intervene in markets in which externalities are present
➤ be familiar with a wide range of examples of externalities
➤ recognise ways in which external costs or benefits may be valued
➤ be familiar with possible solutions to the problem of externalities

Causes of market failure

This chapter and the next explore a number of ways in which markets may fail to bring the best result for society as a whole. In each case, the failure arises because a market settles in a position in which marginal social cost diverges from marginal social benefit. This chapter introduces the most important reasons for market **failure** and examines one common form — externalities. Other forms of market failure are discussed in Chapter 8.

Externalities

If market forces are to guide the allocation of resources, it is crucial that the costs that firms face and the prices to which they respond fully reflect the actual costs and benefits associated with the production and consumption of goods. However, there are a number of situations and markets in which this does not happen because of **externalities**. These cause a divergence between marginal social cost and marginal social benefit in a market equilibrium situation. In the presence of such externalities, a price will emerge that is not equal to the 'true' marginal cost.

> ### Key *terms*
>
> **market failure:** a situation in which the free market mechanism does not lead to an optimal allocation of resources — for example, where there is a divergence between marginal social benefit and marginal social cost
>
> **externality:** a cost or a benefit that is external to a market transaction, and is thus not reflected in market prices

Information failure

If markets are to perform a role in allocating resources, it is extremely important that all relevant economic agents (buyers and sellers) have good information about market conditions; otherwise they may not be able to take rational decisions.

It is important that consumers can clearly perceive the benefits to be gained by their consuming particular goods or services, in order to determine their own willingness to pay. Such benefits may not always be clear. For example, people may not fully perceive the benefits to be gained from education — or they may fail to appreciate the harmfulness of smoking tobacco.

In other market situations, economic agents on one side of the market may have different information from those on the other side: for example, sellers may have information about the goods that they are providing that buyers cannot discern. Chapter 8 explains that such information failure can also lead to a suboptimal allocation of resources.

Public goods

There is a category of goods known as public goods, which because of their characteristics cannot be provided by a purely free market. Street lighting is one example: there is no obvious way in which a private firm could charge all the users of street lighting for the benefits that they receive from it. Such goods are also discussed in Chapter 8.

Labour immobility

Chapter 6 discussed the labour market, and explained how a flexible labour market contributes to the way in which the market mechanism is able to achieve good resource allocation in a society. This occurs when wages act as signals to workers, enabling expanding economic activities to attract the labour that is needed for that

expansion. There may be situations in which this process is impeded by the immobility of labour. For example, it may be that economic activities that are in decline are located in different regions than those that are booming. It may then be difficult to encourage people to move to where the jobs are to be found.

Instability in commodity markets

For markets to be effective in guiding resource allocation, it is important for prices to be able to act as clear signals to both producers and consumers. In some commodity markets, there is an inherent instability that can lead to volatility in prices through time. Where this is the case, the market mechanism may not function effectively, as current prices may not be a reliable guide to market conditions.

Summary

- ➤ Free markets do not always lead to the best possible allocation of resources: there may be market failure.
- ➤ Markets may fail when there is imperfect competition, so that firms are able to utilise market power to disadvantage consumers.
- ➤ When there are costs or benefits that are external to the price mechanism, the economy will not reach allocative efficiency.
- ➤ Markets can operate effectively only when participants in the market have full information about market conditions.
- ➤ Public goods have characteristics that prevent markets from supplying the appropriate quantity.
- ➤ Market failure may also occur if labour is immobile or if commodity prices are instable.

Externalities

Externality is one of those ugly words invented by economists, which says exactly what it means. It simply describes a cost or a benefit that is external to the market mechanism.

An externality will lead to a form of market failure because, if the cost or benefit is not reflected in market prices, it cannot be taken into consideration by all parties to a transaction. In other words, there may be costs or benefits resulting from a transaction that are borne (or enjoyed) by some third party not directly involved in that transaction. This in turn implies that decisions will not be aligned with the best interests of society.

For example, if there is an element of costs that is not borne by producers, it is likely that 'too much' of the good will be produced. Where there are benefits that are not

> **Key terms**
>
> **consumption externality:** an externality that affects the consumption side of a market, which may be either positive or negative
>
> **production externality:** an externality that affects the production side of a market, which may be either positive or negative

included, it is likely that too little will be produced. Later in the chapter, it will be shown that this is exactly what does happen. Externalities can affect either demand or supply in a market: that is to say, they may arise either in **consumption** or in **production**.

In approaching this topic, begin by tackling Exercise 7.1, which offers an example of each type of externality.

Exercise 7.1

Each of the following situations describes a type of externality. Do they affect production or consumption?

a A factory situated in the centre of a town, and close to a residential district, emits toxic fumes through a chimney during its production process. As a result, residents living nearby have to wash their clothes more frequently, and incur higher medical bills as a result of breathing in the fumes.

b Residents living along a main road festoon their houses with lavish Christmas lights and decorations during the month of December, helping passers-by to capture the festive spirit.

Toxic fumes

Example (a) is a negative production externality. The factory emits toxic fumes that impose costs on the residents (third parties) living nearby, who incur high washing and medical bills. The households face costs as a result of the production activities of the firm, so the firm does not face the full costs of its activity.

Thus, the **private costs** faced by the producer are lower than the social costs: that is, the costs faced by society as a whole. The producer will take decisions based only on its private costs, ignoring the **external costs** it imposes on society.

Figure 7.1 illustrates this situation under the assumption that firms operate in a competitive market (i.e. there is not a monopoly). Here, *D* (*MSB*) represents the demand curve, which was characterised in Chapter 4 as representing the marginal social benefit derived from consuming a good. In other words, the demand curve represents consumers' willingness to pay for the good, and thus reflects their marginal valuation of the product.

Key terms

private cost: a cost incurred by an individual (firm or consumer) as part of its production or other economic activities

external cost: a cost that is associated with an individual's (a firm or household's) production or other economic activities, which is borne by a third party

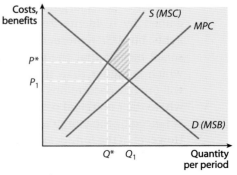

Figure 7.1 *A negative productive externality*

Producers face marginal private costs given by the line *MPC*, but in fact impose higher costs than this on society. Thus *S* represents the supply curve that includes these additional costs imposed on society. This may be regarded as being the marginal social cost (*MSC*) of the firms' production.

If the market is unregulated by the government, firms will choose how much to supply on the basis of the marginal (private) cost they face, shown by *MPC* in Figure 7.1. The market equilibrium will thus be at quantity traded Q_1, where firms just break even on the marginal unit sold; price will be set at P_1.

This is not a good outcome for society, as it is clear that there is a divergence between the price in the market and the 'true' marginal cost — in other words, a divergence between marginal social benefit and marginal social cost. It is this divergence that is at the heart of the market failure. The last unit of this good sold imposes higher costs on society than the marginal benefit derived from consuming it. Too much is being produced.

In fact, the optimum position is at Q^*, where marginal social benefit is equal to marginal social cost. This will be reached if the price is set equal to (social) marginal cost at P^*. Less of the good will be consumed, but also less pollution will be created, and society will be better off than at Q_1.

The extent of the welfare loss that society suffers can be identified: it is shown by the shaded triangle in Figure 7.1. Each unit of output that is produced above Q^* imposes a cost equal to the vertical distance between *MSC* and *MPC*. The shaded area thus represents the difference between marginal social cost and marginal benefit over the range of output between the optimum output and the free market level of output.

Christmas lights

Example (b) in Exercise 7.1 is an example of a positive consumption externality. Residents of this street decorate their homes in order to share the Christmas spirit with passers-by. The benefit they gain from the decorations spills over and adds to the enjoyment of others. In other words, the social benefits from the residents' decision to provide Christmas decorations go beyond the private enjoyment that they receive.

Figure 7.2 illustrates this situation. *MPB* represents the marginal private benefits gained by residents from the Christmas lights; but *MSB* represents the full marginal social benefit that the community gains, which is higher than the *MPB*. Residents will provide decorations up to the point Q_2, where their marginal private benefit is just balanced by the marginal cost of the lights. However, if the full social benefits received are taken into account, Q^* would be the optimum point: the residents do not provide enough décor for the community

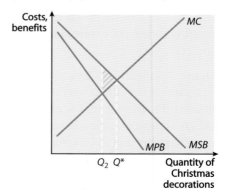

Figure 7.2 *A positive consumption externality*

to reach the optimum. The shaded triangle in Figure 7.2 shows the welfare loss, that is, the amount of social benefit forgone if the outcome is at Q_2 instead of Q^*.

Positive and normative revisited

Example (b) is a reminder of the distinction between positive and normative analysis, which was introduced in Chapter 1. Economists would agree that Figure 7.2 shows the effects of a beneficial consumption externality. However, probably not everyone would agree that the lavish

Christmas lights have a positive consumption externality

Christmas decorations are providing such benefits. This is where a *normative judgement* comes into play. It could equally be argued that the lavish Christmas decorations are unsightly and inappropriate, or that they constitute a distraction for drivers and are therefore likely to cause accidents. After all, not everyone enjoys the garish.

Exercise 7.1 (continued)

Discussion has centred around two examples of externalities: a production externality that had negative effects, and a consumption externality that was beneficial to society. In fact, there are two other possibilities.

c A factory that produces chemicals, which is located on the banks of a river, installs a new water purification plant that improves the quality of water discharged into the river. A trout farm located downstream finds that its productivity increases, and that it has to spend less on filtering the water.

d Liz, a 'metal' enthusiast, enjoys playing her music at high volume late at night, in spite of the fact that she lives in a flat with inadequate sound insulation. The neighbours prefer rock, but cannot escape the metal.

Water purification

Example (c) is a production externality that has positive effects. The action taken by the chemical firm to purify its waste water has beneficial effects on the trout farm, which finds that its costs have been reduced without it having taken any action whatsoever. Indeed, it finds that it has to spend less on filtering the water.

Figure 7.3 shows the position facing the chemical firm. It faces relatively high marginal private costs given by *MPC*. However, its actions have reduced the costs

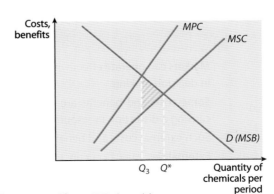

Figure 7.3 A positive production externality

faced by the trout farm, so the 'social' cost of the firm's production activities is lower than its private cost. Thus, in this case marginal social cost, shown by MSC in the figure, is lower than marginal private cost. The firm will produce up to the point where MPC equals marginal social benefit: that is, at Q_3.

In this market position, notice that the marginal benefit that society receives from consuming the product is higher than the marginal social cost of producing it, so too little of the product is being consumed for society's good. Society would be better off at Q^*, where marginal social benefit is equal to marginal social cost.

Again, the shaded triangle in Figure 7.3 represents the extent of the inefficiency: it is given by the excess of marginal social benefit over marginal social cost over the range of output between the market outcome and society's optimum position.

Rock and metal

Example (d) is a negative consumption externality. Liz, the metal fan, gains benefit from listening to her music at high volume, but the neighbours also hear her music and suffer as a result. Indeed, it may be that when they try to listen to rock, the metal interferes with their enjoyment. Their benefit is reduced by having to hear the metal.

Figure 7.4 illustrates this. The situation can be interpreted in terms of the benefits that accrue as a result of Liz's consumption of loud metal music. Liz gains benefit as shown by the line MPB, which represents marginal private benefit. However, the social benefit is lower than this if the vexation suffered by the neighbours is taken into account, so MSB in Figure 7.4 represents the marginal social benefits from Liz's metal.

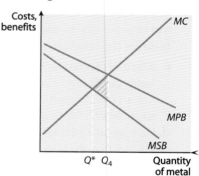

Liz will listen to metal up to the point where her marginal private benefit is just equal to the marginal cost of playing it, at Q_4. However, the optimal position that takes the neighbours into consideration is where marginal social benefit is equal to marginal cost — at Q^*. Thus, Liz plays too much metal for the good of society.

Figure 7.4 A negative consumption externality

Summary

> Markets can operate effectively only if all relevant costs and benefits are taken into account in decision making.

> Some costs and benefits are external to the market mechanism, and are thus neglected, causing a distortion in resource allocation.

> Such external costs and benefits are known as 'externalities'.

> Externalities may occur in either production or consumption, thereby affecting either demand or supply.

> Externalities may be either positive or negative, but either way resources will not be optimally allocated if they are present.

Exercise 7.2

Discuss examples of some externalities that you meet in everyday situations, and classify them as affecting either production or consumption.

Externalities occur in a wide variety of market situations, and constitute an important source of market failure. This means that externalities may hinder the achievement of good resource allocation from society's perspective. The final section of this chapter explores some ways in which attempts have been made to measure the social costs imposed by externalities. First, however, a number of other externalities that appear in various parts of the economy are examined.

Externalities and the environment

Concern for the environment has been growing in recent years, with 'green' lobbyist groups demanding attention, sometimes through demonstrations and protests. There are so many different facets to this question that it is sometimes difficult to isolate the core issues. Externalities lie at the heart of much of the debate.

Some of the issues are international in nature, such as the debate over global warming. At the heart of this concern is the way in which emissions of greenhouse gases are said to be warming up the planet. Sea levels are rising and major climate change seems imminent.

One reason why this question is especially difficult to tackle is that actions taken by one country can have effects on other countries. Scientists argue that the problem is caused mainly by pollution created by transport and industry, especially in the richer countries of the world. However, poorer countries suffer the consequences as well, especially countries such as Bangladesh, where much of the land is low lying and prone to severe flooding — indeed, two-thirds of the country was under water during the floods of 2004.

In principle, this is very similar to example (a) in Exercise 7.1: it is an example of a negative production externality, in which the nations causing most of the damage face only part of the costs caused by their lifestyles and production processes. The inevitable result in an unregulated market is that too much pollution is produced.

When externalities cross international borders in this way, the problem can be tackled only through international cooperation. For example, at the Kyoto World Climate Summit held in Japan in 1997, almost every developed nation agreed to cut greenhouse gas emissions by 6% by 2010. (The USA, the largest emitter of carbon dioxide, withdrew from the agreement in early 2001, fearing the consequences of such a restriction on the US economy.)

Global warming is not the only example of international externality effects. Scandinavian countries have suffered from acid rain caused by pollution in other European countries, including the UK. Forest fires left to burn in Indonesia have caused air pollution in neighbouring Singapore.

Another environmental issue concerns rivers. Some of the big rivers of the world, such as the Nile in Africa, pass through several countries on their way to the sea. For Egypt, through which the river runs at the end of its journey, the Nile is crucial for the livelihood of the economy. If countries further upstream were to increase their usage of the river, perhaps through new irrigation projects, this could have disastrous effects on Egypt. Again, the actions of one set of economic agents would be having damaging effects on others, and these effects would not be reflected in market prices, in the sense that the upstream countries would not have to face the full cost of their actions.

Part of the problem here can be traced back to the difficulty of enforcing property rights. If the countries imposing the costs could be forced to make appropriate payment for their actions, this would help to bring the costs back within the market mechanism. Such a process is known in economics as 'internalising the externality', and will be examined later in this chapter.

Concern has also been expressed about the loss of *biodiversity*, a word that is shorthand for 'biological diversity'. The issue here is that when a section of rainforest is cleared to plant soya, or for timber, it is possible that species of plants, insects or even animals whose existence is not even known at present may be wiped out. Many modern medicines are based on chemicals that occur naturally in the wild. By eradicating species before they have been discovered, possible scientific advances will be forgone. Notice that when it comes to measuring the value of what is being destroyed, biodiversity offers particular challenges — namely, the problem of putting a value on something that might not even be there!

Externalities and transport

With the introduction of the congestion charge in parts of central London, the London authorities have been attempting to tackle congestion. When traffic on the roads reaches a certain volume, congestion imposes heavy costs on road users. This is another example of an externality.

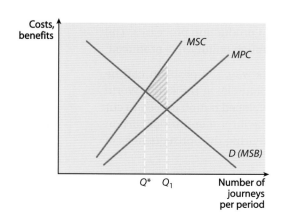

Figure 7.5 *Traffic congestion*

Figure 7.5 illustrates the situation. Suppose that D (MSB) represents the demand curve for car journeys along a particular stretch of road. When deciding whether or not to undertake a journey, drivers will balance the marginal benefit gained from making the journey against the marginal cost that they face. This is given by MPC — the marginal private cost of undertaking journeys. When the road is congested, a motorist who decides to undertake the journey adds to the congestion, and slows the traffic. The MPC curve incorporates the cost to the motorist of joining a congested road, and the chosen number of journeys will be at Q_1.

However, in adding to the congestion the motorist not only suffers the costs of congestion, but also imposes some marginal increase in costs on all other users of the road, as everyone suffers from the slower journeys resulting from the extra congestion. Thus, the marginal social costs (*MSC*) of undertaking journeys are higher than the cost faced by any individual motorist. *MSC* is therefore higher than *MPC*. Society would be better off with lower congestion: that is, with the number of journeys undertaken being limited to *Q**, where marginal social benefit equals marginal social cost. By imposing a charge on motorists entering central London, the authorities are trying to ensure that drivers face at least part of the social costs that they impose on others by using congested roads.

Externalities and health

Healthcare is a sector in which there is often public provision, or at least some state intervention in support of the health services. In the UK, the National Health Service is the prime provider of healthcare, but private healthcare is also available, and the use of private health insurance schemes is on the increase. Again, externalities can help to explain why there should be a need for government to intervene.

There are palpable potential benefits from a vaccination programme

Consider the case of vaccination against a disease such as measles. Suppose an individual is considering whether or not to be vaccinated. Being vaccinated reduces the probability of that individual contracting the disease, so there are palpable potential benefits. However, these benefits must be balanced against the costs. There may be a direct charge for the vaccine; some individuals may have a phobia against needles; or they may be concerned about possible side-effects. Individuals will opt to be vaccinated only if the marginal expected benefit to them is at least as large as the marginal cost.

From society's point of view, however, there are potential benefits that individuals will not take into account. After all, if they do contract measles, there is a chance of their passing it on to others. Indeed, if lots of people decide not to be vaccinated, there is the possibility of a widespread epidemic, which would be costly and damaging to many.

Figure 7.6 illustrates this point. The previous paragraph argues that the social benefits to society of having people vaccinated against measles exceed the private benefits that will be perceived by individuals, so that marginal social benefits exceed marginal private benefits. Private individuals will

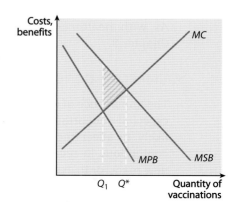

Figure 7.6 *Vaccination*

choose to balance marginal private benefit against marginal private cost at Q_1, whereas society would prefer more people to be vaccinated at Q^*. This parallels the discussion of a positive consumption externality. Chapter 8 returns to consider another aspect of healthcare provision.

Externalities and education

As you are reading this textbook, it is reasonably safe to assume that you are following a course in AS economics. You have decided to demand education. This is yet another area in which externalities may be important.

When you decided to take A-levels (including economics), there were probably a number of factors that influenced your decision. Perhaps you intend to demand even more education in the future, by proceeding to study at university. Part of your decision process probably takes into account the fact that education improves your future earnings potential. Your expected lifetime earnings depend in part upon the level of educational qualifications that you attain. Research has shown that, on average, graduates earn more during their lifetimes than non-graduates. This is partly because there is a productivity effect: by becoming educated, you cultivate a range of skills that in later life will make you more productive, and this helps to explain why you can expect higher lifetime earnings than someone who chooses not to demand education. There is also a signalling effect, as having a degree signals to potential employers that you have the ability to cope with university study and have gained a range of skills.

What does society get out of this? Evidence suggests that not only does education improve productivity, but a *group* of educated workers cooperating with each other become even more productive. This is an externality effect, as it depends on inter-action between educated workers — but each individual perceives only the individual benefit, and not the benefits of cooperation.

In other words, when you decide to undertake education, you do so on the basis of the expected private benefits that you hope to gain from education. However, you do not take into account the additional benefits through cooperation that society will reap. So here is another example of a positive consumption externality. As with healthcare, some other aspects of education will be discussed in Chapter 8.

Social cost–benefit analysis

The importance of externalities in regard to environmental issues means that it is especially important to be aware of externalities when taking decisions that are likely to affect the environment. One area in which this has been especially contentious in recent years is road-building programmes. If decisions to build new roads, or to expand existing ones such as the M25, are taken only by reference to commercial considerations, there could be serious implications for resource allocation.

In taking such decisions, it is desirable to weigh up the costs and benefits of a scheme. If it turns out that the benefits exceed the costs, it might be thought appropriate to go ahead. However, in valuing the costs and the benefits, it is clearly important to include some estimate for the externalities involved in order that the decision can be based on all relevant factors. In other words, it is important to take a 'long and wide view' and not to focus too narrowly on purely financial costs and benefits.

A further complication is that with many such schemes the costs and benefits will be spread out over a long period of time, and it is important to come to a reasonable balance between the interests of present and future generations.

Another example surrounds the costs and benefits associated with hosting major sporting events, such as the Olympics. Here again, the costs and benefits of such an event extend far beyond those associated with the event itself. The need to provide world-class facilities for the wide range of different sporting events that make up the Olympics brings heavy costs in the short run, but may yield long-term benefits, given that those facilities will be available to members of the society for many years in the future. By siting such facilities in areas already in need of regeneration, an event such as the Olympics may offer the opportunity to undertake much-needed investment.

Social cost–benefit analysis is a procedure for bringing together the information needed to make appropriate decisions on such large-scale schemes. This entails a sequence of key steps.

1 Identify relevant costs and benefits

The first step is to identify all relevant costs and benefits. This needs to cover all of the direct costs of the project. These can probably be identified relatively easily, and include the production costs, labour costs and so on. The indirect costs also need to be identified, and this is where externality effects need to be considered. For example, in a road-building scheme, it is important to think in terms not only of the costs of construction, but also of the opportunity cost — how else could the land being used for the road have been used? How will the increase in traffic affect the quality of life enjoyed by local residents? For example, they may suffer from noise from the traffic using the road, or from the traffic fumes. Similarly, direct and indirect benefits need to be identified.

> **Key terms**
>
> **social cost–benefit analysis:** a process of evaluating the worth of a project by comparing its costs and benefits, including both direct and social costs and benefits — including externality effects
>
> **shadow price:** an estimate of the monetary value of an item that does not carry a market price

2 Valuation

If the costs and benefits are to be compared, they all need to be given a monetary valuation. It is likely that some of them will be items that have a market price attached to them. For these, valuation is not a problem. However, for externalities, or for other indirect costs and benefits without a market valuation, it is necessary to establish a **shadow price** — an estimate of the monetary value of each item.

3 Discounting the future

It is also important to recognise that costs and benefits that will flow from the project at some point in the future need to be expressed in terms of their value in the present. From today's perspective, a benefit that is immediate is more valuable than one that will only become relevant in 20 years' time. In order to incorporate this notion into the calculations, we need to **discount** the future at an appropriate rate, and calculate the **net present value** of the future stream of costs and benefits associated with the project under consideration.

Key terms

discount: a process whereby the future valuation of a cost or benefit is reduced (discounted) in order to provide an estimate of its present value

net present value: the estimated value in the current time period of the discounted future net benefit of a project

Summary

➤ Externalities arise in many aspects of economic life.

➤ Environmental issues are especially prone to externality effects, as market prices do not always incorporate environmental issues, especially where property rights are not assigned.

➤ Congestion on the roads can also be seen as a form of externality.

➤ Externalities also arise in the areas of healthcare provision and education, where individuals do not always perceive the full social benefits that arise.

➤ A number of approaches have been proposed to measure externalities. Measurement may enable a social cost–benefit analysis to be made of projects involving a substantial externality element.

Exercise 7.3

Suppose there is a proposal to construct a new industrial estate close to where you live. Identify the costs and benefits of the scheme, including direct costs and benefits and not forgetting externalities.

Exercise 7.4

Discuss the costs and benefits associated with hosting the Olympic Games.

Dealing with externalities

Externalities arise in situations where there are items of cost or benefit associated with transactions, and these are not reflected in market prices. In these circumstances a free market will not lead to an optimum allocation of resources. One approach to dealing with such market situations is to bring those externalities into the market mechanism — a process known as **internalising an externality**. The London congestion charge may be seen as an attempt to internalise

Key term

internalising an externality: an attempt to deal with an externality by bringing an external cost or benefit into the price system

the externality effects of traffic congestion. In the case of pollution this principle would entail forcing the polluting firms to face the full social cost of their production activities. This is sometimes known as the *polluter pays* principle.

Pollution

Figure 7.7 illustrates a negative production externality: pollution. Suppose that firms in the market for chemicals use a production process that emits toxic fumes, thereby imposing costs on society that the firms themselves do not face. In other words, the marginal private costs faced by these firms are less than the marginal social costs that are inflicted on society. As explained earlier in the chapter, firms in this market will choose to produce up to point Q_1 and charge a price of P_1 to consumers. At this point, marginal social benefit is below the marginal cost of producing the chemicals, so it can be claimed that 'too much' of the product is being produced — that society would be better off if production were at Q^*, with a price charged at P^*.

Note that this optimum position is not characterised by *zero* pollution. In other words, from society's point of view it pays to abate pollution only *up to* the level where the marginal benefit of reducing pollution is matched by the marginal cost of doing so. Reducing pollution to zero would be too costly.

How can society reach the optimum output of chemicals at Q^*? In line with the principle that the polluter should pay, one approach would be to impose a tax on firms such that polluters face the full cost of their actions. In Figure 7.7, if firms were required to pay a tax equivalent to the vertical distance between marginal private cost (*MPC*) and marginal social cost (*MSC*), they would choose to produce at Q^*, paying a tax equal to the green line on the figure.

An alternative way of looking at this question is via a diagram showing the marginal benefit and marginal cost of emissions reduction. In Figure 7.8, *MB* represents the marginal social benefits from reducing emissions of some pollutant and *MC* is the marginal costs of reducing emissions. The optimum amount of reduction is found where marginal benefit equals marginal cost, at e^*. Up to this point, the marginal benefit to society of reducing emissions exceeds the marginal cost of the reduction, so it is in the interest of society to reduce pollution. However, beyond that point the marginal cost of reducing the amount of pollution exceeds the benefits that accrue, so society will be worse off. Setting a tax equal to t^* in Figure 7.8 will induce firms to undertake the appropriate amount of emission reduction.

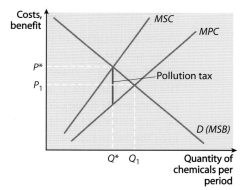

Figure 7.7 *Pollution*

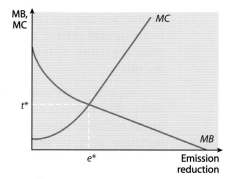

Figure 7.8 *Reducing the emission of toxic fumes*

This is not the only way of reaching the objective, however. Figure 7.8 suggests that there is another possibility — namely, to impose environmental standards, and to prohibit emissions beyond e^*. This amounts to controlling quantity rather than price; and, if the government has full information about marginal costs and marginal benefits, the two policies will produce the equivalent result.

Either of the approaches outlined above will be effective — *if* the authorities have full information about the marginal costs and benefits. But how likely is this? There are many problems with this proviso. The measurement of both marginal benefits and marginal costs is fraught with difficulties.

The marginal social benefits of reducing pollution cannot be measured with great precision, for many reasons. It may be argued that there are significant gains to be made in terms of improved health and lower death rates if pollution can be reduced, but quantifying this is not straightforward. Even if it were possible to evaluate the saving in resources that would need to be devoted to future medical care resulting from the pollution, there are other considerations: quantification of the direct improvements to quality of life; whether or not to take international effects into account when formulating domestic policy; and the appropriate discount rate for evaluating benefits that will be received in the future. Moreover, the environmentalist and the industrialist may well arrive at different evaluations of the benefits of pollution control, reflecting their different viewpoints.

The measurement of costs may also be problematic. For example, it is likely that there will be differences in efficiency between firms. Those using modern technology may face lower costs than those using relatively old capital equipment. Do the authorities try to set a tax that is specific to each firm to take such differences into account? If they do not, but instead set a flat-rate tax, then the incentives may be inappropriate. This would mean that a firm using modern technology would face the same tax as one using old capital. The firm using new capital would then tend to produce too little output relative to those using older, less efficient capital.

Pollution permits

Another approach is to use a *pollution permit system*, under which the government issues or sells permits to firms, allowing them to pollute up to a certain limit. These permits are then tradable, so that firms that are relatively 'clean' in their production methods and do not need to use their full allocation of permits can sell their polluting rights to other firms, whose production methods produce greater levels of pollution.

One important advantage of such a scheme lies in the incentives for firms. Firms that pollute because of their relatively inefficient production methods will find they are at a disadvantage because they face higher costs. Rather than continuing to purchase permits, they will find that they have an incentive to produce less pollution — which, of course, is what the policy is intended to achieve. In this way, the permit system uses the market to address the externality problem — in contrast to direct regulation of environmental standards, which tries to solve pollution by overriding the market.

A second advantage is that the overall level of pollution can be controlled by this system, as the authorities control the total amount of permits that are issued. After all, the objective of the policy is to control the overall level of pollution, and a mixture of 'clean' and 'dirty' firms may produce the same amount of total emissions as uniformly 'slightly unclean' firms.

A system of pollution permits could be effective in regulating pollution

However, the permit system may not be without its problems. In particular, there is the question of enforcement. For the system to be effective, sanctions must be in place for firms that pollute beyond the permitted level, and there must be an operational and cost-effective method for the authorities to check the level of emissions.

Furthermore, it may not be a straightforward exercise for the authorities to decide upon the appropriate number of permits to issue in order to produce the desired reduction in emission levels. Some alternative regulatory systems share this problem, as it is not easy to measure the extent to which marginal private and social costs diverge.

One possible criticism that is unique to a permit form of regulation is that the very different levels of pollution produced by different firms may seem inequitable — as if those firms that can afford to buy permits can pollute as much as they like. On the other hand, it might be argued that those most likely to suffer from this are the polluting firms, whose public image is likely to be tarnished if they acquire a reputation as heavy polluters. This possibility might strengthen the incentives of such firms to clean up their production. Taking the strengths and weaknesses of this approach together, it seems that on balance such a system could be effective in regulating pollution.

Global warming

Global warming is widely seen to require urgent and concerted action at a worldwide level. The Kyoto summit of 1997 laid the foundations for action, with many of the developed nations agreeing to take action to reduce emissions of carbon dioxide and other 'greenhouse' gases that are seen to be causing climate

change. Although the USA withdrew from the agreement in early 2001, apparently concerned that the US economy might be harmed, in November of that year 178 other countries did reach agreement on how to enforce the Kyoto Accord. The absence of US cooperation is potentially significant, however, as the USA is the world's largest emitter of carbon dioxide, responsible for about a quarter of the world's greenhouse gas emissions.

At the heart of the Kyoto Accord is the decision of countries to reduce their greenhouse gas emissions by an agreed percentage by 2010. The method chosen to achieve these targets was based on a tradable pollution permit system. This was seen to be especially demanding for countries such as Japan, whose industry is already relatively energy-efficient. Japan was thus concerned that there should be sufficient permits available for purchase. More explicitly, it was concerned that sloppy compliance by Russia would limit the amount of permits on offer. The issues of monitoring and compliance are thus seen as critical.

A further summit meeting was held in Bali in December 2007 in an attempt to reach agreement on how to proceed when the first phase of the Kyoto protocol expires at the end of 2012. Some progress was made, but countries such as the USA, Canada and Japan remained sceptical, and China is reluctant to negotiate beyond Kyoto. This is significant, as China was soon expected to overtake the USA as the world's largest emitter of greenhouse gases.

The NIMBY syndrome

One problem that arises in trying to deal with externalities is that you cannot please all of the people all of the time. For example, it may well be that it is in society's overall interests to relocate unsightly facilities — it may even be that everyone would agree about this; but such facilities have to be located somewhere, and someone is almost bound to object because they are the ones to suffer. This is the **NIMBY (not in my back yard)** syndrome.

> **Key** *term*
>
> **NIMBY (not in my back yard):** a syndrome under which people are happy to support the construction of an unsightly or unsocial facility, so long as it is not in their back yard

For example, many people would agree that it is desirable for the long-run sustainability of the economy that cleaner forms of energy are developed. One possibility is to build wind farms. People may well be happy for these to be constructed — *as long as* they do not happen to be living near them. This may not be the best example, however, as the effectiveness of wind farms is by no means proven, and there is a strong movement against their use on these grounds.

Exercise 7.5

You discover that your local authority has chosen to locate a new landfill site for waste disposal close to your home. What costs and benefits for society would result? Would these differ from your private costs and benefits? Would you object?

Property rights

The existence of a system of secure property rights is essential as an underpinning for the economy. The legal system exists in part to enforce property rights, and to provide the set of rules under which markets operate. When property rights fail, there is a failure of markets.

One of the reasons underlying the existence of some externalities is that there is a failing in the system of property rights. For example, think about the situation in which a factory is emitting toxic fumes into a residential district. One way of viewing this is that the firm is interfering with local residents' clean air. If those residents could be given property rights over clean air, they could require the firm to compensate them for the costs it was inflicting. However, the problem is that, with such a wide range of people being affected to varying degrees (according to prevailing winds and how close they live to the factory), it is impossible in practical terms to use the assignment of property rights to internalise the pollution externality. This is because the problem of coordination requires high transaction costs in order for property rights to be individually enforced. Therefore, the government effectively takes over the property rights on behalf of the residents, and acts as a collective enforcer.

Nobel Prize winner Ronald Coase argued that externality effects could be internalised in conditions where property rights could be enforced, and where the transaction costs of doing so were not too large.

Summary

➤ In seeking to counter the harmful effects of externalities, governments look for ways of internalising the externality, by bringing external costs and benefits within the market mechanism.

➤ For example, the 'polluter pays' principle argues that the best way of dealing with a pollution externality is to force the polluter to face the full costs of its actions.

➤ Attempts have been made to tackle pollution through taxation, the regulation of environmental standards and the use of pollution permits.

➤ In some cases the allocation of property rights can be effective in curbing the effects of externalities — so long as the transaction costs of implementing it are not too high.

Chapter 8

Other forms of market failure

Externalities are not the only form of market failure. There are also situations where the characteristics of a good or service can affect the effective operation of a market. The chapter explores goods with unusual economic characteristics and markets that may fail as a result of problems with information.

Learning outcomes

After studying this chapter, you should:
➤ understand the nature of public goods and problems that arise in their provision
➤ be able to identify examples of public goods
➤ be aware of the characteristics of merit and demerit goods
➤ be able to give examples of possible merit and demerit goods
➤ appreciate the significance of asymmetric information as a source of market failure

Public goods

Private goods

Most of the goods that individuals consume are **private goods**. You buy a can of Diet Coke, you drink it, and it's gone. You may choose to share it with a friend, but you do not have to: by drinking it you can prevent anyone else from doing so. Furthermore, once it is gone, it's gone: nobody else can subsequently consume that Coke.

The two features that characterise a private good are:
➤ other people can be excluded from consuming it
➤ once consumed by one person, it cannot be consumed by another

> **Key term**
>
> **private good:** a good that, once consumed by one person, cannot be consumed by somebody else; such a good has excludability and is rivalrous

The first feature can be described as *excludability*, whereas the second feature might be described by saying that consumption of a private good is *rivalrous*: the act of consumption uses up the good.

Public goods

Not all goods and services have these two characteristics. There are goods that, once provided, are available to all. In other words, people cannot be excluded from consuming such goods. There are other goods that do not diminish through consumption, so they are non-rivalrous in consumption. Goods that have the characteristics of *non-excludability* and *non-rivalry* are known as **public goods**.

Examples of public goods that are often cited include street lighting, a lighthouse and a nuclear deterrent. For example, once street lighting has been provided in a particular street, anyone who walks along that street at night benefits from the lighting — no one can be excluded from consuming it. So street lighting is non-exclusive. In addition, the fact that one person has walked along the street does not mean that there is less street lighting left for later walkers. So street lighting is also non-rivalrous.

> **Key terms**
>
> **public good:** a good that is non-exclusive and non-rivalrous — consumers cannot be excluded from consuming the good, and consumption by one person does not affect the amount of the good available for others to consume
>
> **free-rider problem:** when an individual cannot be excluded from consuming a good, and thus has no incentive to pay for its provision

The key feature of such a market is that, once the good has been provided, there is no incentive for anyone to pay for it — so the market will fail, as no firm will have an incentive to supply the good in the first place. This is often referred to as the **free-rider problem**, as individual consumers can free-ride and avoid having to pay for the good if it is provided.

Extension material

A key question is how well the market for a public good is likely to operate. In particular, will a free market reach a position where there is allocative efficiency, with price equal to marginal social cost?

Think about the supply and demand curves for a public good such as street lighting. To simplify matters, suppose there are just two potential demanders of the good, a and b. Consider Figure 8.1. If it is assumed that the supply is provided in a competitive market, S represents the supply curve, reflecting the marginal cost of providing street lighting. The curves d_a and d_b represent the demand curves of the two potential demanders. For a given quantity Q_1, a would be prepared to pay P_a and b would pay P_b. If these prices are taken to be the value that each individual places on this amount of the good, then $P_a + P_b = PT$ represents the social benefit derived from consuming Q_1 units of street lighting. Similarly, for any given quantity of street lighting, the marginal social benefit derived from consumption can be calculated as the vertical sum of the two demand curves. This is shown by the curve

MSB. So the optimal provision of street lighting is given by Q^*, at which point the marginal social benefit is equated with the marginal cost of supplying the good. However, if person a were to agree to pay P_a for the good, person b could then consume Q_1 of the good free of charge, but would not be prepared to pay in order for the supply to be expanded beyond this point — as person b's willingness to pay is below the marginal cost of provision beyond this point. So the social optimum at Q^* cannot be reached. Indeed, when there are many potential consumers, the likely outcome is that none of this good will be produced: why should any individual agree to pay if he or she can free-ride on others?

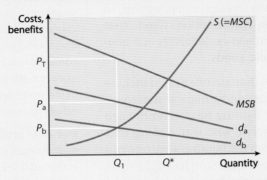

Figure 8.1 *Demand and supply of a public good*

The free-rider problem helps to explain why these sorts of goods have typically been provided through state intervention. This begs the question of how the state can identify the optimal quantity of the good to be provided — in other words, how the government determines Q^*. The extent to which individuals value a particular good cannot be directly observed. However, by including statements about the provision of public goods in their election manifestos, politicians can collect views about public goods provision via the medium of the ballot box. This is an indirect method, but it provides some mandate for the government to take decisions.

The free-rider problem makes it difficult to charge for a public good, so the private sector will be reluctant to supply such goods. In fact, pure public goods are relatively rare, but there are many goods that have some but not all of the required characteristics. On the face of it, the lighthouse service seems to be a good example of a public good. Once the lighthouse has been constructed and is sending out its signal, all boats and ships that pass within the range of its light can benefit from the service: that is, it is non-excludable. Moreover, the fact that one ship has seen the lighthouse signal does not reduce the amount of light available to the next ship, so it is also non-rivalrous.

However, this does not mean that ships cannot be charged for their use of lighthouse services. In 2002 an article in the *Guardian* reported that ships were complaining about the high charges to which they were subjected for lighthouse services. Ships of a certain size must pay 'light dues' every time they enter or leave UK ports, and the fees collected are used to fund lighthouses, buoys and beacons around the coast. In principle, it could be argued that this renders lighthouses excludable, as ships can be prevented from sailing if they have not paid their dues, and so could not consume the lighthouse services. At the heart of the complaints from the shipping companies was the fact that leisure craft below a certain threshold did not have to pay the charges, and they made more use of the lighthouses than the larger vessels. This is one example of the way in which it becomes necessary to design a charging system to try to overcome the free-rider problem associated with the provision of public goods.

In fact, there are many goods that are either non-rivalrous or non-excludable, but not both. One example of this is a football match. If I go to watch a premiership football match, my 'consumption' of the match does not prevent the person sitting next to me from also consuming it, so it is non-rivalrous. However, if I go along without my season ticket (or do not have a ticket), I can clearly be excluded from consuming the match, so it is *not* non-exclusive.

A stretch of road may be considered non-exclusive, as road users are free to drive along it. However, it is not non-rivalrous, in the sense that as congestion builds up consumption is affected. This example is also imperfect as a public good because, by installing toll barriers, users can be excluded from consuming it.

Where goods have some features of a public good, the free market may fail to produce an ideal outcome for society. Exercise 8.1 provides some examples of goods: to what extent may each of these be considered to be non-rivalrous or non-excludable?

Exercise 8.1

For each of the following goods, think about whether they have elements of non-rivalry, non-excludability, both or neither:

a a national park
b a playground
c a theatre performance
d an apple
e a television programme

f a firework display
g police protection
h a lecture
i a DVD recording of a film
j the national defence

Tackling the public goods problem

For some public goods, the failure of the free market to ensure provision may be regarded as a serious problem — for example, in such cases as street lighting or law and order. Some government intervention may thus be needed to make sure that a sufficient quantity of the good or service is provided. Notice that this does not necessarily mean that the government has to provide the good itself. It may be that the government will raise funds through taxation in order to ensure that street lighting is provided, but could still make use of private firms to supply the good through some sort of subcontracting arrangement. In the UK, it may be that the government delegates the responsibility for provision of public goods to local authorities, which in turn may subcontract to private firms.

In some other cases, it may be that changes in technology may alter the economic characteristics of a good. For example, in the case of television programmes,

originally provision was entirely through the BBC, funded by the licence fee. Subsequently, ITV set up in competition, using advertising as a way of funding its supply. More recently, the advent of satellite and digital broadcasting has reduced the degree to which television programmes are non-excludable, allowing private firms to charge for transmissions.

Summary

➤ A private good is one that, once consumed by one person, cannot be consumed by anyone else — it has characteristics of excludability and rivalry.

➤ A public good is non-exclusive and non-rivalrous.

➤ Because of these characteristics, public goods tend to be underprovided by a free market.

➤ One reason for this is the free-rider problem, whereby an individual cannot be excluded from consuming a public good, and thus has no incentive to pay for it.

➤ Public goods, or goods with some of the characteristics of public goods, must be provided with the assistance of the government or its agents.

Merit goods

There are some goods that the government believes everyone should consume, whether or not they wish to, and whether or not they have the means to do so. The key argument is that individuals do not fully perceive the benefits that they will gain from consuming such goods. These are known as **merit goods**.

Clearly, there is a strong political element involved in identifying the goods that should be regarded as merit goods: indeed, there is a subjective or normative judgement involved, since declaring a good to be a merit good requires the decision-maker to make a paternalistic choice on behalf of the population.

> **Key term**
>
> **merit good:** a good that brings unanticipated benefits to its consumers, such that society believes that it should be consumed by individuals regardless of whether they have the means or the willingness to do so

One way of viewing merit goods is that they reflect a divergence between the value that individual members of society place on goods and the decision-maker's views about their value to society as a whole. There is clearly a danger here that the decision-makers will force their views on the rest of society, and again, the ballot box may be the ultimate way of preventing this.

Another aspect of the merit good phenomenon is that the government may be in a better position than individuals to take a long-term view of what is good for society. In particular, governments may need to take decisions on behalf of future generations as well as the present. Resources need to be used wisely in the present in order to protect the interests of tomorrow's citizens. Again, this may require decision-makers to make normative judgements about the appropriate weighting to be given to the present as opposed to the future.

At the heart of the notion of a merit good, therefore, is the decision-maker's perception that there is a divergence between the marginal benefit that individuals perceive to arise from consuming a good, and the social benefit that actually accrues from its consumption. This is reminiscent of the arguments in Chapter 7 about consumption externalities, where a positive consumption externality arises when the marginal social benefit from consuming a good is greater than the marginal private benefit.

Figure 8.2 shows how this situation can be analysed. The example used here is education. In the UK everyone is required to attend school, at least up to age 16. Part of this requirement may be attributed to a merit good argument. It can be argued that education provides benefits to society in excess of those that are perceived by individuals. In other words, society believes that individuals will derive a benefit from education that they will not realise until after they have acquired that education. Thus, the

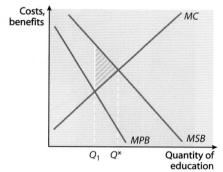

Figure 8.2 *A merit good*

government decrees that everyone must consume education up to the age of 16, whether they want to or not and whether they have the means to do so or not. This is a merit good argument. In Figure 8.2 marginal social benefit (*MSB*) is shown as being higher than marginal private benefit (*MPB*). Thus, society would like to provide Q^* education, where $MSB = MC$ (marginal social cost), but individuals would choose to consume only Q_1 education, where $MPB = MC$, because they do not expect the future benefits to be as high as the government does.

In this case there may be other issues affecting the market for education. Chapter 7 argued that there would also be positive externality effects if educated workers were better able to cooperate with each other. There may be a further argument that individuals may fail to demand sufficient education because of information failure: in other words, they may not perceive the full benefits that will arise from education. The situation may be aggravated if parents have the responsibility of financing their children's education, because they are taking decisions *on behalf of* their children. In the case of tertiary education, there is no guarantee that parents will agree with their children about the benefits of a university education – it could go either way.

Another important issue that arises in the context of education concerns equity in access to higher education. Research has shown that graduates tend to enjoy higher lifetime earnings than non-graduates. However, if some groups have better access to credit markets than others, then those groups may be more able to take advantage of a university education. Specifically, it has been argued that people from low-income households may be discouraged from taking up university places because of failure in credit markets. In other words, the difficulty of raising funds in the present to pay for a university education may prevent people from gaining

Education is often seen as a merit good

the longer-term benefits of having received a university education — hence the launching of student loan schemes, which should help to address this particular form of market failure.

In some societies it has been suggested that the merits of education are better perceived by some groups in society than others. Thus in some less developed countries, individuals in relatively well-off households demand high levels of education, as they realise the long-run benefits that they can receive in terms of higher earnings — and, perhaps, political influence. In contrast, low-income households in remote rural areas may not see the value of education. As a result, drop-out from secondary — and even primary — education tends to be high. This is clearly a merit good argument that may need to be addressed by government, perhaps by making primary education compulsory or free — or both.

Other examples of merit goods are museums, libraries and art galleries. These are goods that are provided or subsidised because someone somewhere thinks that communities should have more of them. Economists are wary of playing the merit good card too often, as it entails such a high normative element. It is also difficult sometimes to disentangle merit good arguments from externality effects.

Demerit goods

In contrast, there is a category of goods that government thinks should not be consumed even if individuals want to do so. These are known as **demerit goods** — or sometimes as 'merit bads'. Obvious examples are hard drugs and tobacco. Here the argument is that individual consumers overvalue the benefits from consuming such a good.

One approach to this problem is to try to remove the information failure; clearly, the government has adopted this approach in seeking to educate people about the dangers of tobacco smoking. As this failed to have the desired effect, the information campaign was eventually reinforced by the ban on smoking in public places that came into effect in mid-2007.

> **Key term**
>
> **demerit good:** a good that brings less benefit to consumers than they expect, such that society believes that it should not be consumed by individuals regardless of whether they wish to do so

Taxing tobacco

Could the problem be tackled through taxation? The market for tobacco is characterised in Figure 8.3. Demand (*MPB*) represents the marginal private benefit that consumers gain from smoking tobacco. However, the government believes that consumers underestimate the damaging effects of smoking, so that the true benefits are given by *MSB* (marginal social benefit). Given the marginal cost (supply) curve, in an unregulated market consumers will choose to smoke up to Q_1 tobacco. The optimum for society, however, is at Q^*.

One way of tackling this problem is through taxation. If the government imposes a tax shown by the red line in Figure 8.3, this effectively shifts the supply curve to the market, as shown in the figure. This raises the price in the market, so consumers are persuaded to reduce their consumption to the optimal level at Q^*. Notice that because the demand curve (*MPB*) is quite steep (relatively inelastic), a substantial tax is needed in order to reach Q^*. Empirical evidence suggests that the demand for tobacco is relatively inelastic — and therefore tobacco taxes have risen to comprise a large portion of the price of a packet of cigarettes.

Conversely, if the government wishes to encourage the consumption of a merit good, it may do so through subsidies. Thus, the museum service is subsidised, and the ballet and opera have enjoyed subsidies in the past. Figure 8.4 shows how such a subsidy might be used to affect the quantity of museum services provided. Demand (*MPB*) again shows the demand for museum services from the public, which is below the marginal social benefit (*MSB*) that the authorities perceive to be

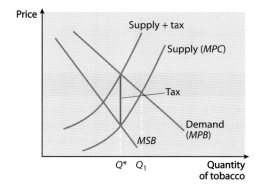

Figure 8.3 *Taxing tobacco*

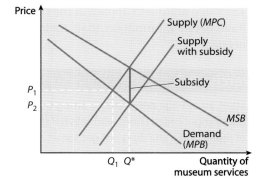

Figure 8.4 *Subsidising museum services*

the true value of museum services. Thus the free market equilibrium position is at Q_1, although the government believes that Q^* is the socially optimum position. By providing a subsidy, the supply curve is shifted to the right, and consumers will choose to demand the optimum quantity at the subsidised price P_2.

Information failures

If markets are to be effective in guiding resource allocation, it is important that economic decision-makers receive full and accurate information about market conditions. Ideally, all traders in a market should have the same information about market conditions — a situation known as *symmetric information.* Consumers need information about the prices at which they can buy and the quality of the products for sale. Producers need to be able to observe how consumers react to prices. Information is thus of crucial significance if markets are to work. However, there are some markets in which not all traders have access to good information, or in which some traders have more or better access to it than others. This is known as a situation of **asymmetric information**, and can be a source of market failure.

 Key *term*

asymmetric information: a situation in which some participants in a market have better information about market conditions than others

Healthcare

One example of asymmetric information is in healthcare. Suppose you go to your dentist for a check-up. He tells you that you have a filling that needs to be replaced, although you have had no pain or problems with it. In this situation the seller in a market has much better information about the product than the buyer. You as the buyer have no idea whether or not the recommended treatment is needed, and without going to another dentist for a second opinion you have no way of finding out. You might think this is an unsatisfactory situation, as it seems to give a lot of power to the seller relative to the consumer. The situation is even worse where the dentist does not even publish the prices for treatment until after it has been carried out! The Office of Fair Trading criticised private dentists for exactly this sort of practice when they reported on this market in March 2003. Indeed, dentists are now required by law to publish prices for treatment.

The same argument applies in the case of other areas of healthcare, where doctors have better information than their patients about the sort of treatment that is needed.

Exercise 8.2

Ethel, an old-age pensioner, is sitting quietly at home when the doorbell rings. At the door is a stranger called Frank, who tells her that he has noticed that her roof is in desperate need of repair, and if she does not get something done about it very soon, there will be problems in the next rainstorm. Fortunately, he can help — for a price. Discuss whether there is a market failure in this situation, and what Ethel (or others) could do about it.

Education

The market for education is similar. Teachers or government inspectors may know more about the subjects and topics that students need to study than the students do themselves. This is partly because teachers are able to take a longer view and can see education provision in a broader perspective. Students taking economics at university may have to take a course in mathematics and statistics in their first year, and some will always complain that they have come to study economics, not maths. It is only later that they come to realise that competence in maths is crucial these days for the economics that they will study later in their course.

How could this problem be tackled? The answer would seem to be obvious — if the problem arises from an information failure, then the answer should be to improve the information flow, in this case to students. This might be achieved by providing a convincing explanation of why the curriculum has been designed in a particular way. It may also be necessary to provide incentives for students to study particular unpopular subjects, perhaps by making success a requirement for progression to the next stage of the course. By understanding the economic cause of a problem, it is possible to devise a strategy that should go some way towards removing the market failure.

Second-hand cars

One of the most famous examples of asymmetric information relates to the second-hand (or 'pre-owned', by the latest terminology) car market. This is because the first paper that drew attention to the problem of asymmetric information, by Nobel laureate George Akerlof, focused on this market.

Akerlof argued that there are two types of car. Some cars are good runners and are totally reliable, whereas some are continually breaking down and needing parts and servicing; the latter are known as 'lemons' in the USA (allegedly from fruit machines, where lemons offer the lowest prize). The problem in the second-hand

The second-hand car market is an example of a market with asymmetric information

car market arises because the owners of cars (potential sellers) have better information about their cars than the potential buyers. In other words, when a car owner decides to sell a car, he or she knows whether it is a lemon or a good-quality car — but a buyer cannot tell.

In this sort of market, car dealers can adopt one of two possible strategies. One is to offer a high price and buy up all the cars in the market, knowing that the lemons will be sold on at a loss. The problem is that, if the lemons make up a large proportion of the cars in the market, this could generate overall losses for the dealers. The alternative is to offer a low price, and just buy up all the lemons to sell for scrap. In this situation, the market for good-quality used cars is effectively destroyed because owners of good quality cars will not accept the low price — an extreme form of market failure!

Again, the solution may be to tackle the problem at its root, by finding a way to provide information. In the case of second-hand cars, AA inspection schemes or the offering of warranties may be a way of improving the flow of information about the quality of cars for sale.

Summary

➤ A merit good is one that society believes should be consumed by individuals whether or not they have the means or the willingness to do so.

➤ There is a strong normative element in the identification of merit goods.

➤ Demerit goods (or 'merit bads') are goods that society believes should not be consumed by individuals even if they wish to do so.

➤ In the case of merit and demerit goods, 'society' (as represented by government) believes that it has better information than consumers about these goods, and about what is good (or bad) for consumers.

➤ Information deficiency can lead to market failure in other situations: for example, where some participants in a market have better information about some aspect(s) of the market than others.

➤ Examples of this include healthcare, education and second-hand cars.

Exercise 8.3

The *Guardian* reported on 27 August 2004 that the pharmaceutical company GlaxoSmithKline had been forced to publish details of a clinical trial of one of its leading antidepressant drugs following a lawsuit that had accused the company of concealing evidence that the drug could be harmful to children. Discuss the extent to which this situation may have led to a market failure because of information problems.

Labour immobility

A characteristic of the way in which an economy evolves over time is that the structure of economic activity changes. As time goes by, the pattern of consumer demand evolves, and so does the pattern of supply. For an economy that engages in international trade, the structure over time needs to evolve not only in response to domestic changes, but also with changes in external demand for British goods and changes in the pattern of world supply of goods and services. New international competitors present new challenges for domestic producers, and domestic firms develop new skills and specialisms.

These changes require firms in the economy to adapt to changing conditions. A critical part of this process is that factors of production need to be redeployed over time, from sectors producing goods that are no longer in strong demand to sectors that are expanding in the face of increasing demand. This is a desirable process for an economy, and an important task for the market mechanism is to enable the reallocation of resources between sectors. There may be barriers to this process if factors of production do not switch readily between activities, and such barriers may constitute another form of market failure.

Labour mobility is one important aspect of this, because if workers cannot transfer from declining to expanding sectors, one result may be **structural unemployment**.

There may be many reasons that make it difficult for labour to move between sectors. One important factor is that different jobs and occupations require different skills. A worker who is made redundant from one sort of job in a declining sector may need training before being equipped for employment in an expanding sector. For the British economy, the decline of manufacturing activity and the expansion of service sectors has required a substantial retraining programme. Coal miners and production

Key *term*

structural unemployment: unemployment arising from changes in the pattern of economic activity in an economy

workers do not become international bankers or ballet dancers overnight. Similarly, in economies such as China, surplus labour from rural areas needs training before being integrated into industrial work in factories.

The situation may be even worse where the expanding sectors are located in a different region to the declining activities. Moving house is costly, and workers may be reluctant to search for jobs that would entail the upheaval of moving to a new environment. Differences in house prices between regions may make it even more difficult, and if there are long queues on council house lists, this will also create problems for would-be migrants. It may also be the case that it is more difficult to find out about job opportunities in other regions — in other words, there may also be an information failure.

Encouraging labour mobility

The sorts of policies that the government could adopt in order to cope with this problem follow naturally from the reasons for immobility. The problem of occupational mobility arises from the inappropriate skills of the workers released from declining sectors. The solution would thus seem obvious — provide retraining programmes so that the released workers can gain the skills that they need to be redeployed. Firms may be reluctant to provide sufficient training themselves, as

there may be a free-rider problem present. This is because once workers have been trained, they may find that other firms will be keen to hire them. There thus may be market failure arguments here that would justify government intervention.

As far as geographic mobility is concerned, there may be a case for the government offering relocation subsidies to encourage workers to move to where they are needed. This would have the effect of reducing the need to pay out unemployment benefits to people who are unable to obtain jobs close to their homes. Such schemes are indeed in place — for example, the subsidies to housing available for key workers, such as nurses and teachers in London and in the southeast and east regions.

Unstable commodity markets

Suppose that weather conditions one season are especially unfavourable, and that the onion crop is ruined. Such a poor harvest means that the supply curve is well to the left of its normal position. Consider Figure 8.5. Suppose that in an average year the harvest produces a supply curve such as S_{av}. Notice that it is relatively steep, reflecting the fact that there are limits to how long the onion sellers can store onions for later sale, or how many more onions they can produce for sale if the price is favourable. In other words, the quantity of onions available at any point in time is constrained by previous decisions about how many onions to plant.

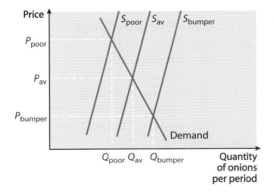

Figure 8.5
The market for onions

Furthermore, notice that the demand curve is relatively price-inelastic ('*relatively*', because elasticity varies along a straight-line demand curve, so is not inelastic throughout its length). It could be expected that the demand for onions would be relatively price-inelastic partly because there are no close substitutes for onions and they are an essential ingredient for many dishes. Furthermore, onions comprise a relatively minor part of a household's spending.

Figure 8.5 can now be used to analyse the market situation. If the harvest is poor, supply will be at S_{poor} instead of at S_{av}, and the equilibrium price will rise to P_{poor} with the quantity traded falling to Q_{poor}. It can be seen that the shortage of onions in the market pushes up the equilibrium price. Furthermore, notice that the inelasticity of both supply and demand in this market means that the price effect is stronger than the quantity effect. You can see this for yourself by sketching a diagram in which the curves are relatively more elastic.

Figure 8.5 also shows what happens in a bumper year, when the harvest is especially good. The supply curve S_{bumper} is now to the right of its normal position at S_{av}. Price falls to P_{bumper}, and quantity traded rises to Q_{bumper}. Again, the price effect is stronger than the quantity effect because of the relatively inelastic supply and demand.

Buffer stock schemes

If the commodity concerned can be stored, a **buffer stock** can be used to try to stabilise prices over time.

Key term

buffer stock: surplus stock that is bought up when the harvest is good with a view to selling when it is poor, in an attempt to stabilise commodity prices

Figure 8.6 illustrates how such a scheme could work for a grain market. Suppose that demand for grain is relatively stable from year to year, but supply varies between S_{poor}, when the weather is unfavourable, and S_{glut}, when conditions are good for agriculture and there is a bumper harvest. This means that the free market price will vary between P_p when the harvest is poor and P_g when the harvest is strong.

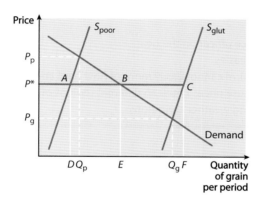

Figure 8.6
A buffer stock scheme

Suppose a buffer stock scheme is set up with the aim of stabilising price at a medium level between the two extremes that occur — say, at P^*. In order to achieve this, grain is bought up as a buffer stock when there is a glut. Notice that, if the scheme buys up the quantity BC, then the remaining quantity is bought by consumers at price P^*. The buffer stock scheme has to pay out the area $BCFE$ as expenditure.

In a poor harvest year, grain is sold via this scheme to prevent the price from rising too high. Thus, if the harvest is at S_{poor} the buffer stock will sell the amount AB. Again, P^* is the price at which the quantity supplied by farmers plus the amount released on to the market from the buffer stock just meets the amount demanded by the market. This time the buffer stock scheme benefits from revenue generated from the sale of past stocks, to the tune of area $ABED$.

This scheme can be effective in stabilising prices; indeed, it can also stabilise the quantity traded through time. The difficulty with such a scheme comes in identifying the level at which prices should be set. If the price is set too high, the buffer

scheme will find itself buying up more grain than it sells, and so grain will accumulate as time goes by. Thus, its expenditure in bumper years could (on average) exceed its revenues in poorer years. This would also become very costly in terms of storage. On the other hand, if the price is set at too low a level, the scheme will not have sufficient stocks to be able to prevent prices rising in times of poor harvests.

Instability in prices has arisen not only as a result of volatility in supply or demand. One of the characteristics of agricultural goods is that there are *inflexibilities* in supply. Farmers take decisions on how much of each crop to plant in advance of knowledge about demand conditions. Once the crop is in the ground, the quantity cannot be varied until the following year. Price signals to producers thus operate with a time lag. This creates sluggishness in the way that producers can respond to changes in market conditions, and farmers may find themselves with an increase in supply at a time when demand has fallen.

Exercise 8.4

Identify the form of market failure associated with each of the following:

a the use of heroin
b the provision of a police officer on the beat
c vaccination against measles
d a situation in which a firm cannot easily monitor how hard an employee is working
e large differences in house prices between different regions of the country
f uncertainty surrounding weather conditions

Summary

> As an economy evolves through time, labour needs to transfer between economic sectors.

> Some sectors need to decline as the pattern of consumer demand changes and as the pattern of international competition alters.

> Similarly, other sectors need to expand to meet consumer demands and to allow the economy to develop new patterns of specialisation.

> If labour is immobile between regions or between occupations, then a result may be structural unemployment.

> This may be tackled by relocation subsidies or training programmes.

> Supply conditions in some commodity markets may lead to volatility in prices from one year to the next.

> A buffer stock scheme is one way of trying to stabilise commodity prices over time.

Chapter 9

Government intervention and government failure

The previous two chapters have examined forms of market failure, and have discussed the sort of policy interventions that might be used to try to correct these market failures. This chapter reminds us of some of these interventions and explores how some well-intentioned interventions by government can sometimes produce unintended results, a situation that may be tantamount to government failure.

Learning outcomes

After studying this chapter, you should:
- ➤ be able to identify areas in which government actions may have unintended distortionary effects
- ➤ be aware of some sources of government failure
- ➤ be familiar with the effects of minimum wage legislation and rent controls
- ➤ be able to analyse the effects of sales taxes and subsidies

Correcting market failure

Markets fail when the price mechanism causes an inefficient allocation of resources within a society. This occurs when price is not set equal to marginal cost, or where marginal social benefit is not equal to marginal social cost. In such circumstances, it seems apparent that by improving the way in which resources are allocated, the society could become better off. In other words, market failure is often viewed as a valid reason for governments to intervene in the economy, in order to tackle the market failures.

Externalities

Chapter 7 looked at the problems caused by externalities, and discussed how these can occur in various different contexts. The final section of that chapter analysed possible policies that a government could adopt to deal with the presence of

externalities in a market. An externality occurs where the price mechanism fails to reflect the true costs or benefits associated with a product. One approach to tackling this problem is to internalise the externality, by bringing its effects into the market mechanism. For example, this might be done by making sure that firms that cause pollution face the true costs of their production activities. An alternative approach is to impose regulation that ensures that the appropriate level of output of a good is produced, perhaps through a pollution permit scheme.

Public goods

The problem with public goods arises from the free-rider problem. When goods are non-exclusive and non-rivalrous, no individual has the incentive to pay. In such circumstances, some form of intervention is needed to ensure that a sufficient quantity of such public goods is produced. These need not be by direct production by the government, but could be through subsidies to local authorities or other bodies.

Imperfect market information

A natural approach to tackling information problems is by providing information. This may take the form of government campaigns to spread information, or by some form of regulation that forces firms to reveal information about their products. One example might be the regulations that require firms to specify ingredient lists on processed food products.

Labour immobility

As discussed in the previous chapter, the solution to cope with labour immobility may depend on the reasons for that immobility. Regional mobility may be tackled by relocation subsidies. Education and training may be able to help to solve problems of occupational mobility. Such measures may enable workers to transfer from declining to expanding sectors, thus improving the efficiency with which resources are allocated to their best use.

Unstable commodity markets

Volatility in prices causes uncertainty in markets, and may obstruct the good functioning of the price mechanism. Schemes that stabilise commodity prices, such as a buffer stock, may enable prices to work more effectively as signals to producers and consumers.

Government failure

Most governments see it as their responsibility to try to correct some of the failures of markets to allocate resources efficiently. As outlined above, this has led to a wide variety of policies being devised to address issues of market failure. Some of these have been discussed already. However, some policies have unintended effects that may not culminate in successful elimination of

> ### Key term
>
> **government failure:** a misallocation of resources arising from government intervention

market failure. Indeed, in some cases government intervention may introduce new market distortions, leading to a phenomenon known as **government failure**. The remainder of this chapter examines some examples of such government failure.

Many of the measures outlined at the beginning of this chapter can cause problems if they are not carefully implemented, or if the government itself does not have sufficient information to take good decisions. For example, in the case of externalities, the government may choose to tackle pollution by a tax, or by regulation. However, if it is not possible to identify the appropriate amount of the tax that is needed to correct the market failure, or if it is not known how many pollution permits need to be issued to reach the optimum outcome for society, then it will not be possible to get the policy exactly right. Similar implementation problems may arise with other attempts to deal with market failure. However, government failure may arise in many other ways.

The minimum wage

Chapter 6 discussed the National Minimum Wage, introduced in the UK in 1999, with the intention of protecting workers on low pay. Figure 9.1 offers a brief reminder of the analysis, using the labour market for office cleaners. Employers demand labour according to the wage rate — the lower the wage, the higher the demand for the labour of office cleaners. On the supply side, more workers will offer themselves for work when the wage rate is relatively high. If the market is unregulated, it will reach equilibrium with a wage rate W^* and quantity of labour L^*.

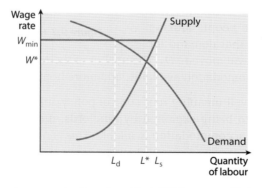

Figure 9.1
A minimum wage

If the government comes to the view that W^* is not sufficiently high to provide a reasonable wage for cleaners, one possible response is to impose a minimum wage, below which employers are not permitted to offer employment — say, W_{min} on the figure. This will have two effects on the market situation. First, employers will demand less labour at this higher wage, so employment will fall to L_d. Second, more workers will be prepared to offer themselves for employment at the higher wage, so labour supply will rise to L_s. However, the net effect of this is that there is an excess supply of labour at this wage and hence unemployment, with more workers offering themselves for work than there are jobs available in the market.

What is happening here is that, with the minimum wage in effect, *some* workers (those who manage to remain in employment) are better off, and now receive a

better wage. However, those who are now unemployed are worse off. It is not then clear whether the effect of the minimum wage is to make society as a whole better off—some people will be better off, but others will be worse off. This is one example of where well-intentioned government intervention may have unintended effects.

Rent controls

Another market in which governments have been tempted to intervene is the housing market. Figure 9.2 represents the market for rented accommodation. The free market equilibrium would be where demand and supply intersect, with the equilibrium rent being R^* and the quantity of accommodation traded being Q^*.

If the government regards the level of rent as excessive, to the point where households on low incomes may be unable to afford rented accommodation, then, given that housing is one of life's necessities, it may regard this as unacceptable.

The temptation for the government is to move this market away from its equilibrium by imposing a maximum level of rent that landlords are allowed to charge their tenants. Suppose that this level of rent is denoted by R_{max} in Figure 9.2. Again, there are two effects that follow. First, landlords will no longer find it profitable to supply as much rental accommodation, and so will reduce supply to Q_s. Second, at this lower rent there will be more people looking for accommodation, so that demand for

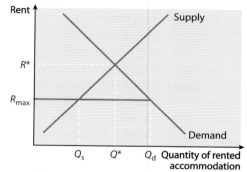

Figure 9.2 Rent controls

rented accommodation will move to Q_d. The upshot of the rent controls, therefore, is that there is less accommodation available, and more homeless people.

It can be seen that the well-meaning rent control policy, intended to protect low-income households from being exploited by landlords, merely has the effect of reducing the amount of accommodation available. This is not what was supposed to happen.

Sales tax

Governments need to raise funds to finance the expenditure that they undertake. One way of doing this is through expenditure taxes such as value added tax (VAT) or excise duties on such items as alcohol or tobacco. You might think that raising money in this way to provide goods and services that would otherwise not be provided would be a benefit to society. But there is a downside to this action, even if all the funds raised by a sales tax are spent wisely.

The effects of a sales tax can be seen in a demand and supply diagram, and were discussed briefly in Chapter 5. An **indirect tax** is paid by the seller, so

> **Key term**
>
> **indirect tax:** a tax levied on expenditure on goods or services (as opposed to a direct tax, which is a tax charged directly to an individual based on a component of income)

it affects the supply curve for a product. Figure 9.3 illustrates the case of a *fixed rate* or *specific* tax — a tax that is set at a constant amount per litre of petrol. Without the tax, the market equilibrium is at the intersection of demand and supply with a price of P_0 and a quantity traded of Q_0. The effect of the tax is to reduce the quantity that firms are prepared to supply at any given price — or, to put it another way, for any given quantity of petrol, firms need to receive the amount of the tax over and above

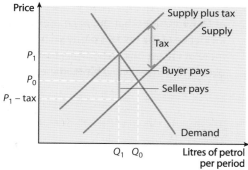

Figure 9.3 *The effects of an indirect tax on petrol*

the price at which they would have been prepared to supply that quantity. The effect is thus to move the supply curve upwards by the amount of the tax, as shown in the figure. We get a new equilibrium with a higher price at P_1 and a lower quantity traded at Q_1.

To what extent is this good for society? The government has raised revenue as a result of the tax, so we might argue that the funds raised can be used in a way that benefits society as a whole. However, the picture is not quite so straightforward. Recall from Chapter 4 that an efficient allocation of resources is achieved when a market reaches an equilibrium such that the price of a product is equal to the marginal cost of producing it. This suggests that the market for petrol shown in Figure 9.3 has been moved away from this ideal state of affairs. It may thus arise that by imposing a tax to raise funds for correcting market failure in one part of the economy, the government introduces a misallocation of resources elsewhere.

Indirect taxes on petrol can be used to reduce consumption

Of course, it may be that in this particular market, the government has some other reason for wanting to reduce the consumption of petrol — perhaps because of congestion or pollution etc. However, this argument cannot be applied to many other markets in which indirect taxes are levied. After all, VAT is applied to almost all goods and services sold in the UK.

Extension material

Is it possible to identify how a sales tax will affect total welfare in society? Consider Figure 9.4, which shows the market for DVDs. Suppose that the government imposes a specific tax on DVDs. This would have the effect of taking market equilibrium from the free market position at P^* with quantity traded at Q^* to a new position, with price now at P_t and quantity traded

at Q_t. Remember that the price rises by less than the amount of the tax, implying that the incidence of the tax falls partly on buyers and partly on sellers. In Figure 9.4 consumers pay more of the tax (the area P^*P_tBE) than the producers (who pay FP^*EG). The effect on society's overall welfare will now be examined.

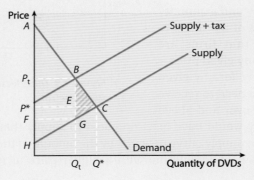

Figure 9.4 A sales tax and economic welfare

Remember that the total welfare that society receives from consuming a product is the sum of consumer and producer surplus. The situation before and after the sales tax is as follows. Before the tax, consumer surplus is given by the area AP^*C and producer surplus is given by the triangle P^*CH. How about afterwards? Consumer surplus is now the smaller triangle AP_tB, and producer surplus is FGH. The area P_tBGF is the revenue raised by the government from the tax, which should be included in total welfare on the assumption that the government uses this wisely. The total amount of welfare is now $ABGH$. If you compare these total welfare areas before and after the tax, you will realise that they differ by the area BCG. This triangle represents a deadweight loss that arises from the imposition of the tax. It is sometimes referred to as the **excess burden** of the tax.

So, even where the government intervenes to raise funding for its expenditure — and spends wisely — a distortion is introduced to resource allocation, and society must bear a loss of welfare.

Prohibition

Another example of how government intervention may have unintended effects is when action is taken to prohibit the consumption of a demerit good. Consider the case of a hard drug, such as cocaine. It can be argued that there are substantial social disbenefits arising from the consumption of hard drugs, and that addicts and potential addicts are in no position to make informed decisions about their consumption of them. One response to such a situation is to consider making the drug illegal — that is, to impose **prohibition**.

Key terms

excess burden of a sales tax: the deadweight loss to society following the imposition of a sales tax

prohibition: an attempt to prevent the consumption of a demerit good by declaring it illegal

Edexcel AS Economics

Figure 9.5 shows how the market for cocaine might look. You may wonder why the demand curve takes on this shape. The argument is that there are two types of cocaine user. There are the recreational users, who will take cocaine if it is available at a reasonable price, but who are not addicts. In addition, there is a hard core of habitual users who are addicts, whose demand for cocaine is highly inelastic. Thus, at low prices demand is relatively elastic because of the presence of the recreational users, who are relatively price-sensitive. At higher prices the recreational users drop away, and demand from the addicts is highly price-inelastic. Suppose that the supply in free market equilibrium is given by S_0; the equilibrium will be with price P_0 and quantity traded Q_0. If the drug is made illegal, this will affect supply. Some dealers will leave the market to trade in something else, and the police will succeed in confiscating a certain proportion of the drugs in the market. However, they are unlikely to be totally successful, so supply could move to, say, S_1.

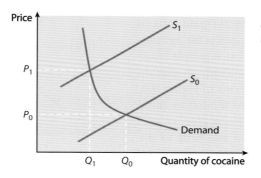

Figure 9.5
Prohibition

In the new market situation, price rises substantially to P_1, and quantity traded falls to Q_1. However, what has happened is that the recreational users have dropped out of the market, leaving a hard core of addicts who will pay any price for the drug, and who may resort to muggings and robberies in order to finance their habit. This behaviour clearly imposes a new sort of externality on society. And the more successful the police are in confiscating supplies, the higher the price will be driven. There may thus be disadvantages in using prohibition as a way of discouraging consumption of a demerit good.

Price instability and the Common Agricultural Policy (CAP)

In the past, many governments have regarded agricultural markets as in need of particular attention, partly because of their strategic significance. For example, in times of war it is important to be able to feed the population, so governments have been reluctant to be dependent on imported food supplies. Within the European Economic Community (EEC), which has now been superseded by the European Union (EU), there was an additional concern to avoid too much migration from the rural areas into the towns.

The Common Agricultural Policy (CAP) was devised to stabilise the incomes of farmers in the EEC/EU. There were two key components of the policy. The first was to provide guaranteed prices to farmers for their crops. However, as the guaranteed prices were typically above the prices that prevailed in world markets, the

second element was a variable tariff designed to prevent Europe from being flooded by cheaper imports.

Figure 9.6 describes this graphically. It represents the market for wheat in the EU. As agricultural products in the EU may be seen as relatively high cost by world standards, suppose that the world price is below the equilibrium price that would obtain in the EU (which would, of course, be at the intersection of demand and supply). P_w represents the world price and, if this price were also to be set within the EU, demand in the market would be given by D_0, of which only a small quantity (S_0) would be produced by EU wheat producers; the remainder ($D_0 - S_0$) would be imported.

Such a situation shows why there might be concern, as wheat production within the EU is on a limited scale and imports seem to make up most of the market. Furthermore, if farmers desert the rural areas for better-paid jobs in the cities, the long-term prospects for agriculture will be even worse, as once people leave the rural areas, it will be difficult to sustain the agricultural sector. In terms of Figure 9.6, the supply curve will drift to the left as more farmers withdraw from the sector — and probably the demand curve will drift to the right as incomes rise, and the dependence on imports will therefore escalate.

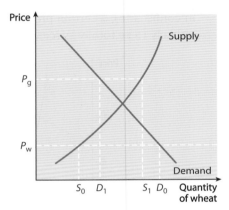

Figure 9.6 *The CAP*

The CAP thus set guaranteed prices for key agricultural commodities, so that farmers could be assured of a certain income. Suppose the guaranteed price for wheat were set at P_g in Figure 9.6. In current market conditions supply would increase to S_1, and demand would fall to D_1. This would maintain the viability of the agricultural sector and eliminate the need for imports. Indeed, at P_g farmers would produce more than consumers would demand at that price, and the EU would have to purchase the excess supply ($S_1 - D_1$).

The second component of the CAP then cuts in, in that a variable levy is imposed on the price of non-European wheat, set at a level that covers the difference between the guaranteed price and the world price. This ensures that foreign producers are not able to undercut prices within the European area. The levy is variable in order to maintain the guaranteed price in the face of varying world prices.

The CAP has come under increasing criticism, especially from producers in less-developed countries, who are desperate to find markets for their produce and feel that it is unfair that European producers should be so heavily subsidised.

In addition, as the EU bought up more and more wheat and other commodities, the costs of storage escalated. This led to the build-up of the now infamous wine 'lakes' and butter 'mountains'. Selling the surplus cheaply elsewhere in the world brought allegations of dumping from governments that did not want their own agricultural sectors to be faced with unfair competition.

Selling surpluses cheaply overseas leads to unfair competition and often attracts allegations of 'dumping'

The CAP has been going through a process of reform in response to these pressures. Milk quotas were introduced in 1984 to limit excess production, and the McSharry reforms of 1992 brought beef quotas and the notion of 'set-aside', under which farmers were paid for setting some of their land aside, i.e. not using it. Guaranteed prices began to be reduced, so that the variable levy could also be reduced — as was required under international agreements on tariff reduction. Additional reforms under Agenda 2000 brought more cuts to guaranteed prices, and rural development schemes were introduced to encourage farmers to engage in other activities within rural areas. In 2003 further measures forced farmers to plan supply in relation to market prices rather than the guaranteed prices. Instead, subsidies are now being provided for a range of environmental and rural development schemes.

Reform has been slow, because there has been much lobbying and political pressure from farmers who felt their interests were being threatened. This is a reminder that economic analysis has to be set into the political context in which it operates.

Subsidies and efficiency

One problem that arises with the use of subsidies to encourage higher production of a commodity relates to the incentives given to producers. If producers are cushioned from having to compete at world prices, there is little incentive for them to achieve cost efficiency. Thus, an indirect effect of a system of subsidies may be a reduction in the efficiency with which production is carried out.

Exercise 9.1

Examine why prices in some markets may be unstable from year to year, and evaluate ways in which more stability might be achieved. How effective would you expect such measures to be?

Costs of intervention

Some roles are critical for a government to perform if a mixed economy is to function effectively. A vital role is the provision by the government of an environment in which markets can operate effectively. There must be stability in the political system if firms and consumers are to take decisions with confidence about the future. And there must be a secure system of property rights, without which markets could not be expected to work.

In addition, there are sources of market failure that require intervention. This does not necessarily mean that governments need to substitute markets with direct action. However, it does mean that they need to be more active in markets that cannot operate effectively, while at the same time performing an enabling role to encourage markets to work well whenever this is feasible.

Such intervention entails costs. There are costs of administering, and costs of monitoring the policy to ensure that it is working as intended. This includes the need to look out for the unintended distortionary effects that some policies can have on resource allocation in a society. It is therefore important to check that the marginal costs of implementing and monitoring policies do not exceed their marginal benefits.

Summary

- Government failure can occur when well-meaning intervention by governments has unintended effects.
- In some circumstances a minimum wage intended to protect the low paid may aggravate their situation by increasing unemployment.
- Rent controls may have the effect of reducing the amount of accommodation available.
- A sales tax imposes an excess burden on society.
- Prohibition may also have unintended effects.
- Governments have often regarded it as desirable to intervene in agricultural markets to sustain food production and stabilise prices.
- In the EU, the Common Agricultural Policy (CAP) involved intervention buying to maintain prices and sustain agriculture.
- Over time this proved costly, in view of the need to store commodities; there was also political pressure from the rest of the world.
- Recent reforms to the CAP have lowered guaranteed prices and redirected subsidies towards environmental goals and the encouragement of rural development.

Edexcel AS Economics

Managing the economy

Part 2

Chapter 10

Measuring economic performance

This part of the book switches attention to macroeconomics. Macroeconomics has much in common with microeconomics, but focuses on the whole economy, rather than on individual markets and how they operate. Although the way of thinking about issues is similar, and although similar tools are used, now it is interactions between economic variables at the level of the whole economy that are studied. This process will introduce some of the major concerns of the media, such as economic growth, inflation and unemployment.

Learning outcomes

After studying this chapter, you should:
- ➤ be aware of the main economic aggregates in a modern economy
- ➤ understand the distinction between real and nominal variables
- ➤ be familiar with the use of index numbers and the calculation of growth rates
- ➤ understand how economic growth is measured and its limitations
- ➤ appreciate the inadequacy of economic growth as a measure of the standard of living
- ➤ be aware of problems of comparison between developed and developing countries
- ➤ appreciate the significance of alternative measurements of inflation and unemployment in the context of the UK economy
- ➤ be familiar with the role and importance of the balance of payments
- ➤ understand the advantages and limitations of the HDI in making comparisons of living standards between countries

Economic performance

Part 1 of the book emphasised the importance of individual markets in achieving allocative and productive efficiency. In a modern economy, there are so many separate markets that it is difficult to get an overall picture of how well the economy is working. When it comes to monitoring its overall performance, the focus thus tends to be on the **macroeconomic** aggregates. 'Aggregate' here means 'totals' — for example, total unemployment in an economy, or total spending on goods and services — rather than, say, unemployed workers in a particular occupation, or spending on a particular good.

> ### Key term
>
> **macroeconomics:** the study of the interrelationships between economic variables at an aggregate (macroeconomic) level

There are a number of dimensions in which the economy as a whole can be monitored. One prime focus of economic policy in recent years has been the inflation rate, as it has been argued that maintaining a stable economic environment is crucial to enabling markets to operate effectively. A second focus has been unemployment, which has been seen as an indicator of whether the economy is using its resources to the full — in other words, whether there are factors of production that are not being fully utilised. In addition, of course, there may be concern that the people who are unemployed are being disadvantaged.

Perhaps more fundamentally, there is an interest in economic growth. Is the economy expanding its potential capacity as time goes by, thereby making more resources available for members of society? In fact, it might be argued that this is the most fundamental objective for the economy, and the most important indicator of the economy's performance.

Other concerns may also need to be kept in mind. In particular, there is the question of how the economy interacts with the rest of the world. The UK is an 'open' economy — one that actively engages in international trade — and this aspect of UK economic performance needs to be monitored too.

The importance of data

To monitor the performance of the economy, it is crucial to be able to observe how the economy is functioning, and for this you need data. Remember that economics, especially macroeconomics, is a non-experimental discipline. It is not possible to conduct experiments to see how the economy reacts to various stimuli in order to learn how it works. Instead, it is necessary to observe the economy, and to come to a judgement about whether or not its performance is satisfactory, and whether macroeconomic theories about how the economy works are supported by the evidence.

So, a reliable measure is needed for tracking each of the variables mentioned above, in order to observe how the economy is evolving through time. The key indicators of the economy's performance will be introduced as this chapter unfolds.

Most of the economic statistics used by economists are collected and published by various government agencies. Such data in the UK are published mainly by the Office of National Statistics (ONS). Data on other countries are published by the International Monetary Fund (IMF), the World Bank and the United Nations, as well

An IMF meeting

national sources. There is little alternative to relying on such sources because the accurate collection of data is an expensive and time-consuming business.

Care needs to be taken in the interpretation of economic data. It is important to be aware of how the data are compiled, and the extent to which they are indicators of what economists are trying to measure. It is also important to remember that the economic environment is ever changing, and that single causes can rarely be ascribed to the economic events that are observed. This is because the ceteris paribus condition that underlies so much economic analysis is rarely fulfilled in reality. In other words, you cannot rely on 'other things remaining constant' when using data about the real world.

It is also important to realise that even the ONS cannot observe with absolute accuracy. Indeed, some data take so long to be assembled that early estimates are provisional in nature and subject to later revision as more information becomes available. Data used in international comparisons must be treated with even greater caution.

Real and nominal measurements

The measurement of economic variables poses many dilemmas for statisticians. Not least is the fundamental problem of what to use as units of measurement. Suppose economists wish to measure total output produced in an economy during successive years. In the first place, they cannot use volume measures. They may be able to count how many computers, passenger cars, tins of paint and cauliflowers the economy produces — but how do they add all these different items together to produce a total?

An obvious solution is to use the money values. Given prices for all the items, it is possible to calculate the money values of all these goods and thus produce a measurement of the total output produced in an economy during a year in terms of pounds sterling. However, this is just the beginning of the problem because, in order to monitor changes in total output between 2 years, it is important to be aware that not only do the volumes of goods produced change, but so too do their prices. In effect, this means that, if pounds sterling are used as the unit of measurement, the unit of measurement will change from one year to the next as prices change.

This is a problem that is not faced by most of the physical sciences. After all, the length of a metre does not alter from one year to the next, so if the length of something is being measured, the unit is fixed. Economists, however, have to make allowance for changing prices when measuring in pounds sterling.

Measurements made using prices that are current at the time a transaction takes place are known as measurements of **nominal values**. When prices are rising, these nominal measurements will always overstate the extent to which an economic variable is growing through time. Clearly, to analyse performance, economists will be more interested in **'real' values** — that is, the quantities produced after having removed the effects of price changes. One way in which these real measures can be obtained is by taking the volumes produced in each year and valuing these quantities at the prices that prevailed in some base year. This then enables allowance to be made for the changes in prices that take place, permitting a focus on the real values. These can be thought of as being measured at *constant prices.*

> **Key terms**
>
> **nominal value:** value of an economic variable based on current prices, taking no account of changing prices through time
>
> **real value:** value of an economic variable taking account of changing prices through time

For example, suppose that last year you bought a tub of ice cream for £2, but that inflation has been 10%, so that this year you had to pay £2.20 for the same tub. Your *real* consumption of the item has not changed, but your spending has increased. If you were to use the value of your spending to measure changes in consumption through time, it would be misleading, as you know that your *real* consumption has not changed at all (so is still £2), although its *nominal* value has increased to £2.20.

Index numbers

In some cases there is no apparent unit of measurement that is meaningful. For example, if you wished to measure the general level of prices in an economy, there is no meaningful unit of measurement that could be used. In such cases the solution is to use **index numbers**, which is a form of ratio that compares the value of a variable with some base point.

> **Key term**
>
> **index number:** a device for comparing the value of a variable in one period or location with a base observation (e.g. the consumer price index measures the average level of prices relative to a base period)

For example, suppose the price of a 250g pack of butter last year was 80p, and this year it is 84p. How can the price between the two periods be compared? One way of doing it is to calculate the percentage change:

$$100 \times (84 - 80) \div 80 = 5\%$$

(Note that this is the formula for calculating any growth rate in percentage terms. The change in the variable is always expressed as a percentage of the initial value, not the final value.)

An alternative way of doing this is to calculate an index number. In the above example, the current value of the index could be calculated as $100 \times 84 \div 80 = 105$. In other words, the current value is divided by the base value and multiplied by 100. The resulting number gives the current value relative to the base value. This turns out to be a useful way of expressing a range of economic variables where you want to show the value relative to a base period.

One particular use for this technique is when you want to show the average level of prices at different points in time. For such a general price index, one procedure is to define a typical basket of commodities that reflects the spending pattern of a representative household. The cost of that bundle can be calculated in a base year, and then in subsequent years. The cost in the base year is set to equal 100, and in subsequent years the index is measured relative to that base date, thereby reflecting the change in

The price of a typical basket of commodities can be used as an index of the cost of living

prices since then. For example, if in the second year the weighted average increase in prices were 2.5%, then the index in year 2 would take on the value 102.5 (based on year 1 = 100). Such a general index of prices could be seen as an index of the *cost of living* for the representative household, as it would give the level of prices faced by the average household relative to the base year.

Summary

> Macroeconomics is the study of the interrelationships between economic variables at the level of the whole economy.

> Some variables are of particular interest when monitoring the performance of an economy — for example, inflation, unemployment and economic growth.

> As economists cannot easily conduct experiments in order to test economic theory, they rely on the use of economic data: that is, observations of the world around them.

> Data measured in money terms need to be handled carefully, as prices change over time, thereby affecting the units in which many economic variables are measured.

> Index numbers are helpful in comparing the value of a variable with a base date or unit.

Economic growth

If the ultimate aim of a society is to improve the well-being of its citizens, then in economic terms this means that the resources available within the economy need to expand through time in order to widen people's choices. This requires a process of economic growth, which as we saw in Chapter 1 is an increase in the productive capacity of the economy.

From a theoretical point of view, economic growth can be thought of as an expansion of the productive capacity of an economy. If you like, it is an expansion of the potential output of the economy.

The notion of economic growth was introduced in Chapter 1 in terms of the production possibility frontier (PPF). Figure 10.1 is a reminder and reproduces Figure 1.4. Economic growth is characterised as an outward movement of the production possibility frontier from PPF_0 to PPF_1. In other words, economic growth enables a society to produce more goods and services in any given period as a result of an expansion in its resources.

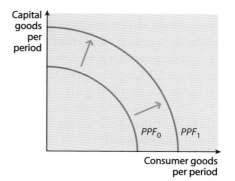

Figure 10.1 Economic growth

Chapter 1 also briefly introduced the notion of **gross domestic product (GDP)** as representing the total output of an economy during a period of time. This can be measured by adding up the total value added produced by all firms in the economy.

Key term

gross domestic product (GDP): a measure of the economic activity carried out in an economy over a period

You might think that it would be possible to measure economic growth by calculating the rate of change of real GDP through time. However, although this provides an estimate of the change in output, this does not necessarily correspond to economic growth. Economic growth has been defined as a change in the productive capacity of the economy: in other words, a change in potential output. If the economy is not always operating at full capacity, then if economists try to measure economic growth using the rate of change of GDP as an indicator, they are not necessarily measuring what they want to.

GDP growth measures the *actual* rate of change of output rather than the growth of the *potential* output capacity of the economy. This can be illustrated with reference to Figure 10.2, where a movement from A to B represents a move on to the *PPF*. This is an increase in actual output resulting from using up surplus capacity in the economy, but it is *not* economic growth in our theoretical sense, as moving from A to B does not entail an increase in productive capacity. On the other hand, a shift of the *PPF* itself,

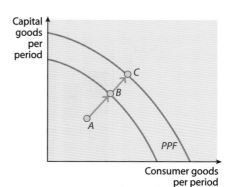

Figure 10.2 Economic growth?

enabling the move from *B* to *C*, *does* represent economic growth. However, when economists observe a change in GDP, they cannot easily distinguish between the two sorts of effect, especially if the economy is subject to a business cycle. It is therefore better to think of economic growth in terms of the underlying trend rate of growth of real GDP.

Figure 10.3 shows real GDP since 1948. You can see that during this period, real GDP has grown in almost every year, but that there are some years where real GDP dipped. It is also important to note that this shows the *level* of real GDP, so to calculate growth it is necessary to compute the annual rate of change. This is done in Figure 10.4, which shows the annual growth rate of real GDP in the UK since 1949. You can see that it is quite difficult to determine the underlying trend because the year-to-year movements are so volatile. Figure 10.5 takes 5-yearly average growth rates over the same period, with the horizontal red line showing the underlying trend rate of growth.

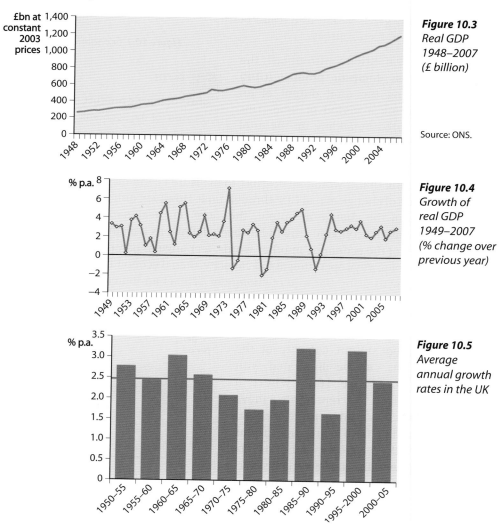

Figure 10.3
Real GDP
1948–2007
(£ billion)

Source: ONS.

Figure 10.4
Growth of
real GDP
1949–2007
(% change over
previous year)

Figure 10.5
Average
annual growth
rates in the UK

The business cycle

In the past it has not been uncommon for economies to go through a regular **business cycle**, where the level of economic activity has varied around an underlying trend. Figure 10.6 shows an economy in which real GDP is trending upwards over time but fluctuating around the trend, so that actual GDP follows a regular cycle around the trend. The point of maximum growth is often referred to as the *peak* of the cycle – or a *boom* period – whereas the low point is known as the *trough* of the cycle. If the growth rate is negative for two consecutive quarters, the economy is considered to be in *recession*.

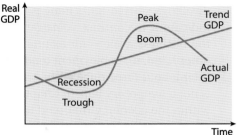

Figure 10.6 *The business cycle*

Key term

business cycle: a phenomenon whereby GDP fluctuates around its underlying trend, following a regular pattern

Figure 10.7 illustrates this in a different way, by showing the growth rates of real GDP in the UK over a cycle from 1984 to 1994. There was evidence in Figure 10.4 that the fluctuations have been less marked in the later years shown.

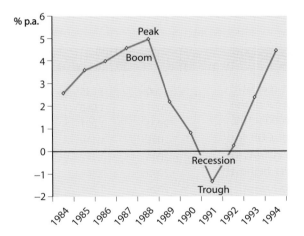

Figure 10.7 *Profile of a cycle: growth of real GDP, 1984–94 (% change over previous year)*

Source: *Economic Trends Annual Supplement.*

A number of explanations have been advanced to explain the business cycle. One suggestion is that some governments engineer the cycle, taking the economy into a boom in the lead-up to an election, only to slow it down again once elected. This has become known as the *political business cycle*. Another suggestion is that cycles arise because of the lagged impact of policy measures on the economy: in other words, it takes time for policies to take effect – sometimes so long that they can destabilise the economy by having unintended effects.

In the past, considerable effort has gone into trying to predict the turning points of the business cycle by looking for *leading indicators* that turn in advance of the cycle – for example, the CBI quarterly survey of business optimism, which is designed to gather firms' views about the cycle. Changes in the number of new

dwellings started and changes in consumer borrowing are also seen as leading indicators. In contrast, *coincident indicators* move in step with the current state of the business cycle — for example, real GDP or the volume of retail sales. On the other hand, unemployment tends to be a *lagging indicator*, as firms may not reduce their labour force right at the start of a recession, preferring first to ensure that it is not a temporary blip. In Chapter 17 it will be seen that there are some responses within the economy that tend to dampen the business cycle automatically; these are known as *automatic stabilisers*.

Summary

➤ Economic growth is a fundamental aspect of the overall performance of an economy, as it is through growth that the citizens of a country can become better off.

➤ From a theoretical point of view, economic growth is an increase in the productive capacity of an economy — in other words, an increase in the potential output of an economy.

➤ GDP is a measure of the total economic activity carried out in an economy during a period by residents living on its territory.

➤ The rate of growth of real GDP informs about the growth in actual output, but not necessarily about the growth of potential output, which is much more difficult to measure.

➤ Economies tend not to grow according to a constant trend, but to fluctuate around the underlying trend, creating the business cycle.

Exercise 10.1

Table 10.1 provides data on real GDP for the period 2000–06. Convert the series to an index based on 2000 = 100. Calculate the growth rate of GDP for each year from 2000/01 to 2005/06. In which year was growth at its highest and in which year was it at its lowest?

Year	Real GDP	
2000	1,035	**Table 10.1** *Real GDP in the UK, 2000–06*
2001	1,060	
2002	1,081	
2003	1,110	
2004	1,147	
2005	1,169	
2006	1,201	

Inflation

Although economic growth may be seen as the most fundamental objective of macro-economic policy, public attention in recent years has focused strongly on the control of inflation. Indeed, it would seem that the government's performance in guiding the economy at the macroeconomic level has been judged in terms of inflation. This being so, it is important to understand how inflation is defined and measured.

Inflation is defined as a change in the overall level of prices in an economy. The first step in measuring inflation is therefore to measure the average level of prices in the economy. Inflation can then be calculated as the percentage rate of change of prices over time.

The consumer price index

The most important general price index in the UK is the **consumer price index (CPI)**, which has been used by the government in setting its inflation target since the beginning of 2004. This index is based on the prices of a bundle of about 650 goods and services measured at different points in time. The information is compiled through the *Family Expenditure Survey*, in which data about the prices of goods and services in the bundle are collected on a monthly basis from a sample of 7,000 households across the country. Some prices are observed directly in randomly selected shops; these are then used to create an index based on 1996 = 100. The weights for the items included in the index are set to reflect the typical spending habits of consumers in the economy, based on the share of each component in their total expenditure. These weights are updated each year, as changes in the consumption patterns of households need to be accommodated if the index is to remain representative.

 Key terms

consumer price index (CPI): a measure of the general level of prices in the UK, the rate of change of which was adopted as the government's inflation target since December 2003

As noted above, it is important to remember that the CPI provides a measurement of the *level* of prices in the economy. This is not inflation: **inflation** is the *rate of change* of prices, and the percentage change in the CPI provides one estimate of the inflation rate.

inflation: the rate of change of the average price level in an economy

Being able to calculate percentage changes is a useful skill. Going back to the example of the ice cream from page 131, remember that you had bought a tub of ice cream for £2 last year, but now have to pay £2.20. The percentage change in the price is obtained by dividing the *change* in price by the original price and multiplying by 100. Thus, the percentage change is 100 × 0.20/2.00 = 10%.

Alternative measurements of inflation

The traditional measure of inflation in the UK for many years was the **retail price index (RPI)**, which was first calculated (under another name) in the early twentieth century to evaluate the extent to which workers were affected by price changes during the First World War. When the Blair government first set an explicit inflation target, it chose the RPIX, which is the RPI excluding mortgage interest payments. This was felt to be a better measure of the effectiveness of macroeconomic policy. It was argued that if interest rates are used to curb inflation, then including mortgage interest payments in the inflation measure will be misleading.

 Key term

retail price index (RPI): a measure of the average level of prices in the UK

The CPI replaced RPIX partly because it is believed to be a more appropriate indicator for evaluating policy effectiveness. In addition, it has the advantage of being calculated using the same methodology as is used in other countries within

the European Union, so that it is more useful than the RPIX for making international comparisons of inflation.

The CPI and RPI are based on a similar approach, although there are some significant differences in the detail of the calculation. Both measures set out to calculate the overall price level at different points in time. Each is based on calculating the overall cost of a representative basket of goods and services at different points in time relative to a base period. Both are produced by combining some 120,000 individual prices, which are collected each month for around 650 representative items. The result of these calculations is an index that shows how the general level of prices has changed relative to the base year. The rate of inflation is then calculated as the percentage rate of change of the price index, whether it be the CPI or the RPI.

The indexes share a common failing, arising from the fixed weights used in calculating the overall index. Suppose the price of a particular item rises more rapidly than other prices during the year. One response by consumers is to substitute an alternative, cheaper, product. As the indexes are based on fixed weights, they do not pick up this substitution effect, and therefore tend to overstate the price level in terms of the cost of living. Some attempt is made to overcome this problem by changing the weights on an annual basis in order to limit the impact of major changes. This includes incorporating new items when appropriate – for example, digital cameras were included in the CPI calculations for the first time in 2004, reflecting a change in consumer spending patterns.

The CPI and RPI differ for a number of reasons, partly because of differences in the content of the basket of goods and services that are included, and partly in terms of the population of people who are covered by the index. For example, in calculating the weights, the RPI excludes pensioner households and the highest-income households, whereas the CPI does not. There are also some other differences in the ways that the calculations are carried out.

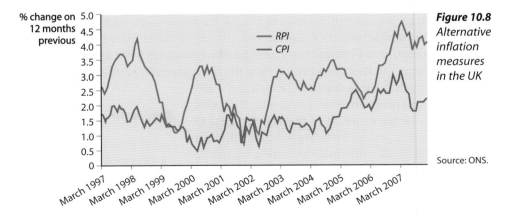

Figure 10.8
Alternative inflation measures in the UK

Source: ONS.

Figure 10.8 shows data for the rates of change of the RPI and the CPI since March 1997. These rates have been calculated on a monthly basis, computing the percentage rate of change of each index relative to the value 12 months previously.

A noticeable characteristic of Figure 10.8 is that for much of the period the CPI has shown a lower rate of change than the RPI. In part this reflects the way in which the prices are combined, but it also reflects the fact that different items and households are covered. The National Statistician, Len Cook, said:

> The CPI's fairly recent development as a macroeconomic indicator of inflation means that it has some distinct advantages over RPIX... Its coverage of spending and households better matches other economic data. The way it combines individual prices also has some clear statistical benefits, and helps us to compare UK inflation with inflation in other countries.

Until the end of 2003, the government's target for inflation was set at 2.5% per annum in the RPIX. After that date, the target for CPI was set at 2% per annum. Since 1997, the Bank of England has had the responsibility of ensuring that inflation remains within one percentage point of this target. You can see from Figure 10.8 that inflation accelerated (on both measures) after March 2006, and in March 2007 the rate of change of CPI went above 3%, thus moving out of the permissible target range for the first time since the inflation target was introduced. You can also see that inflation came back into range very rapidly.

Exercise 10.2

Table 10.2 provides data on consumer prices for the UK, USA and Italy.

a Calculate the annual inflation rate for each of the countries from 1997–2006.
b Plot these three inflation series on a graph against time.
c By what percentage did prices increase in each country over the whole period — that is, between 1996 and 2006?
d Which economy do you judge to have experienced most stability in the inflation rate?

	Consumer price index		
	UK	USA	Italy
1996	89.7	91.1	92.2
1997	92.5	93.2	94.1
1998	95.7	94.7	95.9
1999	97.2	96.7	97.5
2000	100.0	100.0	100.0
2001	101.8	102.8	102.8
2002	103.5	104.5	105.3
2003	106.5	106.8	108.1
2004	109.7	109.7	110.5
2005	112.8	113.4	112.7
2006	116.4	117.1	115.1

Table 10.2 Consumer prices for the UK, USA and Italy

Source: IMF.

Inflation in the UK and throughout the world

Figure 10.9 shows a time path for the rate of change in price levels since 1949. RPI has been used for this purpose, as the CPI was introduced only in 1997, so there

is no consistent long-run series for it. The figure provides the backdrop to understanding the way the UK economy evolved during this period. Apart from the period of the Korean War, which generated inflation in 1951–52, the 1950s and early 1960s were typified by a low rate of inflation, with some acceleration becoming apparent in the early 1970s.

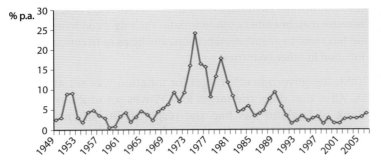

Figure 10.9
RPI inflation,
1949–2007
(% change over
previous year)

Source: ONS.

The instability of the 1970s was due to a combination of factors. Oil prices rose dramatically in 1973–74 and again in 1979–80, which certainly contributed to rising prices, not only in the UK but worldwide. However, inflation was further fuelled by the abandonment of the fixed exchange rate system under which sterling had been tied to the US dollar until 1972. Under a fixed exchange rate system, the government must dedicate the use of monetary policy to maintaining the value of the currency. However, the transition to a floating exchange rate system freed up monetary policy in a way that was perhaps not fully understood by the government of the day. As you can see in Figure 10.9, prices were allowed to rise rapidly — by nearly 25% in 1974/75. The diagram also shows how inflation was gradually reined in during the 1980s, and underlines the relative stability that has now been achieved, with inflation keeping well within the target range set by the government — with the exception of March 2007, as noted above.

Figure 10.10 shows something of the extent to which the UK's experience is typical of the pattern of inflation worldwide. You can see from this how inflation in the industrial countries followed a similar general pattern, with a common accelera-

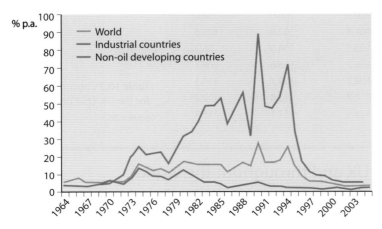

Figure 10.10 *World inflation since 1964 (% change in the consumer price index)*

Source: IMF.

tion in the early 1970s, and a period of gradual control after 1980. However, you can also see that the developing countries in the world experienced inflation at a much higher average level after 1974 because they proved to be less able to bring prices under control after the oil price shocks. Much of this reflects events in Latin America, which suffered especially high rates of inflation in the 1980s and 1990s. This instability in the macroeconomic environment has almost certainly hindered development in the countries affected, and makes it important to understand how inflation is generated and how to curb it.

Unemployment

Unemployment is another important aspect of an economy's performance. If unemployment is seen to be relatively high, then this suggests that the economy is not working as well as it could. There are several aspects to this. It could be argued that high unemployment indicates that the economy is operating below its potential capacity, and that more could be produced if more people could be drawn into work. It could also be argued that high unemployment imposes costs on those who are numbered among the unemployed, and that society could be made better off if those who want to work could find jobs.

The 'claimant count' of unemployment is the number of people claiming the Jobseeker's Allowance

It is important to notice that a rise in unemployment does not necessarily mean that there has been a fall in employment. Migration into an economy, or a change in people's attitudes to work could mean that the size of the labour force can change over time. Equally, an increase in employment could take place without a fall in unemployment if there are immigrant workers taking up jobs, or people joining the workforce who had previously chosen not to work.

The measurement of unemployment in the UK has also been contentious over the years, and the standard definition used to monitor performance has altered several times, especially during the 1980s, when a number of rationalisations were introduced.

Historically, unemployment was measured by the number of people registered as unemployed and claiming unemployment benefit (the Jobseeker's Allowance (JSA)). This measure of employment is known as the **claimant count of unemployment**. People claiming the JSA must declare that they are out of work, capable of, available for and actively seeking work, during the week in which their claim is made.

Key *term*

claimant count of unemployment: the number of people claiming the Jobseeker's Allowance each month

Figure 10.11 shows monthly data on the claimant count since 1971, expressed as a percentage of the workforce. The surge in unemployment in the early 1980s stands out on the graph, when the percentage of the workforce registered as unemployed more than doubled in a relatively short period. Although this seemed to be coming under control towards the end of the 1980s, unemployment rose again in the early 1990s before a steady decline into the new millennium.

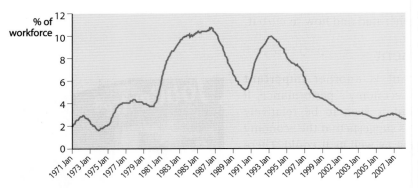

Figure 10.11 *Claimant count 1971–2008*

Source: ONS.

One of the problems with the claimant count is that although people claiming the JSA must declare that they are available for work, it nonetheless includes some people who are claiming benefit, but are not actually available or prepared for work. It also excludes some people who would like to work, and who are looking for work, but who are not eligible for unemployment benefit, such as women returning to the labour force after child birth.

Because of these problems, the claimant count has been superseded for official purposes by the so-called **ILO unemployment rate**, a measure based on the *Labour Force Survey*. This identifies the number of people available for work, and seeking work, but without a job. This definition corresponds to that used by the International Labour Organisation (ILO), and is closer to what economists would like unemployment to measure. It defines as being unemployed those people who are:

Key term

ILO unemployment rate: measure of the percentage of the workforce who are without jobs, but are available for work, willing to work and looking for work

— without a job, want a job, have actively sought work in the last four weeks and are available to start work in the next two weeks; or

— out of work, have found a job and are waiting to start it in the next two weeks

(*Labour Market Statistics*, September 2004)

However, a major difference between the two alternatives from a measurement perspective is that the claimant count is a full count of all those who register, whereas the ILO measure is based on a sample. Figure 10.12 shows both the claimant and ILO measures for the period since 1984. You can see that the difference between the two measures is narrower when unemployment is relatively high, and wider when unemployment is falling. This may be partly because low unemployment encourages more people who are not eligible for unemployment benefit to look for jobs, whereas they withdraw from the workforce when unemployment rises and they perceive that finding a job will be difficult. This is said to affect women in particular, who may not be eligible for the Jobseeker's Allowance because of their partner's earnings.

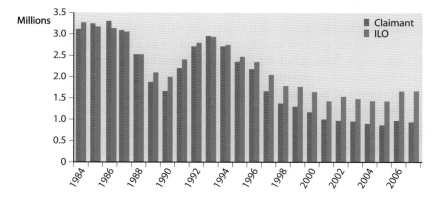

Figure 10.12
Alternative measures of unemployment in the UK, 1984–2007

Note: numbers unemployed in March–May each year (average).

Source: ONS.

Summary

> The retail price index (RPI) is the best-known measure of the average price level in the UK.

> In December 2003 the government adopted the consumer price index (CPI) as its preferred measure of the price level, and inflation is now monitored through the rate of change of CPI.

> Unemployment is measured in two ways. The claimant count is based on the number of people claiming Jobseeker's Allowance. However, the ILO measure, based on the *Labour Force Survey*, is more meaningful.

Exercise 10.3

Visit the website of the Office for National Statistics (at **www.statistics.gov.uk/**) and find out the latest data for inflation and unemployment. Has the performance of the economy in respect of these two variables improved or deteriorated in the last year?

The balance of payments

Another important dimension over which the macroeconomy needs to be monitored is in relation to a country's transactions with the rest of the world. Such transactions involve exports and imports of goods and services, but also assets, not to mention the flow of factor incomes. All of these transactions are monitored through the **balance of payments**, which is a set of accounts designed to identify international transactions between the UK economy and the rest of the world.

 Key term

balance of payments: a set of accounts showing the transactions conducted between residents of a country and the rest of the world

The transactions in the balance of payments are separated into three categories. Transactions in goods and services, together with income payments and transfers,

comprise the *current account.* The *capital account* reflects transactions in fixed assets, and is relatively small; it refers mainly to transactions involving migrants. The *financial account* records transactions in financial assets.

Commentators often focus on the current account. Three main items appear on this account. First, there is the balance of trade in goods and services — in other words, the balance between UK exports and imports of such goods and services. If UK residents buy German cars, this is an import and counts as a negative entry on the current account; on the other hand, if a German resident buys a British car, this is an export and constitutes a positive entry. The trade in goods is normally negative overall. However, this is partly balanced by a normally positive flow in trade in services, where the UK earns strong credits from its financial services.

The second item in the current account is income. Part of this represents employment income from abroad, but the major item of income is made up of profits, dividends and interest receipts arising from UK ownership of overseas assets.

Finally, there are international transfers — either transfers through central government or transfers made or received by private individuals. This includes transactions and grants with international organisations or with the EU. The current balance combines these items together into an overall balance.

Overall, the balance of payments must always be zero, as in some way or other we have to pay for all we consume, and receive payment for all we sell. However, because data can never be entirely accurate, the accounts also incorporate a 'net errors and omissions' item, which ensures that everything balances at the end of the day.

What this really means is that any deficit in the current and capital accounts will always be balanced by a surplus on the financial account. Notice that the financial account incorporates official foreign exchange transactions undertaken by the government. In other words, if British residents buy more goods and services than they sell (i.e. if there is a current account deficit), then they must pay for them by selling financial assets or foreign exchange (i.e. there must be a financial account surplus).

There are a number of ways in which the overall balance can be achieved. 'Balance' could mean that both current and financial accounts are small, or it could mean that a deficit on one is balanced by a surplus on the other. The media tend to focus on the current balance, and a deficit on current account is sometimes seen as a matter of concern. Perhaps this harks back to the fixed exchange rate days, when a current deficit would require authorities to sell foreign exchange reserves in order to balance the accounts. This is no longer the case, as there are other ways of balancing the books. Nonetheless, a persistent deficit on the current account may pose long-term problems that need to be addressed, as it may not be desirable to continue selling UK assets indefinitely.

Table 10.3 presents the components of the balance of payments accounts for 2006. This was a year in which the current account was in deficit, in particular because of a negative balance on trade in goods and services. The financial account was in surplus.

Trade in goods and services	−54 086
Income	22 801
Current transfers	−12 104
Current balance	−43 389
Capital account	**713**
Financial account	**33 726**
Net errors and omissions	8 950
Overall balance of payments	**0**

Table 10.3 The UK balance of payments 2006 (£ million at current prices)

Suppose the Bank of England holds interest rates high compared with other countries, in order to try to control inflation. High UK interest rates will tend to attract financial inflows from abroad, as investors find the UK attractive as a home for their funds. This implies a surplus on the financial account — and hence a deficit on the current account. The downside of such a structure is that UK assets are being sold abroad, which might not be in the best interest of the economy in the long run.

It is this potential long-run difficulty that makes it important to monitor the current balance over time. Figure 10.13 shows the main components of the balance of payments since 1980, in current price terms, which is the form in which the data are published by ONS. This is in the form of a stacked bar chart, and the nature of the balance of payments is that the positive and negative components exactly balance each year. The clear picture that emerges is that the current account has been negative (in deficit) for most of the period since 1980, and that this has been balanced by a positive balance (surplus) on the financial account. In other words, the UK has been importing more goods and services than it has been exporting; but this has been counterbalanced by the surplus on the financial account, i.e. of UK assets sold abroad.

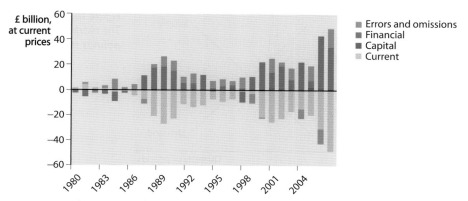

Figure 10.13 The UK balance of payments, 1980–2006
Source: ONS.

The data in Figure 10.13 are measured in current prices, which means that they are *nominal* measurements, which make no attempt to allow for the effects of inflation. It would thus be misleading to infer too much about the magnitude of the

quantities shown. A better perspective on this is provided by Figure 10.14, which shows the current account balance expressed as a percentage of nominal GDP. This helps to put the more recent data into perspective.

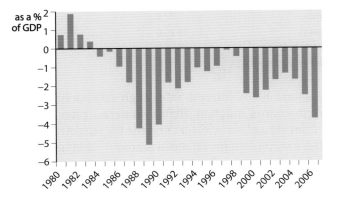

Figure 10.14
The current account of the UK balance of payments

Source: ONS.

Closely associated with the balance of payments is the **exchange rate** — the price of domestic goods in terms of foreign currency. Chapter 5 introduced the notion of the demand and supply of foreign currency, shown in Figure 10.15. The demand for pounds arises from overseas residents (e.g. in the euro area) wanting to purchase UK goods, services or assets,

Key term

exchange rate: the price of one currency in terms of another

whereas the supply of pounds emanates from domestic residents wanting to purchase overseas goods, services or assets. The connection is that the balance of payments accounts itemise these transactions, which entail the demand for and supply of pounds.

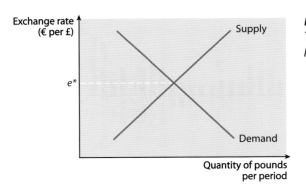

Figure 10.15
The market for pounds sterling

Summary

➤ The balance of payments is a set of accounts that itemises transactions that take place between an economy and the rest of the world, including goods, services, income and assets.

➤ The current account sets out transactions in goods, services, investment income and transfers.

➤ The capital account itemises transactions in fixed assets, and is relatively small.

➤ The financial account covers transactions in financial assets, and includes direct investment and official intervention in the foreign exchange market ('official financing').

➤ The overall balance of payments is always zero.

➤ However, this overall balance has often been achieved in the UK through a persistent deficit on the current account, balanced by a corresponding surplus on the financial account.

➤ This may be a matter for concern in the long run.

Exercise 10.4

Use the data presented in this chapter to evaluate the performance of the UK economy since 1997. If you were the chancellor of the exchequer, which aspects of the economy's performance would you be pleased with, and which ones would concern you?

Chapter 11

Developed and
developing countries

Chapter 10 introduced some important issues relating to the way in which the overall economic performance of an economy can be measured and monitored. In particular, the notion of GDP was introduced as a way of evaluating the total output produced in a country during a period. This chapter examines the extent to which GDP can be viewed as being informative about the standard of living in a country, and whether it can be used to compare standards of living in different countries around the world.

Learning outcomes

After studying this chapter, you should:
- ➤ be aware of the limitations of GDP as a measure of the standard of living
- ➤ be familiar with some of the problems in undertaking international comparisons of living standards
- ➤ be familiar with the most important economic and social indicators that can help to evaluate the standard of living in different societies
- ➤ be aware of significant differences between regions of the world in terms of their level and pace of development
- ➤ recognise the strengths and limitations of such indicators in providing a profile of a country's stage of development
- ➤ be familiar with ways of measuring and monitoring inequality and poverty in the context of less-developed countries

GDP and the standard of living

Chapter 10 introduced GDP as a way of measuring the total output of an economy over a period of time. Although this measure can provide an indicator of the quantity of resources available to citizens of a country in a given period, as an assessment of the standard of living it has its critics.

GDP does have some things going for it. First, it is relatively straightforward and thus is widely understood. Second, it is a well-established indicator and one that is available for almost every country in the world, so that it can be used to compare income levels across countries. For this purpose, it naturally helps to adjust for population size by calculating GDP per person (**GDP per capita**, as it is known). This then provides a measure of average income per head. The World Bank publishes data for countries around the world, using gross national income (GNI), which is a similar measure to GDP.

> **Key term**
>
> **GDP per capita:** the average level of GDP per person

Figure 11.1 provides data on GNI per capita for a selection of countries in different parts of the world in 2006. The extreme differences that exist around the globe are immediately apparent from the data. GNI per capita in Burundi is just $100, whereas in the USA the figure is $44,790. (Luxembourg heads this particular league table, with average income of $76,040 in 2006.) These data seem to suggest that there is a substantial gap in living standards between those countries that have become 'developed', and those which remain 'less-developed', sometimes known as 'developing countries', although for some countries this seems an optimistic label.

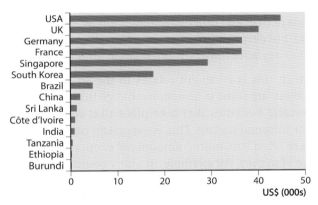

Figure 11.1 GNI per capita, 2006, in US$

Source: *World Development Report 2008.*

In trying to interpret these data, there are a number of issues that need to be borne in mind, as the comparison is not as straightforward as it looks.

Inequality in income distribution

One important point to notice is that looking at the average level of income per person may be misleading if there are wide differences in the way in which income is distributed within countries. In other words, it cannot be assumed that every Burundian receives $100, or that every Luxembourgian receives $76,040. If income is more unequally distributed in some countries, this will affect one's perception of what the term 'average' means. For example, India and Côte d'Ivoire had similar GDP per capita levels in 2006, but the income distribution in India was far more equitable than in Côte d'Ivoire.

The informal sector and the accuracy of data

A further problem with undertaking international comparisons is that it is never absolutely certain that the accuracy with which data are collected is consistent

In many developing countries, substantial economic activity may take place without an exchange of money.

across countries. Definitions of GDP and other variables are now set out in a clear, internationally agreed form, but even when countries are working to the same definitions, some data collection agencies may be more reliable than others.

One particular area in which this is pertinent relates to the so-called 'informal sector'. In every economy there are some transactions that go unrecorded. In most economies, there are economic activities that take place that cannot be closely monitored because of their informal nature. This is especially prevalent in many developing countries, where often substantial amounts of economic activity take place without an exchange of money. For example, in many countries subsistence agriculture remains an important facet of economic life. If households are producing food simply for their own consumption, there is no reason for a money transaction to take place with regard to its production, and thus such activity will not be recorded as a part of GDP. Equally, much economic activity within the urban areas of less-developed countries comes under the category of the 'informal sector'.

Where such activity varies in importance between countries, comparing incomes on the basis of measured GDP may be misleading, as GDP will be a closer indicator of the amount of real economic activity in some countries than in others.

Exchange rate problems
The data presented in Figure 11.1 were expressed in terms of US dollars. This allows economists to compare average incomes using a common unit of measurement. At the same time, however, it may create some problems.

Economists want to compare average income levels so that they can evaluate the standard of living, and compare standards across countries. In other words, it is important to be able to assess people's command over resources in different societies, and to be able to compare the purchasing power of income in different countries.

GDP is calculated initially in terms of local currencies, and subsequently converted into US dollars using official exchange rates. Will this provide information about the relative local purchasing power of incomes? Not necessarily.

One reason for this is that official exchange rates are sometimes affected by government intervention. Indeed, in many of the less-developed countries' exchange rates are pegged to an international currency — usually the US dollar. In these circumstances, exchange rates are more likely to reflect the government's policy and actions than the relative purchasing power of incomes in the countries under scrutiny.

Where exchange rates are free to find their own equilibrium level, exchange rates are likely to be influenced strongly by the price of internationally traded goods — which is likely to be a very different combination of goods than that typically consumed by residents in these countries. Again, it can be argued that the official exchange rates may not be a good reflection of the relative purchasing power of incomes across countries.

The United Nations International Comparison Project has been working on this problem for many years. It now produces an alternative set of international estimates of GDP based on purchasing power parity (PPP) exchange rates, which are designed to reflect the relative purchasing power of incomes in different societies more accurately. Figure 11.2 shows estimates for the same set of countries.

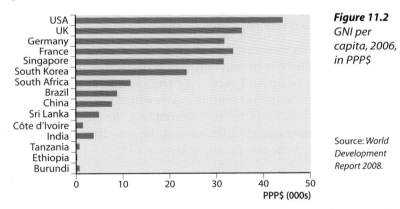

Figure 11.2
GNI per capita, 2006, in PPP$

Source: *World Development Report 2008.*

Comparing this with Figure 11.1, you will notice that the gap between the low-income and high-income countries seems less marked when PPP dollars are used as the unit of measurement. In other words, the US dollar estimates exaggerate the gap in living standards between rich and poor countries. This is a general feature of these measurements — that measurements in US dollars tend to understate real incomes for low-income countries and overstate them for high-income countries compared with PPP-dollar data. Put another way, people in the lower-income countries have a stronger command over goods and services than is suggested by US-dollar comparisons of GDP per capita.

Social indicators

A final question that arises is whether GDP can be regarded as a reasonable indicator of a country's standard of living. You have seen that GDP provides an

indicator of the total resources available within an economy in a given period, calculated from data about total output, total incomes or total expenditure. This focus on summing the transactions that take place in an economy over a period can be seen as a rather narrow view of what constitutes the 'standard of living'. After all, it may be argued that the quality of people's lives depends on more things than simply the material resources that are available.

For one thing, people need to have knowledge if they are to make good use of the resources that are available. Two societies with similar income levels may nonetheless provide very different quality of life for their inhabitants, depending on the education levels of the population. Furthermore, if people are to benefit from consuming or using the available resources, they need a reasonable life span coupled with good health. So, good standards of health are also crucial to a good quality of life.

It is important to remember that different societies tend to set different priorities on the pursuit of growth and the promotion of education and health. This needs to be taken into account when judging relative living standards through a comparison of GDP per capita, as some countries have higher-than-average levels of health and education as compared with other countries with similar levels of GDP per capita.

A reasonable environment in which to live may be seen as another important factor in one's quality of life; indeed, Chapter 16 discusses the possible trade-off that may exist between economic growth and environmental standards.

There are some environmental issues that can distort the GDP measure of resources. Suppose there is an environmental disaster — perhaps an oil tanker breaks up close to a beautiful beach. This reduces the overall quality of life by degrading the landscape and preventing enjoyment of the beach. However, it does not have a negative effect on GDP; on the contrary, the money spent on clearing up the damage actually adds to GDP, so that the net effect of an environmental disaster may be to *increase* the measured level of GDP.

Summary

- GDP is a widely used measure of the total amount of economic activity in an economy over a period of time.
- The trend rate of change of GDP may thus be an indicator of economic growth.
- GDP is a widely understood and widely available measure, but it does have some drawbacks.
- Average GDP per person neglects the important issue of income distribution.
- There may be variation in the effectiveness of data collection agencies in different countries, and variation in the size of the informal sector.
- Converting from a local currency into US dollars may distort the use of GDP as a measure of the purchasing power of local incomes.
- GDP may neglect some important aspects of the quality of life.

Exercise 11.1

Below are some indicators for two countries, A and B.

a Discuss the extent to which GDP (here measured in PPP$) provides a good indication of relative living standards in the two countries.

b Discuss what other indicators might be useful in this evaluation.

	Country A	Country B
GDP per capita (PPP$)	10,276	11,192
Life expectancy (in years at birth)	73.4	47.0
Adult literacy rate (%)	88.7	82.4
People living with HIV/AIDS (% of adults aged 15–49)	0.5	18.8
Infant mortality rate (per 1,000 live births)	12	54

Table 11.1 *Indicators for two countries*

Note: all data is for 2004.

Source: *Human Development Report 2006.*

Economic growth: international experience

The growth performance of different regions around the world has shown contrasting patterns in recent years. As early as the 1950s, a gap had opened up between the early developing countries in North America, Western Europe and Japan and the late developers in sub-Saharan Africa and Latin America.

Between 1960 and 1980, this gap began to widen, except for a small group of countries, mainly in East Asia, where it had begun to close. Figure 11.3 gives some data for countries in different regions. Tanzania and Ethiopia (in sub-Saharan Africa), together with Sri Lanka and India (in South Asia) grew relatively slowly in this period, with only Sri Lanka achieving an average growth rate above 2% per annum. Latin America showed a diverse experience: the examples shown in the figure are Colombia, which grew at about 3% per annum, and Brazil, which achieved growth of above 5% per annum. However, East Asia (represented here by South Korea and Singapore) took off during this period, growing at an average rate of 7% per year and more. Japan also grew rapidly at this time, while the UK and the USA grew at a more sedate pace of just above 2% per annum.

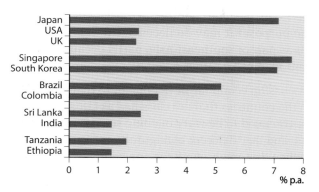

Figure 11.3 *Growth of GNP per capita 1960–80 (annual average)*

Source: *World Development Report 1982.*

Figure 11.4 presents some more recent data, this time by region, for the period 1975–2005 (and for 1990–2005). This reveals some important patterns. The high-income OECD member countries continued to grow at a rather sedate rate of around 2% per annum, and less in the 1990s. Countries in East Asia and the Pacific maintained their impressive high growth of nearly 6% per annum, but again slowed a bit in the 1990s. South Asia showed some improvement, and even accelerated in the 1990s, as indeed did Latin America and the Caribbean. However, sub-Saharan African countries went through a dismal period in which their GDP per capita growth was negative – in other words, GDP per capita was lower in 2005 than it had been in 1975. This is serious indeed. The transition economies of Central and Eastern Europe offer data only for the 1990s. This was the decade in which they went through a painful process of transition, with negative growth rates.

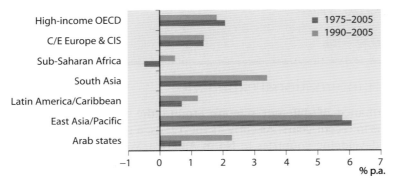

Figure 11.4
Growth of GDP per capita

Note: data represent growth rates of real GDP per capita measured in local currency.

Source: *Human Development Report 2007/08.*

Which are the less-developed countries?

In its *Human Development Report 2004*, the United Nations Development Programme (UNDP) identified 137 countries or areas as 'developing'. In addition, there are 27 transition economies in Central and Eastern Europe and the Commonwealth of Independent States (CIS). However, the range of countries that fall within this definition is very wide, including countries such as Singapore and South Korea, which were also classified as being in the 'high-income' bracket. Figure 11.5 shows average income levels in countries around the world.

In broad terms, the countries regarded as less developed countries (LDCs) are concentrated in four major regions: sub-Saharan Africa, Latin America, South Asia and Southeast Asia. This excludes some countries in the 'less-developed' range, but relatively few. For some purposes it may be necessary to treat China separately, rather than including it as part of Southeast Asia, partly because of its sheer size, and partly because it has followed a rather different development path.

It is important when discussing economic development to remember that there is wide diversity between the countries that are classified as LDCs, and although it is tempting to generalise, you need to be wary of doing so. Different countries have different characteristics, and face different configurations of problems and opportunities. Therefore, a policy that might work for one country may fail totally in a different part of the world.

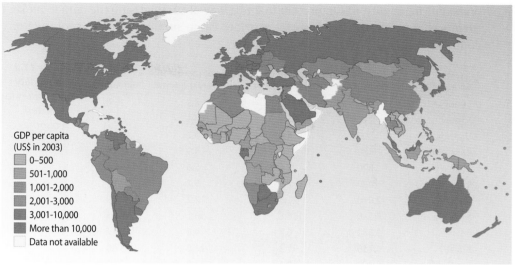

GDP per capita (US$ in 2003)
- 0–500
- 501-1,000
- 1,001-2,000
- 2,001-3,000
- 3,001-10,000
- More than 10,000
- Data not available

Figure 11.5 *Average income levels around the world*

Other indicators of development

The discussion in this chapter so far has suggested that GDP per capita is flawed as a measure of living standards for a variety of reasons. If this is the case, is it possible to devise alternative measures that will cast light on the way in which the standard of living varies between countries?

Income distribution

One important limitation of GDP per capita as a measure of living standards is that it is an *average* measure, and so does not reveal information about how income is distributed among groups in society. Is it possible to measure the extent of inequality in a society?

In Brazil, the poorest 10% of households received less than 1% of total income in the country in 2004, whereas the richest 10% received nearly half. In Belarus, on the other hand, the poorest 10% received 5% of income and the richest 10% received 20%. These are extreme examples of the degree of inequality in the distribution of income within countries.

These data are produced by first ranking the households in order of household income, and then calculating the share of household income going to the poorest 10%, the poorest 20% and so on. The groups of 10% of the population are referred to as **deciles**; thus, the poorest 10% is the first decile, the next 10% is the second decile, and so on. Similarly, the poorest 20% is the first **quintile**.

These data are not very easy to assimilate, especially for a large number of countries, and to explore the question

> **Key terms**
>
> **decile:** when data are presented in rank order, a decile marks boundaries between 10% band widths; similarly, a **quintile** marks boundaries between 20% band widths

of income inequality, it is important to find a way of summarising the data to make them easier to interpret. Table 11.2 provides some summary data for a range of countries.

Country	GNI per capita 2006	Ratio of top decile to poorest decile	Ratio of top quintile to poorest quintile	Gini index
Ethiopia	200	6.6	4.3	30.0
Sierra Leone	240	87.2	57.6	62.9
Uganda	300	16.6	9.2	45.7
Bangladesh	480	7.5	4.9	33.4
India	820	8.6	5.6	36.8
Indonesia	1,420	7.8	5.2	34.3
China	2,010	21.6	12.2	46.9
Namibia	3,230	128.8	56.1	74.3
Belarus	3,380	6.9	4.5	29.7
Brazil	4,730	51.3	21.8	57.0
South Africa	5,390	33.1	17.9	57.8
Malaysia	5,490	22.1	12.4	49.2
Hungary	10,950	5.5	3.8	26.9
Singapore	29,320	17.7	9.7	42.5
Japan	38,410	4.5	3.4	24.9
United Kingdom	40,180	13.8	7.2	36.0
United States	44,970	15.9	8.4	40.8

Table 11.2
Inequality measures for selected countries

Source: *Human Development Report 2007/08.*

By looking at the ratio of the richest decile or quintile to the poorest, it is possible to get some impression of the gap between the poorest and richest households. For example, in Namibia the richest 10% of households receive 128.8 times more income than the poorest 10%, whereas in Hungary the gap is only just over five-fold.

One thing to notice about this table is that the countries are listed in ascending rank order of average income. If you cast your eye down the columns of the table, you will see that there is no very strong relationship between average income and the decile and quintile ratios. The contrast in the pattern of the income shares between Sierra Leone and Bangladesh is striking, but average income levels are not too different.

The Lorenz curve

It would be useful to have a way of presenting such data visually. Although conventional types of graph are not well suited to this purpose, an alternative graphical technique is the **Lorenz curve**. Some of these are shown in Figure 11.6.

Key term

Lorenz curve: a graphical way of depicting the distribution of income within a country

Lorenz curves are constructed as follows. Using data provided in Table 11.3, the first step is to convert the numbers in the table into *cumulative* percentages. In other words (using Brazil as an example), the poorest 20% receives 2.5% of total household income, the poorest 40% receives 2.5% + 5.5% = 8%, the poorest 60%

receives 8% + 10% = 18%, and so on. These cumulative percentages are then plotted to produce the Lorenz curve, as in Figure 11.6.

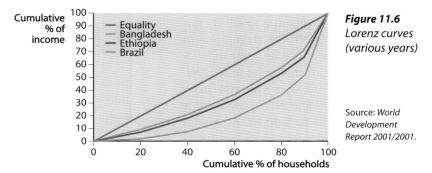

Figure 11.6
*Lorenz curves
(various years)*

Source: *World
Development
Report 2001/2001.*

Country	Lowest 10%	Lowest 20%	Second 20%	Third 20%	Fourth 20%	Highest 20%	Highest 10%
Ethiopia	3.0	7.1	10.9	14.5	19.8	47.7	33.7
Bangladesh	3.9	8.7	12.0	15.7	20.8	42.8	28.6
Brazil	0.9	2.5	5.5	10.0	18.3	63.8	47.6

Table 11.3 Income distribution in Ethiopia, Bangladesh and Brazil, various years

Suppose that income is perfectly equally distributed between households – in other words, suppose the poorest 10% of households receive exactly 10% of income, the poorest 20% receive 20% and so on. The Lorenz curve would then be a straight line going diagonally across the figure.

This is a help in interpreting the country curves. The closer a country's Lorenz curve is to the diagonal equality line, the more equal is the distribution. You can see on the figure how unequal the income distribution is in Brazil as compared with that in Bangladesh or Ethiopia.

The Gini index

The Lorenz curve is fine for comparing income distribution in just a few countries. However, it would also be helpful to have an index that can summarise the relationship in a numerical way. The **Gini index** does just this. It is a way of quantifying the equality of income distribution, and is obtained by calculating

> **Key** *term*
>
> **Gini index:** a measure of the degree of inequality in a society

the ratio of the area between the equality line and a country's Lorenz curve to the whole area under the equality line. This is normally expressed as a percentage, although sometimes you may find data that treat it as a proportion (i.e. with values between 0 and 1). The closer the Gini index is to 100 (or to 1), the further the Lorenz curve is from equality, and thus the more unequal the income distribution. The values for the Gini index are shown in the final column of Table 11.2.

The Kuznets hypothesis

The economist Simon Kuznets argued that there is expected to be a relationship between the degree of inequality in the income distribution and the level of

development that a country has achieved. He claimed that in the early stages of economic development income is fairly equally distributed, with everyone living at a relatively low income level. However, as development begins to take off there will be some individuals at the forefront of enterprise and development, and their incomes will rise more rapidly. So in this middle phase the income distribution will tend to worsen. At a later stage of development, society will eventually be able to afford to redistribute income to protect the poor, and all will begin to share in the benefits of development.

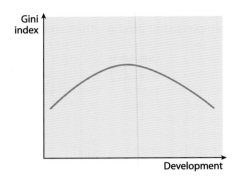

Figure 11.7 *The Kuznets curve*

This can be portrayed as the relationship between the Gini index and the level of development. The thrust of the Kuznets hypothesis is that this should reveal an inverted U-shaped relationship, as shown in Figure 11.7. Although the data in Table 11.2 do not strongly support this hypothesis, there is some evidence to suggest that the relationship does hold in some regions of the world.

The Human Development Index

Another criticism of GDP per capita as a measure of living standards is that it fails to take account of other dimensions of the quality of life. In 1990 the United Nations Development Programme (UNDP) devised an alternative indicator, known as the **Human Development Index (HDI)**, which was designed to provide a broader measure of the stage of development that a country had reached.

Key term

Human Development Index (HDI): a composite indicator of the level of a country's development, reflecting resources, knowledge and longevity; varying between 0 and 1

The basis for this measure is that there are three key aspects of human development: resources, knowledge of how to make good use of those resources, and a reasonable life span in which to make use of those resources (see Figure 11.8). The three components are measured by, respectively, GDP per capita in PPP$, indicators of education

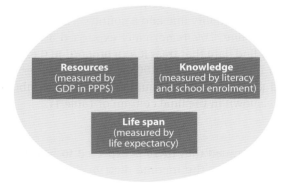

Figure 11.8
Components of the Human Development Index

(adult literacy and school enrolment) and life expectancy. The measurements are then combined to produce a composite index ranging between 0 and 1, with higher values reflecting higher human development.

Values of the HDI for 2005 are charted in Figure 11.9 for the selected countries. You can see that the broad ranking of the countries is preserved, but the gap between low and high human development is less marked. An exception is India, which is ranked more highly on the basis of the HDI than on GDP per capita; in other words, India seems to have achieved relatively high levels of human development for its GDP per capita level. There are other countries in the world that share this feature.

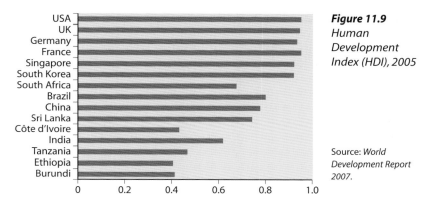

Figure 11.9
Human Development Index (HDI), 2005

Source: *World Development Report 2007.*

In part, this diversity reflects differing priorities that governments have given to different aspects of development. Countries such as Brazil have aimed primarily at achieving economic growth, while those such as Sri Lanka have given greater priority to promoting education and healthcare.

There is a view that growth should be the prime objective for development, since by expanding the resources available the benefits can begin to trickle down through the population. An opposing view claims that, by providing first for basic needs, more rapid economic growth can be facilitated. The problem in some cases is that growth has not resulted in the trickle-down effect, and inequality remains. It may be significant that countries such as Brazil and South Africa, where the GDP per capita ranking is high relative to the HDI ranking, are countries in which there remain high levels of inequality in the distribution of income.

Summary

> Less-developed countries (LDCs) are largely located in four major regions: sub-Saharan Africa, Latin America, South Asia and Southeast Asia.

> These regions have shown contrasting patterns of growth and development.

> Different countries have different characteristics, and face different configurations of problems and opportunities.

> GDP per capita is one measure of the standard of living in a country, but it has a number of shortcomings for LDCs.

➤ In particular, it neglects the importance of the informal sector, and fails to take into account inequality in the distribution of income.

➤ The Human Development Index (HDI) recognises that human development depends on resources, knowledge and health, and therefore combines indicators of these key aspects.

Exercise 11.2

Discuss the relative merits of GDP per capita and the HDI as alternative measures of the standard of living in different countries.

Chapter 12

Income, wealth and the circular flow

Gross domestic product (GDP) has been discussed as a way of measuring total income in an economy, and some of its limitations have been analysed. Income can be seen as a flow of resources in the economy. As a concept, it can be seen to be closely associated with total expenditure and total output, and this chapter begins by exploring the relationship between these three notions. There is also some discussion of the important distinction to be drawn between income and wealth.

Learning outcomes

After studying this chapter, you should:

➤ understand that national income can be represented as a circular flow of income, output and expenditure
➤ be aware of the distinction between income and wealth
➤ be familiar with the notion of injections and withdrawals within the circular flow
➤ appreciate the potential impact and importance of investment in affecting productive capacity

The circular flow of income, expenditure and output

Previous chapters have introduced the notion of *gross domestic product* (GDP), which was described as the total output of an economy. It is now time to examine this concept more closely, and how it can help to highlight the way that macro-economic variables can interact.

Consider a simplified model of an economy. Assume for the moment that there are just two types of economic agent in an economy: households and firms. In other words, ignore the government and assume there is no international trade. (These agents will be brought back into the picture soon.) We also assume that all factors of production are owned and supplied to firms by households.

In this simple world, assume that firms produce goods and hire labour and other factor inputs from households. Households supply their labour (and other factor inputs) and buy consumer goods. In return for supplying factor inputs, households receive income, which they spend on consumer goods.

If you examine the monetary flows in this economy, you can see how the economy operates. In Figure 12.1 the blue arrow shows the flow of income that goes from firms to households as payment for their factor services (labour, land and capital). The orange arrow shows that output produced by firms goes to households in the form of consumer goods. The green arrow show that the expenditure flows back to firms. This model is sometimes known as the **circular flow model**.

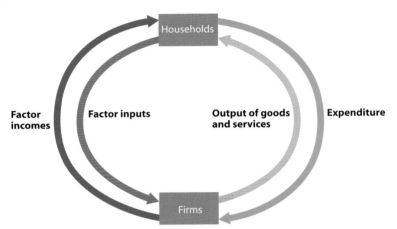

Figure 12.1
The circular flow of income, expenditure and output

As this is a closed system, these flows must balance. This means that there are three ways in which the total amount of economic activity in this economy can be measured: by the incomes that firms pay out, by the total amount of output that is produced, or by total expenditure. Whichever method is chosen, it should give the same result.

An economy such as the UK's is more complicated than this, so it is also necessary to take into account the economic activities of government and the fact that the UK engages in international trade, so that some of the output produced is sold abroad and some of the expenditure goes on foreign goods and services. Furthermore, some of the output produced by firms is made up of investment goods purchased by firms, and some household income is used for saving. However, the principle of measuring total economic activity is the same: GDP can be measured in three ways. These issues will be considered later in the chapter.

In practice, when the ONS carries out the measurements the three answers are never quite the same, as it is impossible to measure with complete accuracy. The published data for GDP are therefore calculated as the

Key term

circular flow of income, expenditure and output: a model of the economy which shows the movement of goods and services between households and firms and their corresponding payments in money terms

average of these three measures, each of which gives information about different aspects of a society's total resources.

The expenditure-side estimate describes how those resources are being used, so that it can be seen what proportion of society's resources is being used for consumption and what for investment etc.

The income-side estimate reports on the way in which households earn their income. In other words, it tells something about the balance between rewards to labour (e.g. wages and salaries), capital (profits), land (rents), enterprise (self-employment) and so on.

The output-side estimate focuses on the economic structure of the economy. One way in which countries differ is in the balance between primary production such as agriculture, secondary activity such as manufacturing, and tertiary activity such as services. Service activity has increased in importance in the UK in recent years, with financial services in particular emerging as a strong part of the UK's comparative advantage.

Summary

➤ The circular flow of income, expenditure and output describes the relationship between these three key variables.

➤ The model suggests that there are three ways in which the total level of economic activity in an economy during a period of time can be measured: by total income, by total expenditure and by total output produced.

➤ In principle, these should give the same answers, but in practice data measurements are not so accurate.

Income and wealth

In everyday parlance, it is not uncommon to use income and wealth as words that mean virtually the same. In economic analysis, it is important to realise that the two things are very different. **Income** has been described as a *flow*; it is the amount of income that is earned during a period. **Wealth** is a *stock* — it is the accumulated amount of assets that have been built up from past income.

Wealth is considerably less evenly distributed than income. In 2001, the most wealthy 1% of households in the UK owned 23% of the marketable wealth (33% if the value of dwellings is omitted), and the most wealthy 50% of households owned 95% of the country's marketable wealth.

Key terms

income: a flow concept — the amount of income that is earned during a period

wealth: a stock concept — the accumulation of assets, such as property or shares

Figure 12.2 charts the percentage of wealth owned by the wealthiest 1% of the UK population in various years. You can see that there was an increase in the concentration of wealth between 1991 and 2002, and a levelling out after then. The

distribution has been strongly influenced by rising house prices in recent years, but was also affected by the fall in share prices following the September 2001 terrorist attacks. Figure 12.3 shows a similar pattern looking at the most wealthy 25% in the population.

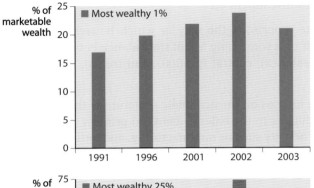

Figure 12.2
The distribution of wealth in the UK

Source: Inland Revenue, cited in *Social Trends 37*.

Figure 12.3
The distribution of wealth in the UK

Source: Inland Revenue, cited in *Social Trends 37*.

Notice that, although wealth and income are not the same thing, inequality in wealth can *lead to* inequality in income, as wealth (the ownership of assets) creates an income flow — from rents and profits — which then feeds back into a household's income stream.

A significant change in the pattern of owner-ship of assets in recent decades has been the increase in home ownership and the rise in house prices. For those who continue to rent their homes, and in particular for those who rent council dwellings, this is a significant source of rising inequality.

The rise in home ownership has led to rising inequality

Measuring poverty

One aspect of inequality is poverty. If there is a wide gap between the richest and poorest households, it is important to evaluate just how poor those poorest house-holds are, and whether they should be regarded as being 'in poverty'. This requires a definition of poverty.

One way of defining poverty is to specify a basket of goods and services that is regarded as the minimum required to support human life. Households that are seen to have too low an income to allow them to purchase everything in that basic bundle of goods would be regarded as being in **absolute poverty**.

Globally, the UN Development Programme regards households in which income is below $1 per day per person as being in absolute poverty, as this is their declared *poverty line*.

For a country like the UK, this absolute poverty line is not helpful, as so few people fall below it. Thus poverty is defined in *relative* terms. If a household has insufficient income for its members to participate in the normal social life of the country, it is said to be in **relative poverty**. This too is defined in terms of a poverty line, set at 50% of the median adjusted household disposable income. (The median is the income of the middle-ranked household.)

Key terms

absolute poverty:
situation describing a household if its income is insufficient to allow it to purchase the minimum bundle of goods and services needed for survival

relative poverty:
situation applying to a household whose income falls below 50% of median adjusted household disposable income

Figure 12.4 presents some data for a range of developed countries. The proportion of people below the relative poverty line varies substantially across these countries, from 4.9% in the Czech Republic to 18.8% in the Russian Federation.

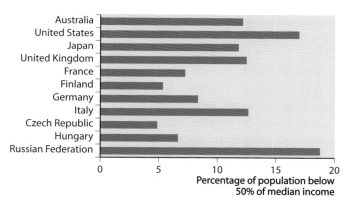

Figure 12.4
Poverty in some developed countries

Source: *Human Development Report.*

The percentage falling below the poverty line is not a totally reliable measure on its own: it is also important to know *how far* below the poverty line households are falling. The *income gap* (the distance between household income and the poverty line) is a useful measure of the intensity of poverty as well as of its incidence.

It is interesting to note that many people remain unaware of where they fit into the income distribution of their country. A survey in the USA in 2000 found that 19% of Americans believed that they were in the top 1% of earners.

One way in which people are able to accumulate wealth is through their saving activity. In other words, not all of household income is used for expenditure on consumer goods, but may be used to purchase assets, which may then be regarded as an addition to wealth. In order to analyse the effect of this, it is necessary to return to the circular flow diagram and introduce some additional elements.

Summary

➤ Income is a flow, but wealth is a stock.

➤ Wealth is less evenly distributed than income in the UK.

➤ Inequality in wealth can lead to inequality in income.

➤ Inequality can give rise to poverty.

➤ Relative poverty is present to some extent in every society.

Exercise 12.1

Imagine that you are the Minister for Poverty Alleviation in a country in which the (absolute) poverty line is set at $500. Of the people living below the poverty line, you know that there are two distinct groups, each made up of 50 individuals. The people in group 1 have an income of $450, whereas those in group 2 have only $250. Suppose that your budget for poverty alleviation is $2,500.

a Your prime concern is with the most needy: how would you use your budget?

b Suppose instead that your prime minister instructs you to reduce the percentage of people living below the poverty line: do you adopt the same strategy for using the funds?

c How helpful is the poverty line as a strategic target of policy action?

Injections and withdrawals

The circular flow diagram in Figure 12.1 was a simple of model of the economy that analysed the three-way flow of resources around an economy. Households supplied factor inputs in exchange for income, which was then spent on goods and services produced by firms. This model has limited applicability from a real world perspective because it was a *closed* system, whereas in practice this is not the case, as there are **withdrawals** (or leakages) from the system and **injections** into it. These arise because of the economic activities of government and through an economy's international trade with the rest of the world.

Key terms

withdrawals: where money flows out of the circular flow in the form of savings, taxation and imports

injections: where money flows into the circular flow in the form of investment, government spending and exports

The government affects the circular flow in two important ways. First, the government spends money on goods and services. For example, it may spend on the provision of public goods, and has to spend in order to carry out its other governmental obligations. In order to finance these activities, the government must raise revenue — which it can do through taxation.

International trade also affects the circular flow. Part of the expenditure on goods and services in the economy comes from abroad in the form of exports. In addition, part of the expenditure undertaken by households is on imported goods and services.

The saving activity of households also affects the circular flow, as there is a part of household income that is saved instead of being spent on goods and services. It is also important to realise that firms also contribute to expenditure when they buy investment goods to add to their productive capacity.

Figure 12.5 adds all of these effects on to the circular flow diagram. The flow of expenditure is no longer just made up on household consumption expenditure on consumer goods, but is augmented by investment expenditure by firms (I), export expenditure from overseas (X) and government expenditure (G). These can be regarded as injections into the circular flow.

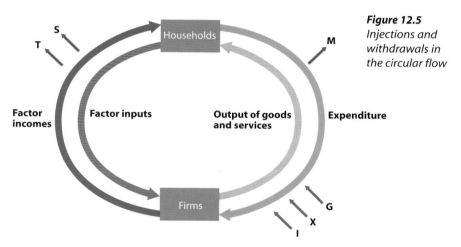

Figure 12.5
Injections and withdrawals in the circular flow

On the other side of the coin, there are withdrawals from the circular flow, made up of imports from the rest of the world (M), household savings (S) and taxes raised by the government from households (T). The overall economy will be in balance when planned injections are equal to planned withdrawals.

Investment plays an important role within the macroeconomy. Investment is expenditure by firms on machinery, buildings and other productive resources. By undertaking investment expenditure, firms add to the productive capacity of the economy, and thus enable economic growth to take place. A change in the balance between investment and consumption activity therefore has an effect on the long-run path of the economy.

An increase in expenditure on investment by firms may have other effects as well. In order to meet the additional demand for machinery, other firms need to expand production. This will mean that they need to hire extra workers — and pay them of course. The additional workers will then spend part of their income on consumer goods, thus unleashing a second round of expenditure. This phenomenon will be examined in Chapter 13.

The circular flow diagram is useful in emphasising the importance of the inter-actions between households, firms and other economic factors in the macro-economy. The next chapter begins to analyse these interactions more carefully.

Exercise 12.2

Identify each of the following as an injection to or a withdrawal from the circular flow:

a household saving
b expenditure by government on goods and services
c imports of goods and services
d income tax
e exports of goods and services
f investment expenditure by firms
g VAT

Summary

➤ In reality, the circular flow diagram needs to be expanded to accommodate injections and withdrawals.

➤ The government affects the circular flow through expenditure (an injection) and taxation (a withdrawal).

➤ International trade is important because of exports (an injection) and imports (a withdrawal).

➤ The circular flow is also affected by household savings (a withdrawal) and by firms' investment expenditure (an injection).

➤ Investment is also important because it affects the productive capacity of the economy in the long run, and is thus important for economic growth.

Chapter 13

Aggregate demand

Now that you are familiar with the main macroeconomic aggregates, it is time to start thinking about how economic analysis can be used to explore the way in which these variables interact. The starting point is to consider the components of aggregate demand. The way in which the levels of these components are determined in practice is an important key to the operation of the economy when considered at the aggregate level.

Learning outcomes

After studying this chapter, you should:
- ➤ understand what is meant by aggregate demand
- ➤ be able to identify the components of aggregate demand and their determinants
- ➤ be aware of the possibility of multiplier effects
- ➤ be familiar with the notion of the aggregate demand curve

The components of aggregate demand

Chapter 12 introduced the notion of the circular flow of income, expenditure and output. If aggregate demand were considered in that model, it would comprise the combined spending of households (on consumer goods) and firms (on investment goods). It was noted that in the real world it is also necessary to include international trade (exports and imports) and spending by government in this measure. The full version of aggregate expenditure can be written as:

$$AD = C + I + G + X - M$$

where AD denotes aggregate demand, C is consumption, I is investment, G is government spending, X is exports and M is imports.

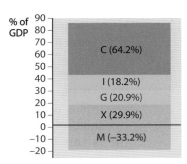

Figure 13.1 *The breakdown of real GDP in 2006*

Note: C includes spending by non-profit institutions serving households; I includes changes in inventory holdings; the statistical discrepancy is not shown.

Source: ONS.

Figure 13.1 shows the expenditure-side breakdown of real GDP in the UK in 2006. This highlights the relative size of the components of aggregate demand. Consumption is by far the largest component, amounting to more than 64% of real GDP in 2006. Government current expenditure accounted for about 20%, but you should realise that this somewhat understates the importance of government in overall spending, as it excludes public spending on investment, which is treated together with private sector investment in the data. Combined public and private sector investment made up just over 18% of total GDP; this includes changes in the inventory holdings of firms. Notice that imports were rather higher than exports, indicating a negative balance of trade in goods and services.

In the circular flow model it was noted that total expenditure should be the same as total income and total output if all were measured fully. This seems to suggest that the macroeconomy is always in a sort of equilibrium, in the sense that expenditure and output are always the same. However, this is misleading. When you observe the economy, you should find that expenditure and output are the same *after* the event, but this does *not* mean that equilibrium holds in the sense that all economic agents will have found that their plans were fulfilled. In other words, it is not necessarily the case that *planned* expenditure equals *planned* output.

This is the significance of the inclusion of inventory changes as part of investment. If firms find that they have produced more output than is subsequently purchased, their inventory holdings increase. Thus, although after the event expenditure always equals output, this is because any disequilibrium is reflected in unplanned inventory changes.

Exercise 13.1

Suppose there is an economy in which the values in Table 13.1 apply.

a Calculate the level of aggregate demand.
b Calculate the trade balance.

Consumption	75	**Table 13.1** Values in an economy (all measured in $ million)
Profits	60	
Investment	30	
Government expenditure	25	
Exports	50	
Private saving	50	
Imports	55	

When in the next chapter you come to consider the conditions under which a macroeconomy will be in equilibrium, you will need to think in terms of the factors that will influence *ex ante* (planned) aggregate demand. The first step is to consider each component in turn.

Consumption

Consumption is the largest single component of aggregate demand. What factors could be expected to influence the size of total spending by households? John Maynard Keynes, in his influential book

Key terms

consumption: total planned household spending

disposable income: the income that households have to devote to consumption and saving, taking into account payments of direct taxes and transfer payments

Edexcel AS Economics

The General Theory of Employment, Interest and Money, published in 1936, suggested that the most important determinant is **disposable income**.

In other words, as real incomes rise, households will tend to spend more. However, he also pointed out that they would not spend all of an increase in income, but would save some of it. Remember that this was important in the circular flow model. Keynes defined the **average propensity to consume** as the *ratio* of consumption to income, and the **marginal propensity to consume** as the proportion of an *increase* in disposable income that households would devote to consumption.

Key terms

average propensity to consume: the proportion of income that households devote to consumption

marginal propensity to consume: the proportion of additional income devoted to consumption

Extension material

Later writers argued that consumption does not necessarily depend on current income alone. For example, Milton Friedman put forward the *permanent income hypothesis*, which suggested that consumers take decisions about consumption based on a notion of their permanent, or normal, income levels — that is, the income that they expect to receive over a 5- or 10-year time horizon. This suggests that households do not necessarily vary their consumption patterns in response to changes in income that they perceive to be only transitory. An associated theory is the *life-cycle hypothesis*, developed by Ando Modigliani, who suggested that households smooth their consumption over their lifetimes, on the basis of their expected lifetime incomes. Thus, people tend to borrow in their youth against future income; then in middle age, when earning more strongly, they pay off their debts and save in preparation to fund their consumption in retirement. Consumption thus varies by much less than income, and is based on expected lifetime earnings rather than on current income.

However, income will not be the only influence on consumption. Consumption may also depend partly on the *wealth* of a household. Notice that income and wealth are not the same. Income accrues during a period as a reward for the supply of factor services, such as labour. Wealth, on the other hand, represents the stock of accumulated past savings. If you like, wealth can be thought of in terms of the asset holdings of households. If households experience an increase in the value of their asset holdings, this may influence their spending decisions.

Furthermore, if part of household spending is financed by borrowing, the rate of interest may be significant in influencing the total amount of consumption spending. An increase in the rate of interest that raises the cost of borrowing may deter consumption. At the same time it may encourage saving, as the return on saving is higher when the interest rate is higher. The rate of interest may also have an indirect effect on consumption through its effect on the value of asset holdings. In addition, households may be influenced in their consumption decisions by their expectations about future inflation. Notice that some of these effects may not be instantaneous: that is, consumption may adjust to changes in its determinants only after a time lag.

This **consumption function** can be portrayed as a relationship between consumption and income. This is shown in Figure 13.2, which focuses on the relationship between consumption and household income, ceteris paribus: in other words, in drawing the relationship between consumption and income, it is assumed that the other determinants of consumption, such as wealth and the interest rate, remain constant. A change in any of these other influences will affect the *position* of the line. Notice that the marginal propensity to consume (*MPC*) is the slope of this line. For example, if the *MPC* is 0.7, this means that for every additional £100 of income received by households, £70 would be spent on consumption and the remaining £30 would be saved.

consumption function: the relationship between consumption and disposable income; its position depends on the other factors that affect how much households spend on consumption

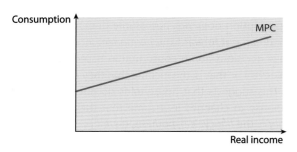

Figure 13.2 The consumption function

In practice, it is not expected that the empirical relationship between consumption and income will reveal an exact straight line, if only because over a long time period there will be changes in the other influences on consumption, such as interest rates and expected inflation. However, Figure 13.3 shows that the hypothesis is not totally implausible.

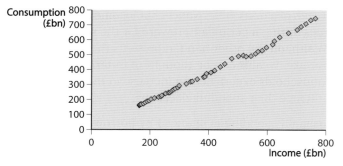

Figure 13.3 Real consumption and disposable income in the UK, 1948–2006

Source: ONS.

Investment

The rate of interest is also likely to be influential in affecting firms' decisions about investment spending. Again, this is because the interest rate represents the cost of borrowing; so, if firms need to borrow in order to undertake **investment**, they may be discouraged from spending on investment goods when the rate of interest is relatively high.

investment: expenditure undertaken by firms to add to the capital stock

Investment leads to an increase in the productive capacity of the economy, by increasing the stock of capital available for production. This capital stock comprises plant and machinery, vehicles and other transport equipment, and buildings, including new dwellings, which provide a supply of housing services over a long period.

Although important, the rate of interest is not likely to be the only factor that determines how much investment firms choose to undertake. First, not all investment has to be funded from borrowing — firms may be able to use past profits for this purpose. However, if firms choose to do this, they face an opportunity cost. In other words, profits can be used to buy financial assets that will provide a rate of return dependent on the rate of interest. The rate of interest is thus still important, as it represents the opportunity cost of an investment project.

In considering an investment project, firms will need to form expectations about the future stream of earnings that will flow from the investment. Their expectations about the future state of the economy (and of the demand for their products) will thus be an important influence on current investment. This is one reason why it is argued that inflation is damaging for an economy, as a high rate of inflation increases uncertainty about the future and may dampen firms' expectations about future demand, thereby discouraging investment.

Figure 13.4 shows the relationship between investment and the rate of interest. The investment demand function I_{D0} is downward sloping because investment is relatively low when the rate of interest is relatively high. An improvement in business confidence for the future would result in more investment being undertaken at any given interest rate, so the investment function would move from I_{D0} to I_{D1}.

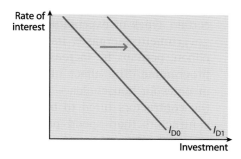

Figure 13.4 *Investment and the rate of interest*

Government expenditure

By and large, you might expect government expenditure to be decided by different criteria from those influencing private sector expenditures. Indeed, some aspects of government expenditure might be regarded as part of macroeconomic policy, as will be seen in Chapter 17. Some other aspects of government expenditure may vary automatically with variations in the overall level of economic activity over time. For example, unemployment benefit payments are likely to increase during recessionary periods. The effects of this will be examined in Chapter 17.

From the point of view of investigating macroeconomic equilibrium, however, government expenditure can be regarded as mainly *autonomous*: that is, independent of the variables in the model that will be constructed in this chapter and the following one.

Trade in goods and services

Finally, there are the factors that may influence the level of exports and imports. One factor that will affect both of these is the exchange rate between sterling and other currencies. This affects the relative prices of UK goods and those produced overseas. Other things being equal, an increase in the sterling exchange rate makes UK exports less competitive and imports into the UK more competitive.

However, the demand for exports and imports will also depend on the relative prices of goods produced in the UK and the rest of the world. If UK inflation is high relative to elsewhere, again, this will tend to make UK exports less competitive and imports more competitive. These effects will be examined more carefully in Chapter 18, when it will be shown that movements in the exchange rate tend to counteract changes in relative prices between countries.

In addition, the demand for imports into the UK will depend partly upon the level of domestic aggregate income, and the demand for UK exports will depend partly upon the level of incomes in the rest of the world. Thus, a recession in the European Union will affect the demand for UK exports.

The multiplier

In his *General Theory*, Keynes pointed out that there may be **multiplier** effects in response to certain types of expenditure. Suppose that the government increases its expenditure by £1 billion, perhaps by increasing its road-building programme. The effect of this is to generate incomes for households — for example, those of the contractors hired to build the road. Those contractors then spend part of the additional income (and save part of it). By spending part of

Key *term*

multiplier: the ratio of a change in equilibrium real income to the autonomous change that brought it about; it is defined as 1 divided by the marginal propensity to withdraw

the extra money earned, an additional income stream is generated for shopkeepers and café owners, who in turn spend part of *their* additional income, and so on. Thus, the original increase in government spending sparks off further income generation and spending, causing the multiplier effect. In effect, equilibrium output may change by more than the original increase in expenditure.

The size of this multiplier effect depends on a number of factors. Most importantly, it depends on the size of *withdrawals* or *leakages* from the system. In particular, it depends on how much of the additional income is saved by households, how much is spent on imported goods, and how much is returned to the government in the form of direct taxes. These items constitute withdrawals from the system, in the sense that they detract from the multiplier effect. For example, if households save a high proportion of their additional income, then this clearly reduces the multiplier effect, as the next round of spending will be that much lower. This seems to go against the traditional view that saving is good for the economy.

However, there are also *injections* into the system in the form of autonomous government expenditure, investment and exports. One condition of macro

Government spending on road building may increase spending in other areas of the economy due to the multiplier effect

economic equilibrium is that total withdrawals equal total injections. The fact that injections can have this multiplied effect on equilibrium output and income seems to make the government potentially very powerful, as by increasing its expenditure it can have a multiplied effect on the economy.

Extension point

A numerical value for the multiplier can be calculated with reference to the withdrawals from the circular flow. First, define the *marginal propensity to withdraw* (*MPW*) as the sum of the marginal propensities to save, tax and import. The multiplier formula is then 1 divided by the marginal propensity to withdraw (1/*MPW*). If the value of the multiplier is 2, then for every £100 million injection into the circular flow, there will be a £200 million increase in equilibrium output.

It is worth noting that the size of the withdrawals may depend in part upon the domestic elasticity of supply. If domestic supply is inflexible, and therefore unable to meet an increase in demand, more of the increase in income will spill over into purchasing imports, and this will dilute the multiplier effect.

Exercise 13.2

Identify each of the following as an injection or a leakage, and state whether it increases or decreases the impact of the multiplier:

a saving by households
b expenditure by central government
c spending by UK residents on imported goods and services
d expenditure by firms on investment
e spending by overseas residents on UK goods and services
f income tax payments

The aggregate demand curve

The key relationship to carry forward is the **aggregate demand curve**, which shows the relationship between aggregate demand and the overall price level. Formally, this curve shows the total amount of goods and services demanded in an economy at any given overall level of prices.

Key term

aggregate demand (AD) curve: the relationship between the level of aggregate demand and the overall price level; it shows planned expenditure at any given possible overall price level

It is important to realise that this is a very different sort of demand curve from the microeconomic demand curves that were introduced in Chapter 2, where the focus was on an individual product and its relationship with its own price. Here the relationship is between the *total* demand for goods and services and the overall price level. Thus, aggregate demand is made up of all the components discussed above, and price is an average of all prices of goods and services in the economy.

Figure 13.5 shows an aggregate demand curve. The key question is why it slopes downwards. To answer this, it is necessary to determine the likely influence of the price level on the various components of aggregate demand that have been discussed in this chapter, as prices have not been mentioned explicitly (except for how expectations about inflation might influence consumer spending). First, however, the discussion needs to be cast in terms of the price *level*.

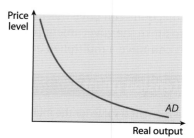

Figure 13.5 *An aggregate demand curve*

When the overall level of prices is relatively low, the purchasing power of income is relatively high. In other words, low overall prices can be thought of as indicating relatively high real income. Furthermore, when prices are low, this raises the real value of households' wealth. For example, suppose a household holds a financial asset such as a bond with a fixed money value of £100. The relative (real) value of that asset is higher when the overall price level is relatively low. From the above discussion, this suggests that, ceteris paribus, a low overall price level means relatively high consumption.

A second argument relates to interest rates. When prices are relatively low, interest rates also tend to be relatively low, which, it was argued, would encourage both investment and consumption expenditure, as interest rates can be seen as representing the cost of borrowing.

A third argument concerns exports and imports. It has been argued that, ceteris paribus, when UK prices are relatively low compared with the rest of the world, this will increase the competitiveness of UK goods, leading to an increase in foreign demand for UK exports, and a fall in the demand for imports into the UK as people switch to buying UK goods and services.

All of these arguments support the idea that the aggregate demand curve should be downward sloping. In other words, when the overall price level is relatively low, aggregate demand will be relatively high, and when prices are relatively high, aggregate demand will be relatively low.

Other factors discussed above will affect the *position* of the *AD* curve. This point will be explored after the introduction of the other side of the coin — the aggregate supply curve.

Summary

> Aggregate demand is the total demand in an economy, made up of consumption, investment, government spending and net exports.

> Consumption is the largest of these components and is determined by income and other influences, such as interest rates, wealth and expectations about the future.

> Investment leads to increases in the capital stock and is influenced by interest rates, past profits and expectations about future demand.

> Government expenditure may be regarded as largely autonomous.

> Trade in goods and services (exports and imports) is determined by the competitiveness of domestic goods and services compared with the rest of the world, which in turn is determined by relative inflation rates and the exchange rate. Imports are also affected by domestic income, and exports are affected by incomes in the rest of the world.

> Autonomous spending, such as government expenditure, may give rise to a magnified impact on equilibrium output through the multiplier effect.

> The aggregate demand curve shows the relationship between aggregate demand and the overall price level.

part **2**

Chapter 14

Aggregate supply and macroeconomic equilibrium

Having seen what is meant by aggregate demand, it is now time to investigate aggregate supply and the factors that will influence it. This chapter explores the notion of macro-economic equilibrium. As in microeconomics, this relates to the process by which balance can be achieved between the opposing forces of demand and supply. However, there are some important differences in these concepts when applied at the macro-economic level.

Learning outcomes

After studying this chapter, you should:
- ➤ understand what is meant by aggregate supply
- ➤ be able to identify the factors that influence aggregate supply
- ➤ be familiar with the notion of the aggregate supply curve
- ➤ understand the nature of equilibrium in the macroeconomy
- ➤ be able to undertake comparative static analysis of external shocks affecting aggregate demand and aggregate supply

The aggregate supply curve

The previous chapter discussed the notion of aggregate demand and introduced the aggregate demand curve. In order to analyse the overall macroeconomic equilibrium, it is necessary to derive a second relationship: that between aggregate supply and the price level. It is important to remember that the level of aggregate supply covers the output of all sorts of goods and services that are produced within an economy during a period of time. However, it is not simply a question of adding up all the individual supply curves from individual markets. Within an individual market, an increase in price may induce higher supply of a good because firms will switch from other markets in search of higher profits. What you now need to be looking for is a relationship between the *overall* price level and the total amount supplied, which is a different kettle of fish.

The total quantity of output supplied in an economy over a period of time depends on the quantities of inputs of factors of production employed: that is, the total amounts of labour, capital and other factors used. The ability of firms to vary output in the short run will be influenced by the degree of flexibility the firms have in varying inputs. This suggests that it is necessary to distinguish between short-run and long-run aggregate supply.

In the short run, firms may have relatively little flexibility to vary their inputs. Money wages are likely to be fixed, and if firms wish to vary output, they may need to do so by varying the intensity of utilisation of existing inputs. For example, if a firm wishes to expand output, the only way of doing so in the short run may be by paying its existing workers overtime, and it will be prepared to do this only in response to higher prices. This suggests that in the short run, aggregate supply may be upward sloping, as shown in Figure 14.1, where *SAS* represents **short-run aggregate supply**.

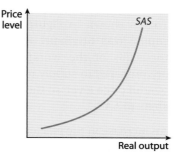

Figure 14.1 *Aggregate supply in the short run*

Firms will not want to operate in this way in the long run. It is not good practice to be perma-nently paying workers overtime. In the long run, therefore, firms will adjust their working practices and hire additional workers to avoid this situation.

Key *term*

short-run aggregate supply curve: a curve showing how much output firms would be prepared to supply in the short run at any given overall price level

The position of the aggregate supply curve

What factors influence the position of aggregate supply? Given that aggregate supply arises from the use of inputs of factors of production, one important influence is the availability and effectiveness of factor inputs. Factors that influence the costs faced by firms will also be important.

The quantity of inputs

As far as labour input is concerned, an increase in the *size* of the workforce will affect the position of aggregate supply. In practice, the size of the labour force tends to change relatively slowly unless substantial international migration is taking place. The expansion of membership of the EU in May 2004 led to significant migration into the UK, which chose to impose fewer restrictions on the movement of workers than other existing EU members.

An increase in the quantity of capital will also have this effect, by increasing the capacity of the economy to produce. However, such an increase requires firms to have undertaken investment activity. In other words, the balance of spending between consumption and investment may affect the position of the aggregate supply curve in future periods.

The effective use of inputs

The effectiveness with which inputs are utilised is another important influence on the position of the aggregate supply curve. For example, an increase in the skills that workers have will increase the amount of aggregate output that can be produced and lead to a shift in the aggregate supply curve. This is shown in Figure 14.2, where aggregate supply was originally at SAS_0. An increase in the skills of the workforce means that firms are prepared to supply more output at any given overall price level, so the aggregate supply curve shifts to SAS_1.

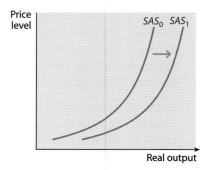

Figure 14.2 *A shift in aggregate supply*

An increase in the efficiency of capital, perhaps arising from improvements in technology, would have a similar effect, enabling greater aggregate supply at any given overall price level, and raising the productive capacity of the economy.

The costs faced by firms

Underlying the aggregate supply curve are the decisions taken by firms about production levels at any given price. A change in the costs faced by firms may induce them to choose to supply more (or less) output. There are several factors that could influence costs in this way. It might be that there is a change in the cost of raw materials. If a key raw material becomes more limited in supply, perhaps because reserves are exhausted, then prices will tend to rise, thus raising firms' costs of production. They may then choose to supply less output at any given price — and the aggregate supply curve would shift to the left. A change in the exchange rate could have similar effects, by affecting the domestic price of imported inputs. This could be favourable, of course. It may be that the exchange rate moves to reduce the domestic price of imports. Firms may then be prepared to supply more output at any given price, so the aggregate supply curve would shift to the right.

It may be that changes in the domestic production environment could affect the costs faced by firms — either for better or worse. An increase in regulation that forced firms to spend more on health and safety measures would raise costs, as would an increase in congestion on the roads that raised transport costs. These effects would tend to result in a leftward shift of the aggregate supply curve. On the other hand, improvements to infrastructure in the domestic economy, such as improvements to the transport system, would have the opposite effect of reducing the costs faced by firms, which could then lead to a rightward shift of the aggregate supply curve.

Exercise 14.1

For each of the following, state whether the aggregate supply curve would shift to the left or to the right:

a the discovery of a new source of a raw material, reducing its price
b an increase in the rate of emigration from a country
c an increase in the exchange rate
d improvements to the transportation system in a country
e a technological advance that improves efficiency
f an increase in investment by firms

Macroeconomic equilibrium

Bringing aggregate demand and aggregate supply together, the overall equilibrium position for the macroeconomy can be identified. In Figure 14.3, with aggregate supply given by *SAS* and aggregate demand by *AD*, equilibrium is reached at the real output level *Y*, with the price level at *P*.

This is an equilibrium, in the sense that if nothing changes then firms and households will have no reason to alter their behaviour in the next period. At the price *P*, aggregate supply is matched by aggregate demand.

Can it be guaranteed that the macroeconomic equilibrium will occur at the full employment level of output? For example, suppose that in Figure 14.4 the output level Y^* corresponds to the full employment level of output — that is, the level of output that represents productive capacity when all factors of production are fully employed. It may be possible to produce more than this in the short run, but only on a temporary basis, perhaps by the use of overtime. If aggregate demand is at AD^*, the macroeconomic equilibrium is at this full employment output Y^*. However, if the aggregate demand curve is located at AD_1 the equilibrium will occur at Y_1, which is below the full employment level, so there is surplus capacity in the economy.

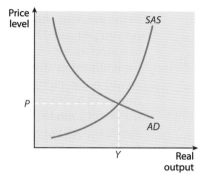

Figure 14.3 *Macroeconomic equilibrium*

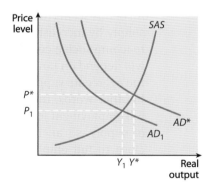

Figure 14.4 *Macroeconomic equilibrium at full employment*

Summary

➤ The aggregate supply (*SAS*) curve shows the relationship between aggregate supply and the overall price level.

➤ Macroeconomic equilibrium is reached at the intersection of *AD* and *AS*.

An increase in aggregate demand

Having identified macroeconomic equilibrium, it is possible to undertake some comparative static analysis. The position of the aggregate demand curve depends on the components of aggregate demand: consumption, investment, government spending and net exports. Factors that affect these components will affect the position of aggregate demand.

Consider Figure 14.5. Suppose that the economy begins in equilibrium with aggregate demand at AD_0. The equilibrium output level is Y_0, and the price level is at P_0. An increase in government expenditure will affect the position of the aggregate demand curve, shifting it to AD_1. The economy will move to a new equilibrium position, with higher output level Y_1 and a higher price level P_1.

In the previous chapter, the notion of the multiplier was introduced. This was the idea that an increase in autonomous expenditure, such as government expenditure or investment expenditure by firms, would have *multiplier* effects through successive rounds of additional expenditure. In the context of the AD/AS model, this would affect the extent to which the AD curve shifts to the right following an increase in autonomous expenditure. In other words, the initial shift of AD would be augmented in following periods by further shifts as the successive rounds of additional expenditure work themselves through the system.

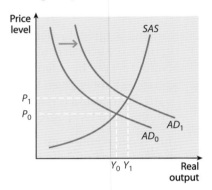

Figure 14.5 *A shift in aggregate demand*

All of this seems to suggest that the government can always reach full employment, simply by increasing its expenditure. However, you should be a little cautious in reaching such a conclusion, as the effect on equilibrium output and the price level will depend on how close the economy is to the full employment level. Notice that the aggregate supply curve becomes steeper as output and the price level increase.

In other words, the closer the economy is to the full employment level, the smaller is the elasticity of supply, so an increase in aggregate demand close to full employment will have more of an effect on the price level (and hence potentially on inflation) than on the level of real output.

Indeed, it might be argued that the aggregate supply curve becomes vertical at some point, as there is a maximum level of output that can be produced given the availability of factors of production. Such a curve is shown in Figure 14.6, where Y^* represents the full employment level of real output. In this case, the economy has settled into an equilibrium that is below potential

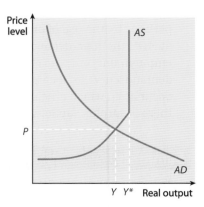

Figure 14.6 *Macroeconomic equilibrium in the longer run*

capacity output. We may regard this as a longer-run aggregate supply curve (AS), since the only way that real output can be beyond Y^* is through the temporary use of overtime, which could not be sustained in the long run.

The effect of a supply shock

The AD/AS model can also be used to analyse the effects of an external shock that affects aggregate supply. For example, suppose there is an increase in oil prices arising from a disruption to supplies in the Middle East. This raises firms' costs, and leads to a reduction in aggregate supply. Comparative static analysis can again be employed to examine the likely effects on equilibrium.

Figure 14.7 analyses the situation using the long-run AS curve. The economy begins in equilibrium with output at Y_0 and the overall level of prices at P_0. The increase in oil prices causes a movement of the aggregate supply curve from AS_0 to AS_1, with aggregate demand unchanged at AD. After the economy returns to equilibrium, the new output level has fallen to Y_1 and the overall price level has increased to P_1.

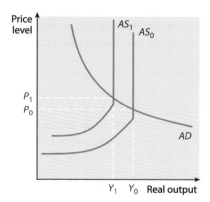

Figure 14.7 A supply shock

At the time of the first oil price crisis back in 1973/74, the UK government of the day tried to maintain the previous level of real output by stimulating aggregate demand. This had the effect of pushing up the price level, but did not have any noticeable effect on real output. Such a result is not unexpected, given the steepness of the aggregate supply curve. Indeed, in Figure 14.7 the previous output level Y_0 cannot be reached with aggregate supply in its new position. You can see the effects of the oil shock on the UK economy by looking back at Figure 10.9.

The cost of oil drove up world prices of goods in the 1970s

Exercise 14.2

For each of the following, decide whether the change affects aggregate demand or aggregate supply, and sketch a diagram to illustrate the effects on equilibrium real output and overall price level. Undertake this exercise first for a starting position in the steep part of the *AS* curve, and then repeat the exercise for an initial position further to the left, where *AS* is more elastic:

a an advancement in technology that improves the efficiency of capital
b a financial crisis in Asia that reduces the demand for UK exports
c an improvement in firms' expectations about future demand, such that investment expenditure increases
d the introduction of new health and safety legislation that raises firms' costs

Shifts of and movements along *AD* and *AS*

It is important to be aware of the distinction between shifts *of* the *AD* and *AS* curves, and movements *along* them. Typically, if a shock affects the position of one of the curves, it will lead to a movement *along* the other. For example, if the *AS* curve shifts as a result of a supply shock, the response is a movement *along* the *AD* curve, and vice versa. Thus, in trying to analyse the effects of a shock, the first step is to think about whether the shock affects *AD* or *AS*, and the second is to analyse whether the shock is positive or negative: that is, which way the relevant curve will shift. The move towards a new equilibrium can then be investigated.

Exercise 14.3

For each of the changes that you analysed in Exercise 14.2, indicate whether the result is a shift of or a movement along the *AD* and *AS* curves.

Summary

➤ Comparative static analysis can be used to analyse the effects of changes in the factors that influence aggregate demand and aggregate supply.

➤ Changes in the components of aggregate demand shift the aggregate demand curve. Within the vertical segment of *AS*, changes in *AD* affect only the overall price level, but below full employment both price and real output will be affected.

➤ Changes in the factors affecting aggregate supply alter the long-run potential productive capacity of the economy.

Chapter 15

Economic growth

One of society's prime responsibilities is to provide a reasonable standard of living for its citizens and to promote their well-being. Hence one of the major objectives for economic policy in the long run is to enable improvements in well-being and, in order to do this, it is first necessary to expand the resources available within society. A key element in this process is to achieve economic growth, which is the subject of this chapter. However, there may be more to well-being than just growth, and the chapter also explores some of the limitations of a strategy that aims to maximise GDP growth.

Learning outcomes

After studying this chapter, you should:
- ➤ be able to understand the meaning of economic growth and productivity
- ➤ be familiar with factors that can affect the rate of economic growth, in particular the role of investment
- ➤ evaluate the importance to a society of economic growth and the costs that such growth may impose
- ➤ understand the meaning and significance of sustainable growth

Defining economic growth

From a theoretical point of view, **economic growth** can be thought of as an expansion of the productive capacity of an economy. If you like, it is an expansion of the potential output of the economy.

Earlier, this was discussed in terms of a shift in the production possibility frontier (*PPF*); economic growth enables a society to produce more goods and services in any given period as a result of an expansion in its resources.

A second way of thinking about economic growth is to use the *AD/AS* model. For example, in Figure 15.1, an increase in the skills of the workforce will enable firms to produce more output at any given price, so that the aggregate supply curve will

Key *term*

economic growth: the expansion of the productive capacity of an economy

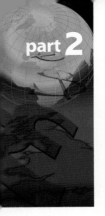

shift outwards from AS_0 to AS_1. This entails an increase in full employment output (or capacity output) from Y^* to Y^{**}. This again can be characterised as economic growth. Chapter 17 investigates policies that might be introduced to affect aggregate supply. In this chapter the focus is on a broader perspective within which long-run growth can be achieved.

As was pointed out before, if economists try to measure economic growth using the rate of change of GDP as an indicator, they are not necessarily measuring what they want to. GDP growth measures the *actual* rate of change of output rather than the growth of the *potential* output capacity of the economy.

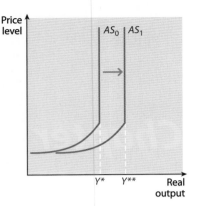

Figure 15.1 *A shift in aggregate supply*

Exercise 15.1

In Figure 15.2, which of the following represent(s) genuine economic growth?

a a shift from A to B
b a shift from B to C
c a shift from C to A
d a shift from C to D
e none of the above

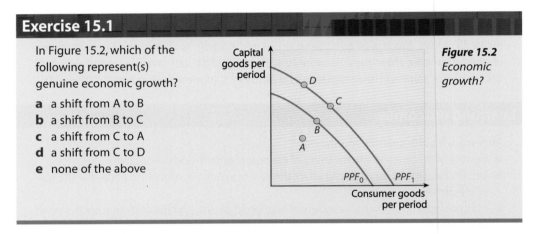

Figure 15.2 *Economic growth?*

Figure 15.3 shows the actual time path of real GDP in the UK since 1948, together with its underlying trend. Although the two series do not diverge by very much, you can see the way in which the actual path of real GDP fluctuates around the

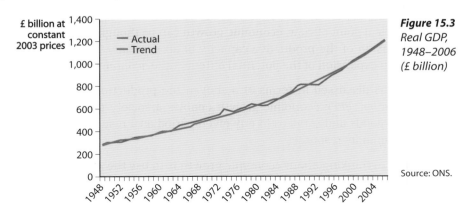

Figure 15.3 *Real GDP, 1948–2006 (£ billion)*

Source: ONS.

trend, especially in the middle part of the period. You might think that the **output gap**, that is, the difference between actual real GDP and potential GDP could be calculated as the difference between these two series, but that is not the case. After all, it could be that the economy never reaches full capacity, in which case it is never possible to observe potential output directly.

Key term

output gap: the difference between actual real GDP and potential real GDP

However, this could be important when trying to interpret the performance of the economy. Look at Figure 15.3. You can see how in the 1970s there were several years in which real GDP was above its underlying trend. This could mean that the economy is trying to operate above its potential. The likely outcome of such a situation is that there will be upward pressure on the price level in the economy — in other words, the economy could be 'overheating' and running the risk of high inflation. On the other hand, there are also periods in which real GDP falls below trend, which could well be periods in which there is spare capacity in the economy — in other words, there could be unemployment.

Economists at the OECD have attempted to estimate the potential level of real output for OECD economies. Figure 15.4 shows their estimates of the output gap for the UK since 1989 (and projected to 2008), defined as the deviations of actual output from potential. This shows that there was a period in the early 1990s when the output gap was significantly negative. In other words, this was a period in which there was spare capacity in the economy. If you look back at Figure 10.12, you will see that this period coincided with an increase in unemployment — one of the measures of spare capacity. Knowledge of the output gap helps policy-makers in determining the priorities for macroeconomic policy.

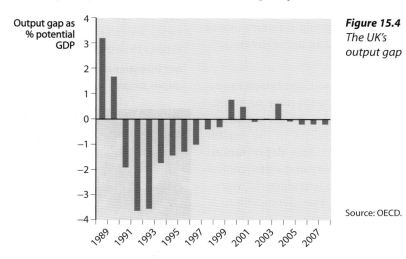

Figure 15.4
The UK's output gap

Source: OECD.

Sources of economic growth

At a basic level, production arises from the use of factors of production — capital, labour, entrepreneurship and so on. Capacity output is reached when all factors of production are fully and efficiently utilised. From this perspective, an increase in capacity output

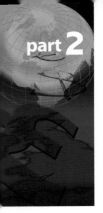
can come either from an increase in the quantity of the factors of production, or from an improvement in their efficiency or productivity. **Productivity** is a measure of the efficiency of a factor of production. For example, **labour productivity** measures output per worker, or output per hour worked. The latter is the more helpful measure, as clearly total output is affected by the number of hours worked, which does vary somewhat across countries. **Capital productivity** measures output per unit of capital. **Total factor productivity** refers to the average productivity of all factors, measured as the total output divided by the total amount of inputs used.

An increase in productivity raises aggregate supply and the potential capacity output of an economy, and thus contributes to economic growth.

Capital

Capital is a critical factor in the production process. An increase in capital input is thus one source of economic growth. In order for capital to accumulate and increase the capacity of the economy to produce, **investment** needs to take place.

Notice that in economics 'investment' is used in this specific way. In common parlance the term is sometimes used to refer to investing in shares or putting money into a deposit account at the bank. Do not confuse these different concepts. In economics 'investment' relates to a firm buying new capital, such as machinery or factory buildings. If you put money into a bank account, that is an act of saving, not investment.

In the national accounts, the closest measurement that economists have to investment is 'Gross Fixed Capital Formation'. This covers net additions to the capital stock, but it also includes **depreciation**. Some of the machinery and other capital purchased by firms is to replace old, worn-out capital, i.e. to offset depreciation. It does not therefore represent an addition to capital stock. As depreciation cannot be observed easily, the convention in the accounts is to measure gross investment (i.e. including depreciation) and then make an adjustment for depreciation to arrive at **net investment**.

> ### Key terms
>
> **productivity:** measure of the efficiency of a factor of production
>
> **labour productivity:** measure of output per worker, or output per hour worked
>
> **capital productivity:** measure of output per unit of capital
>
> **total factor productivity:** the average productivity of all factors, measured as the total output divided by the total amount of inputs used
>
> **investment:** an increase in the capital stock
>
> **depreciation:** the fall in value of physical capital equipment over time as it is subject to wear and tear
>
> **net investment:** gross investment *minus* depreciation

Capital stock includes machinery, a critical factor in the production process

Figure 15.5 shows the time path for gross investment in the UK since 1950, expressed as a percentage of GDP. You can see that the share of investment in GDP has fluctuated a little over the years, but it has settled at about 17% in recent years, which is relatively high by historical standards.

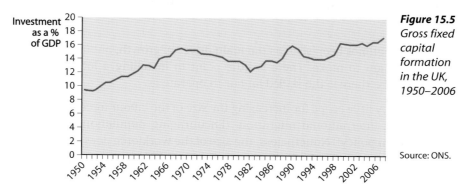

Figure 15.5
Gross fixed capital formation in the UK, 1950–2006

Source: ONS.

The choice that any society makes here is between using resources for current consumption and using resources for investment. Investment thus entails sacrificing present consumption in order to have more resources available in the future.

Different countries give investment very different priorities. Something of this can be seen in Figure 15.6, which shows gross capital formation in a selection of countries around the world in 2006. The diversity is substantial, ranging from just 12% in Côte d'Ivoire to 41% in China. Given this high rate of investment, it is perhaps not surprising to discover that China is among the fastest growing economies in the world in the early twenty-first century – but it must also be remembered that there is a cost to this, as it means sacrificing present consumption in China.

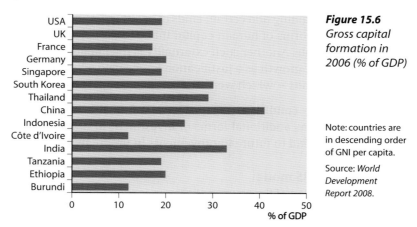

Figure 15.6
Gross capital formation in 2006 (% of GDP)

Note: countries are in descending order of GNI per capita.

Source: *World Development Report 2008.*

The contribution of capital to growth is reinforced by technological progress, as the productivity of new capital is greater than that of old capital that is being phased out. For example, the speed and power of computers has increased enormously over recent years, which has had a great impact on productivity. Effectively, this

means that technology is increasing the contribution that investment can make towards enlarging capacity output in an economy.

Innovation can also contribute, through the invention of new forms of capital and new ways of using existing capital, both of which can aid economic growth.

Labour

Capital has sometimes been seen as the main driver of growth, but labour too has a key contribution to make. There is little point in installing a lot of high-tech equipment unless there is the skilled labour to operate it.

There is relatively little scope for increasing the size of the labour force in a country, except through international migration. (Encouraging population growth is a rather long-term policy!) Nonetheless, the size of the workforce does contribute to the size of capacity output. A number of sub-Saharan African countries have seen this effect in reverse in recent years, with the impact of HIV/AIDS. The spread of this epidemic has had a devastating impact in a number of countries in the region;

Key term

human capital: the stock of skills and expertise that contribute to a worker's productivity; can be increased through education and training

in some countries the percentage of adults affected is over 30% — nearly 40% in Botswana. This has a serious impact on capacity output, because the disease affects people of working age disproportionately, diminishing the size of the workforce and the productivity of workers.

The quality of labour input is more amenable to policy action. Education and training can improve the productivity of workers, and can be regarded as a form of investment in **human capital**.

Chapter 7 discussed how education and healthcare may have associated externalities. In particular, individuals may not perceive the full social benefits associated with education, training and certain kinds of healthcare, and thus may choose to invest less in these forms of human capital than is desirable from the perspective of society as a whole. Another such externality is the impact of human capital formation on economic growth as a justification for viewing education and healthcare as being merit goods — which were discussed in Chapter 8.

For many developing countries, the provision of healthcare and improved nutrition can be seen as additional forms of investment in human capital, since such investment can lead to future improvements in productivity.

Growth and the *AD/AS* model

Notice that this discussion of the sources of economic growth has focused on factors that affect aggregate supply, as in Figure 15.1. This is because economic growth has been defined in terms of an increase in the productive capacity of the economy, which can only increase when the *AS* curve shifts to the right. An increase in aggregate demand can lead to higher real output in the economy if the initial equilibrium is below full capacity output, but this is equivalent to a move towards the *PPF*, so is not true economic growth. The only exception to this is where the increase in aggregate demand is due to an increase in investment expenditure that will later enable an increase in productive capacity. This will be important in Chapter 17, which analyses policy instruments available to the government.

Summary

➤ Economic growth is the expansion of an economy's productive capacity.

➤ This can be envisaged as a movement outwards of the production possibility frontier, or as a rightward shift of the aggregate supply curve.

➤ Economic growth can be seen as the underlying trend rate of growth in real GDP.

➤ Economic growth can stem from an increase in the inputs of factors of production, or from an improvement in their productivity, i.e. the efficiency with which factors of production are utilised.

➤ Investment contributes to growth by increasing the capital stock of an economy, although some investment is to compensate for depreciation.

➤ The contribution of capital is reinforced by the effects of technological progress.

➤ Labour is another critical factor of production that can contribute to economic growth; for instance, education and training can improve labour productivity. This is a form of human capital formation.

Exercise 15.2

Which of the following represent genuine economic growth, and which may just mean a move to the *PPF*?

a an increase in the rate of change of potential output
b a fall in the unemployment rate
c improved work practices that increase labour productivity
d an increase in the proportion of the population joining the labour force
e an increase in the utilisation of capital
f a rightward shift in the aggregate supply curve

The importance of economic growth

Expanding the availability of resources in an economy enables the standard of living of the country to increase. For developing countries this may facilitate the easing of poverty, and may allow investment in human capital that will improve standards of living further in the future. In the industrial economies, populations have come to expect steady improvements in incomes and resources. For households, economic growth may bring higher incomes, for firms it may bring higher profits, for governments it may bring higher tax revenue, and an improved capacity to provide public goods.

Thus for any society economic growth is likely to be seen as a fundamental objective — perhaps even the most important one. It may be argued that other

policy objectives should be regarded as subsidiary to the growth target. In other words, the control of inflation, the maintenance of full employment and the achievement of stability in the current account of the balance of payments are seen as important short-run objectives, because their achievement facilitates long-run economic growth.

In some less-developed countries the perspective may be different, and there has been a long-running debate about whether a society in its early stages of development should devote its resources to achieving the growth objective or to catering for basic needs. By making economic growth the prime target of policy, it may be necessary in the short run to allow inequality of incomes to continue, in order to provide the incentives for entrepreneurs to pursue growth. With such a 'growth-first' approach, it is argued that eventually, as growth takes place, the benefits will trickle down; in other words, growth is necessary in order to tackle poverty and provide for basic needs. However, others have argued that the first priority should be to deal with basic needs, so that people gain in human capital and become better able to contribute to the growth process.

For the industrial countries, growth has become embedded as the main long-run objective of the economy, although the short-run objective of inflation control sometimes dominates media discussion. Nonetheless, the long-run growth rate of GDP is monitored on a regular basis, to assess how the UK is performing relative to other industrial countries. If you would like to see how the UK is doing, Figure 15.7 shows some growth rates for 2001–06 for a selected group of OECD countries.

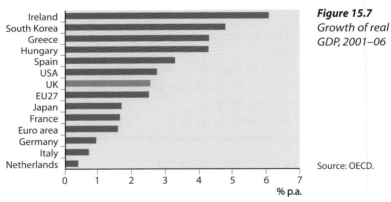

Figure 15.7
Growth of real GDP, 2001–06

Source: OECD.

The costs of economic growth

Economic growth also brings costs, perhaps most obviously in terms of pollution and degradation of the environment. In designing long-term policy for economic growth, governments need to be aware of the need to maintain a good balance between enabling resources to increase and safeguarding the environment. Pollution reduces the quality of life, so pursuing economic growth without regard to this may be damaging. This means that it is important to consider the long-term effects of economic growth — it may even be important to consider the effects not only for today's generation of citizens, but also for future generations.

These costs have been highlighted in recent years by the growing concerns that have been expressed about global climate change and the pressures on non-renewable resources such as oil and natural gas. For example, the rapid growth rates being achieved by large emerging economies such as China and India have raised questions about the sustainability of economic growth in the long run. China in particular has experienced a period of unprecedented growth since 1978, which is shown in Figure 15.8. This shows the average growth between 1978 and 1985 (when reforms began to affect the economy), and for each five-year period afterwards. No other economy in recent history has been able to achieve an average growth rate of 9.64% per annum over a 27-year period.

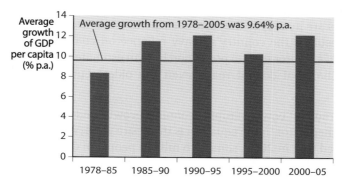

Figure 15.8
China's economic growth

Source: Calculated from IMF data.

Economic growth may thus have important effects on the environment, and in pursuing growth, countries must bear in mind the need for **sustainable development**, safeguarding the needs of future generations as well as the needs of the present.

Another aspect of environmental degradation concerns *biodiversity*. This refers to the way in which misuse of the environment is contributing to the loss of plant species — not to mention those of birds, insects and mammals — which are becoming extinct as their natural habitat is destroyed. Some of the lost species may not even have been discovered yet. Given the natural healing properties of many plants, this could mean the destruction of plants that might provide significant new drugs for use in medicine. But how can something be valued when its very existence is as yet unknown?

 Key *term*

sustainable development:
'development that meets the needs of the present without compromising the ability of future generations to meet their own needs' (Brundtland Commission, 1987)

One way of viewing the environment is as a factor of production that needs to be used effectively, just like any other factor of production. In other words, each country has a stock of *environmental* capital that needs to be utilised in the best possible way.

However, if the environmental capital is to be used appropriately, it must be given an appropriate value and this can be problematic. If property rights are not firmly established — as they are not in many LDCs — it is difficult to enforce legis-

lation to protect the environment. Furthermore, if the environment (as a factor of production) is underpriced, then 'too much' of it will be used by firms.

There are externality effects at work here too, in the sense that the loss of bio-diversity is a global loss, and not just something affecting the local economy. In some cases there have been international externality effects of a more direct kind, such as when forest fires in Indonesia caused the airport in Singapore to close down because of the resulting smoke haze.

In August 2004, *The Economist* reported that 16 of the world's most polluted cities are now located in China, and that around half of China's population (i.e. some 600 million people) have water supplies that are contaminated by animal and human waste. River systems are heavily polluted, and air pollution is becoming a serious issue, partly as a result of the country's heavy reliance on coal-fired electricity generation. Shanghai's environmental protection bureau estimated that 70% of the 1 million cars in Shanghai do not reach even the oldest European emission standard.

This illustrates the trade-off between rapid economic growth and protection of the environment. The other factor in the equation is the desire to alleviate poverty. The World Bank estimated that in 2003, some 216 million people in China were living in poverty — defined as living on less than $1 per day. The need to bring so many people out of extreme poverty lends urgency to the drive for economic growth. However, this needs to be balanced against the need to ensure sustainable development. In other words, economic growth must be achieved in such a way that it does not destroy the environment for future generations.

There are many aspects to this issue, of which protecting the environment is just one. Sustainable development also entails taking account of the depletion rates of

A coal-fired power plant in Shenyang, China. Rapid economic growth may not be sustainable in the long run

non-renewable resources, and ensuring that renewable resources *are* renewed in the process of economic growth.

So, although economic growth is important to a society, the drive for growth must be tempered by an awareness of the possible trade-offs with other important objectives.

There may be other kinds of concerns about the desirability of economic growth. It is possible that economic growth could increase inequality in society, if the benefits from growth are restricted to some groups. If economic growth entails structural change in the economy, there may be workers who are displaced from declining sectors who find that they do not have the right skills for redeployment in expanding sectors. In other words, there may be structural unemployment, although hopefully this could be a transitional problem. There may also be times when economic growth has an effect on the balance of payments, if the marginal propensity to import is high — in other words, if rising incomes lead to a rapid increase in imports.

Exercise 15.3

Discuss with your fellow students the various benefits and costs associated with economic growth, and evaluate their relative importance.

Summary

➤ The experience of economic growth has varied substantially in different regions of the world.

➤ There is a gap in living standards between countries that industrialised early and countries that are now classified as being less developed.

➤ A few countries, mainly in East Asia, went through a period of rapid growth from the 1960s that has allowed them to close the gap. This was achieved partly through export-led growth, although other factors were also important.

➤ However, countries in sub-Saharan Africa have stagnated, and remain on very low incomes.

➤ Economic growth remains important for all countries, at whatever stage of development.

➤ There may be costs attached to economic growth, particularly in respect of the environment.

Chapter 16

Macroeconomic policy objectives

Inevitably, there is a policy dimension to the study of the performance of the macro-economy. Indeed, in evaluating such performance, it is the success of macroeconomic policy that is under scrutiny. However, the success of macroeconomic policy can be judged only if you are aware of what it is that the policy is trying to achieve. This chapter introduces and analyses the main objectives of policy at the macroeconomic level and explores the possibility that there may be conflict between some of the targets.

Learning outcomes

After studying this chapter, you should:

➤ be familiar with the principal objectives of macroeconomic policy
➤ understand the reasons for setting these policy objectives
➤ be aware of some potential obstacles that may inhibit the achievement of the targets
➤ appreciate that the targets may sometimes conflict with each other

Targets of policy

Chapter 10 introduced a number of ways in which economists try to monitor and evaluate the performance of the economy at the macroeconomic level. If macro-economic performance is found to be wanting in some way, then it is reasonable to ask whether some policy intervention might improve the situation. This chapter considers aspects of the macroeconomy that might be regarded as legitimate targets for policy action. Chapter 17 analyses the policy actions that might be introduced, and evaluates their possible effectiveness. Chapter 18 examines the possibility that the policies themselves may conflict with each other.

Chapter 10 discussed some key measures of an economy's performance, particularly inflation, unemployment, GDP and the balance of payments. In addition, it is pertinent to ask whether governments should be concerned about inequality of income distribution within a society. These areas all raise policy questions that need to be addressed. Furthermore, there is a growing concern about the need to preserve the environment in which we live; Chapter 7 pointed out that an externality element in connection with the environment may be a cause of market failure, and commented that there may be international externalities that need to be considered. As this issue has a macroeconomic dimension to it, it will also need to be analysed in conjunction with the discussion of macroeconomic policy. Each of these objectives will now be considered in turn.

Price stability

One of the most prominent objectives of macroeconomic policy in recent years has been the need to control inflation. Indeed, this has been at the heart of governments' stated policy objectives since 1976.

Causes of inflation

Chapter 10 defined inflation as a rise in the general price level. However, it is important to distinguish between a one-off increase in the price level and a sustained rise over a long period of time. For example, a one-off rise in the price of oil may have an effect on the price level by shifting aggregate supply, thus affecting the equilibrium price level — as shown in Figure 16.1 (reproducing Figure 14.7). However, this takes the economy to a new equilibrium price level, and if nothing else were to change, there would be no reason for prices to continue to rise beyond P_1.

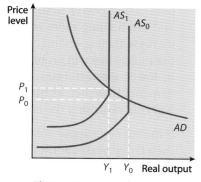

Figure 16.1 *A supply shock*

Nonetheless, this is one reason why prices may *begin* to increase. Inflation thus may be initiated on the supply side of the macroeconomy, arising from an increase in the costs faced by firms. This is sometimes referred to as **cost-push inflation**, as the increase in the overall level of prices is cost-driven.

In terms of the *AD/AS* model, it is clear that an alternative explanation of a rise in the general price level could come from the demand side, where an increase in aggregate demand leads to a rise in prices, especially if the *AS* curve becomes so

Key terms

cost-push inflation: inflation initiated by an increase in the costs faced by firms, arising on the supply side of the economy

demand-pull inflation: inflation initiated by an increase in aggregate demand

steep in the long run as to become vertical, as some macroeconomists believe. This is shown in Figure 16.2, where the increase in aggregate demand from AD_0 to AD_1 leads to a rise in the overall price level from P_0 to P_1 with no change at all in real output. An increase in the price level emanating from the demand side of the macroeconomy is some times referred to as **demand-pull inflation**.

But why should there be *persistent* increases in prices over time? One-off movements in either aggregate demand or aggregate supply may lead to one-off changes in the overall price level, but unless the movements continue in subsequent periods there is no reason to suppose that inflation will continue. One explanation is provided by changes in the supply of money circulating in an economy.

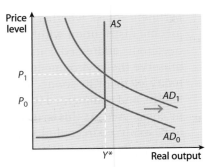

Persistent inflation can take place only when the **money stock** grows more rapidly than real output. This can be shown in terms of aggregate demand and aggregate supply. If the money supply increases, firms and households in the economy find they have excess cash balances: that is, for a given price level they have more purchasing power than they expected to have,

Figure 16.2 *An increase in aggregate demand*

Key **term**

money stock: the quantity of money in the economy

and are holding more money than they intended. Their impulse will thus be to increase their spending, which will cause the aggregate demand curve to move to the right. They will probably also save some of the excess, which will tend to result in lower interest rates — which will then reinforce the increase in aggregate demand. However, as the *AD* curve moves to the right, the equilibrium price level will rise, returning the economy to equilibrium.

If the money supply continues to increase, the process repeats itself, with prices then rising persistently. One danger of this is that people will get so accustomed to the process that they speed up their spending decisions, which simply accelerates the whole process.

To summarise, the analysis suggests that, although a price rise can be triggered on either the supply side or the demand side of the macroeconomy, persistent inflation can arise only through persistent excessive growth in the money stock, which can be seen in terms of persistent movements of the aggregate demand curve.

Costs of inflation

A crucial question is why it matters if an economy experiences inflation. The answer is that very high inflation gives rise to a number of costs.

The fact that firms have to keep amending their price lists raises the costs of undertaking transactions. These costs are often known as the *menu costs* of inflation; however, this should not be expected to be significant unless inflation really is very high. A second cost of very high inflation is that it discourages people from holding money because, at the very high nominal interest rates that occur when inflation is high, the opportunity cost of holding money becomes great. People therefore try to keep their money in interest-bearing accounts for as long as possible, even if it means making frequent trips to the bank — for which reason these are known as the *shoe leather costs* of inflation.

Prices continually change in every economy, normally upwards

This reluctance to use money for transactions may inhibit the effectiveness of markets. For example, there was a period in the early 1980s when inflation in Argentina was so high that some city parking fines had to be paid in litres of petrol rather than in cash. Markets will not work effectively when people do not use money and the economy begins to slip back towards a barter economy. The situation may be worsened if taxes or pensions are not properly indexed so that they do not keep up with inflation. If pensions do not keep up with inflation, this then means that pensioners lose out, and income inequality worsens. If tax revenue fails to keep up with government expenditure, then the authorities may be drawn into printing even more money in order to finance their spending plans.

These costs are felt mainly when inflation reaches the *hyperinflation* stage. This has been rare in developed countries in recent years, although many Latin American economies were prone to hyperinflation for a period in the 1980s, and some of the transition economies also went through very high inflation periods as they began to introduce market reforms; one example of this was the Ukraine, where inflation reached 10,000% per year in the early 1990s. Another example is the African country of Zimbabwe, where *The Economist* in February 2008 claimed that inflation had reached 150,000%.

However, there may be costs associated with inflation even when it does not reach these heights, especially if inflation is volatile. If the rate of change of prices cannot be confidently predicted by firms, the increase in uncertainty may be damaging, and firms may become reluctant to undertake the investment that would expand the economy's productive capacity. This is important for economic growth.

Furthermore, as Chapter 5 emphasised, prices are very important in allocating resources in a market economy. Inflation may consequently inhibit the ability of prices to act as reliable signals in this process, leading to a wastage of resources and lost business opportunities.

It is these last reasons that have elevated the control of inflation to being one of the central planks of UK government macroeconomic policy. However, it should be noticed that the target for inflation has not been set at zero. During the period when the inflation target was set in terms of RPIX (as explained in Chapter 10), the inflation target was 2.5%; from 2004 the target for CPI inflation was 2%. The reasoning here is twofold. One argument is that it has to be accepted that measured inflation will overstate actual inflation, partly because it is so difficult to take account of quality changes in products such as PCs, where it is impossible to distinguish accurately between a price change and a quality change. Second, wages and prices tend to be sticky in a downward direction: in other words, firms may be reluctant to reduce prices and wages. A modest rate of inflation (e.g. 2%) thus allows relative prices to change more readily, with prices in some sectors rising by more than in others. This may help price signals to be more effective in guiding resource allocation.

Summary

> The control of inflation has been the major focus of macroeconomic policy in the UK since about 1976.

> Inflation can be initiated on either the supply side of an economy or the demand side.

> However, sustained inflation can take place only if there is also a sustained increase in money supply.

> High inflation imposes costs on society and reduces the effectiveness with which markets can work.

> Low inflation reduces uncertainty, and may encourage investment by firms.

Exercise 16.1

Suppose that next year inflation in the UK economy suddenly takes off, reaching 60% per annum — in other words, prices rise by 60% — but so do incomes. Discuss how this would affect your daily life. Why would it be damaging for the economy in the future?

Full employment

For an economy to be operating on the production possibility frontier, the factors of production need to be fully employed. From society's point of view, surplus capacity in the economy represents waste. In the macroeconomic policy arena, attention in this context focuses on unemployment. For example, Figure 16.3 shows that it is possible for the economy to be in macroeconomic equilibrium at a level of output Y_1 that is below the potential full employment

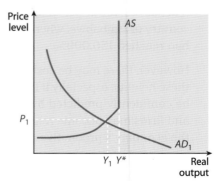

Figure 16.3 Macroeconomic equilibrium below full employment

level at Y^*. This may be seen as an unnecessary waste of potential output. In addition, there may be a cost suffered by the people who are unemployed in this situation and who could have been productively employed.

Causes of unemployment

There will always be some unemployment in a dynamic economy. At any point in time, there will be workers transferring between jobs. Indeed, this needs to happen if the pattern of production is to keep up with changing patterns of consumer demand and relative opportunity cost. In other words, in a typical period of time there will be some sectors of an economy that are expanding and others that are in decline. It is crucial that workers are able to transfer from those activities that are in decline to those that are booming. Accordingly, there will be some unemployment while this transfer takes place, and this is known as **frictional unemployment**.

In some cases, this transfer of workers between sectors may be quite difficult to accomplish. For example, coal mining may be on the decline in an economy, but international banking may be booming. It is clearly unreasonable to expect coal miners to turn themselves into international bankers overnight. In this sort of situation there may be some longer-term unemployment while workers retrain for new occupations and new sectors of activity. Indeed, there may be workers who find themselves redundant at a relatively late stage in their career and for whom the retraining is not worthwhile, or who cannot find firms that will be prepared to train them for a relatively short payback time. Such unemployment is known as **structural unemployment**. It arises because of the mismatch between the skills of workers leaving sectors that are in decline and the skills required by expanding sectors in the economy.

Figure 16.3 showed a different form of unemployment, one that arises because the economy is trapped in an equilibrium position that is below full employment. This is sometimes referred to as **demand-deficient unemployment** — and a solution to it might be to boost aggregate demand. This possibility will be discussed in Chapter 17.

A further reason for unemployment concerns the level of wages. Figure 16.4 shows a labour market in which a free market equilibrium

> ### Key terms
>
> **frictional unemployment:** unemployment associated with job search: that is, people who are between jobs
>
> **structural unemployment:** unemployment arising because of changes in the pattern of economic activity within an economy
>
> **demand-deficient unemployment:** unemployment that arises because of a deficiency of aggregate demand in the economy, so that the equilibrium level of output is below full employment

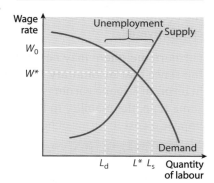

Figure 16.4 *Unemployment in a labour market*

would have wage W^* and quantity of labour L^*. If for some reason wages were set at W_0, there would be disequilibrium between labour supply (at L_s) and labour demand (at L_d). Expressing this in a different way, here is a situation in which there are more workers seeking employment at the going wage (L_s) than there are firms prepared to hire at that wage (L_d). The difference is unemployment.

There are a number of reasons why this situation might arise. Trade unions may have been able to use their power and influence to raise wages above the equilibrium level, thereby ensuring higher wages for their members who remain in employment, but denying jobs to others. Alternatively, it could be argued that wages will be inflexible downwards. Thus, a supply shock that reduced firms' demand for labour could leave wages above the equilibrium, and they may adjust downwards only slowly. Chapter 9 mentioned that in some situations the imposition of a minimum wage in a low-wage competitive labour market could also have the effect of institutionally setting the wage rate above its equilibrium level.

Finally, if unemployment benefits are set at a relatively high level compared with wages in low-paid occupations, some people may choose not to work, thereby creating some **voluntary unemployment**. From the point of view of those individuals, they are making a rational choice on the basis of the options open to them. From society's point of view, however, there needs to be a balance between providing appropriate social protection for those unable to obtain jobs and trying to make the best use of available resources for the benefit of society as a whole.

Costs of unemployment

The costs of unemployment were mentioned earlier. From society's perspective, if the economy is operating below full capacity, then it is operating within the production possibility frontier, and therefore is not making the best possible use of society's resources. In other words, if those unemployed workers were in employment, society would be producing more aggregate output; the economy would be operating more efficiently overall.

Key terms

voluntary unemployment:
situation arising when an individual chooses not to accept a job at the going wage rate

involuntary unemployment:
situation arising when an individual who would like to accept a job at the going wage rate is unable to find employment

Furthermore, there may be costs from the perspective of prospective workers, in the sense that **involuntary unemployment** carries a cost to each such individual in terms of forgone earnings and the need to rely on social security support. At the same time, the inability to find work and to contribute to the family budget may impose a cost in terms of personal worth and dignity.

Summary

> Full employment occurs when an economy is operating on the production possibility frontier, with full utilisation of factors of production.

> An economy operating below full capacity is characterised by unemployment.

➤ Some unemployment in a dynamic economy is inevitable, as people may have to undergo short spells of unemployment while between jobs — this is known as frictional unemployment.

➤ Structural unemployment occurs when there is a mismatch between the skills that workers have to offer and the skills that employers want. This occurs when the economy is undergoing structural change, with some sectors expanding and some contracting.

➤ Demand-deficient unemployment may occur if the macroeconomy is in equilibrium below full employment.

➤ If wages are held above the equilibrium level — for example, by minimum wage legislation or trade union action — then unemployment may occur.

➤ High levels of unemployment benefit may encourage some workers not to accept jobs as the opportunity cost of not working is low.

Exercise 16.2

Classify each of the following types of unemployment as arising from frictional, structural, demand-deficient or other causes, and decide whether they are voluntary or involuntary:

a unemployment arising from a decline of the coal mining sector and the expansion of financial services

b a worker leaving one job to search for a better one

c unemployment that arises because the real wage rate is held above the labour market equilibrium

d unemployment arising from slow adjustment to a fall in aggregate demand

e unemployment arising because workers find that low-paid jobs are paying less than can be obtained in unemployment benefit

The balance of payments

Lists of macroeconomic policy objectives invariably include equilibrium on the balance of payments as a key item. Unlike inflation and unemployment, it is not so obvious why disequilibrium in the balance of payments is a problem that warrants policy action.

Figure 16.5 shows the market for pounds relative to euros. Here the demand for pounds arises from residents in the euro area wanting to buy UK goods, services and assets, whereas the supply arises from UK residents wanting to buy goods, services and assets from the euro area. If the exchange rate is at its equilibrium level, this implies that the demand for pounds (i.e. the foreign demand for UK goods, services and assets) is equal to the supply of pounds (i.e. the domestic demand for goods, services and assets from the euro area).

In a free foreign exchange market, the exchange rate can be expected to adjust in order to bring about this equilibrium position. Even under a fixed exchange rate system in which the government pledges to hold the exchange rate at a particular level, any discrepancy between the demand and supply of pounds would have to be met by the monetary authorities buying or selling foreign exchange reserves.

Thus, the overall balance of payments is always in equilibrium. So why might there be a problem?

The problem arises not with the *overall* balance of payments, but with an imbalance between components of the balance of payments. In particular, attention focuses on the balance of the current account, which shows the balance in the trade in goods and services together with investment income flows and current transfers.

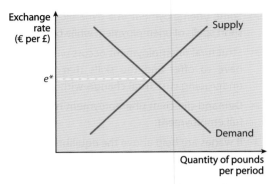

Figure 16.5 *The market for pounds sterling*

If the current account is in deficit, UK residents are purchasing more in imports of goods and services than the economy is exporting. Another way of expressing this is that UK earnings from exports are not sufficient to pay for UK imports. This is a bit like a household spending beyond its income, which can be sustained only by selling assets or by borrowing.

The concern for the economy is that a large and sustained deficit on the current account implies that the financial account must be experiencing a large and sustained surplus. This in turn means that the UK is effectively exporting assets. And this means that overseas residents are buying up UK assets, which in turn may mean a leakage of investment income in the future. Alternatively, overall balance could be achieved through the sale of foreign exchange reserves. This soaks up the excess supply of pounds that arises because UK residents are supplying more pounds in order to buy imports than overseas residents are demanding in order to buy UK exports.

However the current account deficit is financed, a large deficit cannot be sustained indefinitely. This begs the question of what is meant by a 'large' deficit. Figure 10.14 showed the current account balance as a percentage of GDP, which gives some idea of the relative magnitude of the deficit. This shows that, although the current account has been in deficit every year since 1984, the deficit has been less than 4% of GDP since 1990. This might be regarded as tolerable.

A critical issue is whether UK assets remain attractive to foreign buyers. Running a sustained deficit on current account requires running a surplus on financial account. If foreign buyers of UK assets become reluctant to buy, UK interest rates might have to rise in order to make UK assets more attractive. A by-product of this would be a curb in spending by UK firms and consumers. Given that part of this reduction in spending would have an impact on imports, this would begin to reduce the current account deficit.

One way in which the balance of payments is important from a policy perspective occurs when a government wishes to stimulate the economy, perhaps because it regards the level of unemployment as being excessive. An expansionary policy may be intended to increase domestic aggregate demand. However, in designing such a policy it is vital to remember that some of the increased demand will go not on domestic goods, but on imports, which is likely to dilute the effect of the expansion.

A major concern during the early years of the twenty-first century has been the large and persistent current account deficit being run by the US economy. This has been associated in part with the sizeable government spending of the Bush administration, which was forecast to reach a level that could have global repercussions.

Causes of a deficit on current account

The quantity of exports of goods and services from the UK depends partly on income levels in the rest of the world and partly on the competitiveness of UK goods and services, which in turn depends partly on the sterling exchange rate and partly on relative price levels in the UK and elsewhere. Similarly, the level of imports depends partly on domestic income and partly on the international competitiveness of UK and foreign goods and services.

This suggests that a fundamental cause of a deficit on the current account is a lack of competitiveness of UK goods and services, arising from an overvalued exchange rate or from high relative prices of UK goods and services. Alternatively, UK incomes may be rising more rapidly than those in the rest of the world.

Summary

> If the exchange rate is free to reach its equilibrium value, the overall balance of payments will always be zero.

> However, a deficit on the current account of the balance of payments must always be balanced by a corresponding surplus on the financial account.

> A persistent deficit on the current account means that in the long run domestic assets are being sold to overseas buyers, or that foreign exchange reserves are being run down. Neither situation can be sustained in the long run.

> A key cause of a deficit on the current account is the lack of competitiveness of domestic goods and services.

Economic growth

If the ultimate aim of a society is to improve the well-being of its citizens, then in economic terms this means that the resources available within the economy need to expand through time in order to widen people's choices. This requires a process of economic growth, which as we saw in Chapter 15 is an increase in the productive capacity of the economy. If you like, it is an expansion of the potential output of the economy.

This is such an important policy objective for an economy that the whole of Chapter 15 was devoted to it. Recall that the nearest measure that economists have of the resources available to members of a society is GDP; so in looking for economic growth, they are looking for sustained growth in real potential GDP over time.

As has been argued, economic growth may be regarded as the most fundamental of all macroeconomic policy objectives, with other policy objectives being subsidiary to it. For example, one of the key reasons for maintaining low inflation is to encourage firms to undertake investment — because this enables economic growth. Maintaining full employment ensures the best possible use of a society's resources, enabling it to reach the production possibility frontier — and failure to do this may have indirect consequences for economic growth. Running a

Wide choice for high street shoppers is a sign of economic growth

sustained current account deficit on the balance of payments that requires the sale of UK assets may limit the future growth prospects of the economy.

Concern for the environment

International externalities pose problems for policy design because they require coordination across countries. If pollution caused by the UK manufacturing sector causes acid rain elsewhere in Europe, the UK is imposing costs on other countries that are not fully reflected in market prices. Furthermore, there may be effects that are felt across generations. If the environment today is damaged, it may not be enjoyed by future generations — in other words, there may be intergenerational externality effects.

The growing concerns about global warming have drawn attention to the possible harm caused by rapid economic growth. It is this relationship between the environment and the rate of economic growth that has highlighted the macro-economic dimension to concern for the environment, and the growing calls for growth to be sustainable — as was pointed out in the previous chapter.

Income redistribution

The final macroeconomic policy objective to be considered concerns attempts to influence the distribution of income within a society. This may entail transfers of income between groups in society — that is, from richer to poorer — in order to protect the latter. Income redistribution may work through progressive taxation (whereby those on high incomes pay a higher proportion of their income in tax) or through a system of social security benefits such as the Jobseeker's Allowance or Income Support.

Causes of inequality

Some degree of inequality in the income distribution within a society is inevitable. People have different innate talents and abilities, and choose to undergo different types and levels of education and training, such that they acquire different sets of skills. Market forces imply that different payments will be made to people in different sectors of economic activity and different occupations. Income inequality also arises because of inequality in the ownership of assets. However, people in identical circumstances and with identical skills and abilities *may* receive identical income. This notion is sometimes known as *horizontal equity*, which most people would agree is desirable.

One category of policy measures is designed to encourage horizontal equity. Equal opportunities legislation tries to ensure that members of society do not suffer discrimination that might deny them equal pay for equal work, or equal access to employment. Nonetheless, there remain significant differences in earnings and employment between ethnic groups and between men and women.

Setting this aside, the key question remaining is the extent to which the government needs to intervene at the macroeconomic level in order to influence the distribution of income and protect vulnerable groups by redistributing from richer to poorer. Indeed, are there economic effects of inequality suggesting that redistribution of income is needed for reasons other than the purely humanitarian objective of alleviating poverty and protecting the vulnerable?

Equal opportunities legislation tries to ensure equal pay for equal work

The costs of inequality

In a society where there is substantial inequality in the distribution of income, there are likely to be groups of people who are disadvantaged in various ways: for example, they may find it more difficult to obtain education for themselves or for their children. In the UK it remains the case that a lower proportion of students from low-income families go to university. It may also be that some potential entrepreneurs find it more difficult to obtain the credit needed to launch their business ideas.

If this is so, it suggests that there are people in society who are inhibited from developing their productive potential — which in turn implies that economic growth in the future will be lower than it might be. This could provide a justification for redistributing income — or at least for trying to ensure that there is equality of opportunity for all members of society. However, it might be argued that redistribution can be taken too far. If the higher-income groups in society face too high a marginal tax rate on their income — in other words, if additions to income are very heavily taxed for the rich — this could remove their incentive to exploit income-earning opportunities, which could have a damaging impact on economic growth.

Getting the right balance between protecting the vulnerable and providing appropriate incentives for enterprise is a tricky task for policy-makers.

Too much inequality may also lead to high crime rates and social discontent, which in turn may lead to political instability in a society. This could affect the security of property rights and inhibit economic growth.

There is some evidence that inequality has been widening in many countries in recent years. In particular, the way that technology has been progressing places a higher premium on skills, so that the gap between the earnings of skilled and unskilled workers has been widening.

Summary

➤ Economic growth is the most important long-run macroeconomic policy objective, as this enables improvements in the well-being of society's citizens.

➤ However, there may be a need to moderate the pursuit of economic growth in order to protect the environment.

➤ Macroeconomic policy may also encompass the redistribution of income within society, on grounds of equity and also because extreme inequality may inhibit economic growth.

Exercise 16.3

Discuss which of the objectives of macroeconomic policy *you* think to be of most importance.

Conflicts between policy objectives

Having reviewed the main macroeconomic policy objectives, it should be clear that the designing of economic policy is likely to be something of a juggling act. This is especially so because there may be conflict and trade-offs between some of the targets of policy.

For example, it has already been noted that there may be a conflict between economic growth and the environment, so that the pursuit of economic growth may need to be tempered by concern for the environment. Policy must therefore be designed bearing in mind that there may be a trade-off between these two objectives — at some point, it could be that more economic growth is possible only by sacrificing environmental objectives, or that protecting the environment can only be achieved at the cost of a slower rate of economic growth.

Unemployment and inflation

This notion of trade-off between conflicting objectives applies in other areas too. One important trade-off was discovered by the Australian economist Bill Phillips. In 1958 Phillips claimed that he had found an 'empirical regularity' that had existed for almost a century and that traced out a relationship between the rate of unemployment, and the rate of change of money wages. This was rapidly generalised into a relationship between unemployment and inflation (by arguing that firms pass on increased wages in the form of higher prices).

Figure 16.6 shows what became known as the **Phillips curve**. Although Phillips began with data, he also came up with an explanation of why such a relationship should exist. At the heart of his argument was the idea that when the demand for labour is high (and unemployment is low) firms will be prepared to bid up wages in order to attract labour. To the extent that higher wages are then passed on in the form of higher prices, this would imply a relationship between unemployment and inflation: when unemployment is low, inflation will tend to be higher, and vice versa.

From a policy perspective, this suggests a trade-off between unemployment and inflation objectives. If the Phillips curve relationship holds, attempts to reduce the rate of unemployment are likely to raise inflation. On the other hand, a reduction in inflation is likely to result in higher unemployment. This suggests that it might be difficult to maintain full employment and low inflation at the same time. For example, Figure 16.7 shows a Phillips curve that is drawn

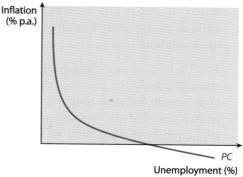

Figure 16.6 *The Phillips curve*

> ### Key *term*
>
> **Phillips curve:** an empirical relationship suggesting that there is a trade-off between unemployment and inflation

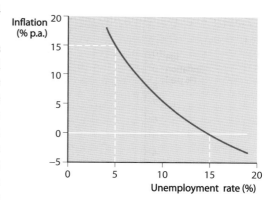

Figure 16.7 *The Phillips curve inflation–unemployment trade-off*

such that to achieve an unemployment rate of 5%, inflation would need to rise to 15% per annum; this would not be acceptable these days, when people have become accustomed to much lower inflation rates. Furthermore, to bring inflation down to zero would require an unemployment rate of 15%. Having said that, as recently as 1990 the UK economy was experiencing inflation of nearly 10% and unemployment of 7%, which is not far from this example.

Nonetheless, the Phillips curve trade-off offers a tempting prospect to policy-makers. For example, if an election is imminent it should be possible to reduce unemployment by allowing a bit more inflation, thereby creating a feel-good factor. After the election the process can be reversed. This suggests that there could be a political business cycle induced by governments seeking re-election. In other

words, the conflict between policy objectives could be exploited by politicians who see that in the short run an electorate is concerned more about unemployment than inflation.

The 1970s provided something of a setback to this theory, when suddenly the UK economy started to experience both high unemployment and high inflation simultaneously, suggesting that the Phillips curve had disappeared. This combination of stagnation and inflation became known as **stagflation**. One possibility that was put forward was that the Phillips curve had not in fact disappeared, but had moved. Suppose that wage bargaining takes place on the basis of *expectations* about future rises in retail prices. As inflation becomes embedded in an economy, and people come to expect it to continue, those expectations will be built into wage negotiations. Another way of viewing this is that expectations about price inflation will influence the *position* of the Phillips curve.

 Key term

stagflation: a situation describing an economy in which both unemployment and inflation are high at the same time

Figure 16.8 shows some empirical data for the UK since 1986. From 1986 until 1993 (or even until 1995), the pattern seems consistent with a Phillips curve relationship. However, after that time inflation seems to have stabilised, and unemployment is gradually falling — as if, with stable inflation, people's expectations have kept adjusting and allowed unemployment to fall.

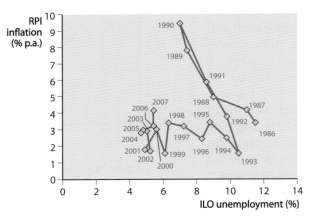

Figure 16.8
Unemployment and inflation in the UK, 1986–2007

Source: ONS.

Figures 16.9 and 16.10 show the pattern of the relationship between unemployment and inflation for two other countries, Sweden and France. Sweden shows a classic Phillips curve pattern; France has experienced less variation in the unemployment rate.

Economic growth and sustainability

It is clear that there may be conflict between achieving economic growth and the environment. Nowhere is this better seen than in the case of China in the early part of the twenty-first century. China's persistently rapid growth has had consequences for the quality of the environment. Figure 16.11 shows one aspect of this

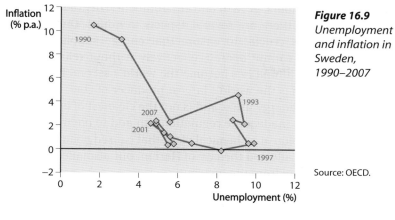

Figure 16.9
Unemployment and inflation in Sweden, 1990–2007

Source: OECD.

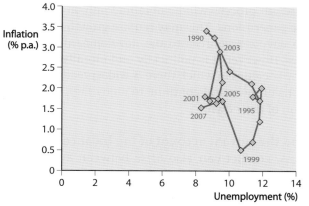

Figure 16.10
Unemployment and inflation in France, 1990–2007

Source: OECD.

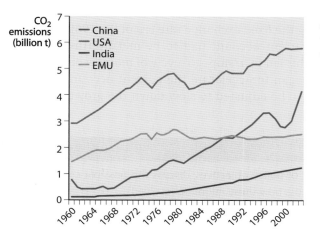

Figure 16.11
Carbon dioxide emissions

— the emissions of carbon dioxide, which is one of the key so-called greenhouse gases that contribute to the process of global warming. The acceleration of emissions in China in the early years of the century is very apparent in the figure, and China is expected to overtake USA to become the largest emitter of carbon dioxide in about 2009.

The link between economic growth and environmental degradation is a clear one. In the case of China, there are several aspects to notice. During the process of industrialisation, it is crucial to ensure that energy supplies keep pace with demand, as factories cannot operate effectively without reliable electricity and other energy sources. China has become the world's second biggest oil importer (behind the USA), and is the world's largest producer of coal, which accounts for some 80% of its total energy use — and is not the cleanest of energy technologies. It is also possible that inadequate regulation can add to environmental degradation, such as an explosion at a chemical plant that caused pollution in the Songhua River, which not only affected the city of Harbin, but also affected part of Russia, which was downstream from the incident.

For economic growth to be sustainable, these environmental effects must be taken into account, or there is a real danger that the improved standard of living that flows from the growth process will be obtained only at the expense of the quality of life of future generations. This may require growth to be slowed in the short run in order to devote resources to the development of renewable and cleaner energy sources. However, it is politically and morally difficult to impose this on newly emerging societies in which there is widespread poverty, especially when the richer nations of the world continue to enjoy high standards of living while causing pollution of their own.

Economic growth and the current account of the balance of payments

In some circumstances, conflict can also arise between achieving economic growth, and attaining equilibrium on the current account of the balance of payments. An increase in economic growth resulting in higher real incomes could lead to an increase in imports of goods and services, if UK residents spent a high proportion of their additional income abroad. This was seen as a major problem during the fixed exchange rate era of the 1950s and 1960s, when any deficit on the current account had to be met by running down foreign exchange reserves. This led to a 'stop–go' cycle of macroeconomic policy, where every time growth began to accelerate the current account went into deficit, and policy then had to be adjusted to slow down the growth rate to deal with the deficit.

Exercise 16.4

Given the following list of policy objectives, discuss the possible conflicts that may arise between them, and discuss how these might be resolved:

➤ low inflation
➤ low unemployment
➤ high economic growth
➤ a low deficit on the current account of the balance of payments
➤ maintenance of a high environmental quality
➤ equity in the distribution of income

Summary

➤ There may be conflict and trade-offs between policy objectives.

➤ The Phillips curve describes a trade-off between unemployment and the inflation rate, which suggests that in the short run, lower unemployment can only be achieved at the expense of a higher rate of inflation.

➤ There may also be a conflict between attaining a high rate of economic growth and sustainability, although some forms of growth may be less problematic in this respect.

➤ Economic growth may also lead to problems with the current account of the balance of payments in some circumstances.

Chapter 17

Macroeconomic policy instruments

Previous chapters have shown that there may be a range of macroeconomic policy objectives, from economic growth, full employment, the control of inflation and equilibrium on the current account of the balance of payments, to concerns for the environment and for the distribution of income. Attention now turns to the sorts of policy that might be implemented to try to meet these targets. Policies at the macroeconomic level are designed to affect either aggregate demand or aggregate supply, and each will be examined in turn.

Learning outcomes

After studying this chapter, you should:

➤ understand and be able to evaluate policies that affect aggregate demand, including fiscal, monetary and exchange rate policies
➤ understand and be able to evaluate policies that affect aggregate supply
➤ be able to appraise the relative merits of policies applied to the demand and supply sides of the macroeconomy
➤ be familiar with how macroeconomic policy has been conducted in the UK in recent years

Macroeconomic policy objectives revisited

Chapter 16 identified a number of objectives that might be seen as desirable for the macroeconomy. These can be interpreted in terms of Figure 17.1, which shows an economy in macroeconomic equilibrium.

Price stability

The first objective discussed related to the control of inflation, where it was pointed out that prices can increase because of shifts in either aggregate demand or aggregate supply. However, it was also pointed out that *persistent* inflation would arise only in a situation in which money stock was growing more rapidly than real output. This seems to suggest that one policy response to control persistent inflation would be to control the growth of the money stock.

An increase in money stock affects aggregate demand, shifting the aggregate demand curve to the right and causing prices to rise in an attempt to regain macroeconomic equilibrium. Thus, attempts to control inflation can be interpreted as attempts to create stability in the overall equilibrium price level.

Full employment

A second macroeconomic policy objective is full employment, which occurs at Y^* in Figure 17.1. If the aggregate demand curve were to be positioned further to the left in Figure 17.1, macroeconomic equilibrium would occur at less than the full employment level of real output. This suggests that, to restore full employment, policy should be aimed at altering the position of the aggregate demand curve in order to bring the economy back to Y^*. Notice that policy-makers need to be sure that the *AD* curve really is positioned in the upward segment of the *AS* curve. If *AD* cuts *AS* in the vertical section of the *AS* curve — as it does in Figure 17.1, then any rightward shift of the *AD* curve would lead to an increase in the overall price level, but no change in real output.

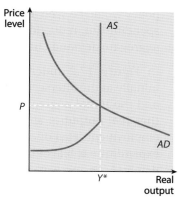

Figure 17.1 *Macroeconomic policy objectives*

Balance of payments

Policy-makers need to be aware of the dangers of a prolonged and substantial deficit on the balance of payments current account, which can have long-run effects on the ownership pattern of UK assets. If these assets are sold to foreigners, their sale will have a long-run effect on the aggregate supply curve. However, the deficit is caused by an imbalance between the components of aggregate demand, so in a sense the current account objective is related to both aggregate supply and aggregate demand. In effect, the need to achieve current account balance acts as a constraint on attempts to meet other policy objectives, so the trade-offs between objectives are of the greatest importance in this case.

Economic growth

The achievement of economic growth is a long-term objective, the aim of which is to increase the economy's productive capacity. With respect to Figure 17.1, this can be interpreted in terms of policies affecting the *position* of the long-run aggregate supply curve. Economic growth occurs when the aggregate supply curve shifts to the right. Thus, in order to influence the economic growth rate of a country, economists need to look for policies that can affect aggregate supply.

Demand-side policies

Policies that aim to influence an economy's aggregate demand are designed either to stabilise the level of output and employment or to stabilise the price level. The prime focus is thus on the short-run position of the macroeconomy. The two major categories of policy are fiscal policy and monetary policy.

Fiscal policy

The term **fiscal policy** covers a range of policy measures that affect government expenditures and revenues. For example, an expansionary fiscal policy would be seen as an increase in government spending (or reduction in taxes) that shifts the aggregate demand curve to the right.

In Figure 17.2 macroeconomic equilibrium is initially at the intersection of aggregate supply (*AS*) and the initial aggregate demand curve (*AD*$_0$), so that real output is at Y_0, which is below the full employment level of output at Y^*. As government expenditure is one of the components of aggregate demand, an increase in such expenditure moves the aggregate demand curve from *AD*$_0$ to *AD*$_1$. In response, the economy moves to a new equilibrium, in which the overall price level has risen to P_1 but real output has moved to Y_1, which is closer to the full employment level Y^*.

> **Key** *term*
>
> **fiscal policy:** decisions made by the government on its expenditure, taxation and borrowing

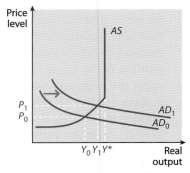

Figure 17.2 *The use of fiscal policy*

In this scenario, government expenditure is treated as an injection into the circular flow, and it will be reinforced by the multiplier effect. In the present context, an increase in government expenditure is effective in raising the level of real output in the economy, although some of the increase is dissipated in the form of an increase in the overall level of prices. Notice that such a move cannot be interpreted as 'economic growth' *per se*, as this term is reserved for a situation in which there is an increase in the full employment (potential capacity) level of real output. It is also important to be aware that, if the multiplier is relatively low, the reinforcement of fiscal policy through this route will also be relatively weak. Remember that the strength of the multiplier effect depends on the size of withdrawals from the circular flow. For example, if consumers have a high propensity to import, this will weaken the impact of the multiplier.

This kind of policy is effective only if the aggregate demand curve intersects the aggregate supply curve in the upward-sloping segment of *AS*. If the economy is already at the full employment level of output, an increase in aggregate demand merely results in a higher overall level of prices. The effective use of such policy thus requires policy-makers to have good information about the current state of the economy; in particular, they need to know whether the economy is at or below full employment. Otherwise, the results could be damaging for the price stability target. In other words, there is a danger that an expansionary fiscal policy will lead to inflation, but not affect output very much if the *AS* curve is relatively steep.

The effect on the balance of payments must also be borne in mind. Part of an increase in aggregate demand is likely to be spent on imports, but there is no immediate reason for exports to change, so in the short run there is likely to be an increase in the current account deficit on the balance of payments.

Although the focus of the discussion so far has been on government expenditure, fiscal policy also refers to taxation. In fact, the key issue in considering fiscal policy is the *balance* between government expenditure and government revenue, as it is this balance that affects the position of aggregate demand directly.

An increase in the **government budget deficit** (or a decrease in the **government budget surplus**) moves the aggregate demand curve to the right. The budget deficit may arise either from an increase in expenditure or from a decrease in taxation, although the two have some differential effects.

To a certain extent, the government budget deficit changes automatically, without active intervention from the government. If the economy goes into a period of recession, unemployment benefit payments will rise, thereby increasing government expenditure. At the same time, tax revenues will decrease, partly because people who lose their jobs no longer pay income tax. In addition, people whose income is reduced — perhaps because they no longer work overtime — also pay less tax. This is reinforced by the progressive nature of the income tax system, which means that people pay lower rates of tax at lower levels of income. Furthermore, VAT receipts will fall if people are spending less on goods and services.

Key terms

government budget deficit (surplus): the balance between government expenditure and revenue

automatic stabilisers: effects by which government expenditure adjusts to offset the effects of recession and boom without the need for active intervention

The opposite effects will be evident in a boom period, preventing the economy from overheating. For example, tax revenues will tend to increase during the boom, and the government will need to make fewer payments of social security benefits. By such **automatic stabilisers,** government expenditure automatically rises during a recession and falls during a boom.

In the past there was a tendency for governments to use fiscal policy in a *discretionary* way in order to influence the path of the economy. A government might use its discretion to increase government expenditure to prevent a recession, for example. Indeed, there have been accusations that governments have sometimes, in some countries, used fiscal policy to create a 'feel-good' factor in the run-up to a general election, by allowing the economy to boom as the election approaches, only to impose a clampdown afterwards.

The government budget deficit will change regardless of government intervention

Such intervention has been shown to be damaging to the long-run path of the economy because of its effect on inflation. Furthermore, there are other problems with using fiscal policy in this way. Apart from anything else, it takes time to collect data about the performance of the economy, so its *current* state is never known for certain. Because the economy responds quite sluggishly to policy change, it is often the case that the policy comes into effect just when the economy is already turning around of its own accord. This is potentially destabilising, and can do more harm than good.

Exercise 17.1

Use *AD/AS* analysis to consider the effect of an expansionary fiscal policy on the equilibrium level of real output and the overall price level. Undertake this exercise with different initial positions along the aggregate supply curve, first analysing an economy that begins at full employment and then one in which aggregate demand creates an equilibrium that is below full employment. Discuss the differences in your results.

Fiscal policy in the UK

If the government spends more than it raises in revenue, the resulting deficit has to be financed in some way. The government deficit is the difference between public sector spending and revenues, and is known as the *public sector net cash requirement* (PSNCR), which until 1999 was known as the *public sector borrowing requirement* (PSBR). Part of the PSNCR is covered by borrowing, and the government closely monitors its *net borrowing*. Over time, such borrowing leads to *net debt*, which is the accumulation of past borrowing. Figure 17.3 shows public sector net debt as a percentage of GDP. The Labour government has aimed to keep this below 40% — and has been successful in achieving this after 1998.

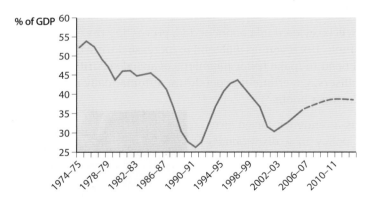

Figure 17.3
Public sector net debt (% of GDP)

Source: HM Treasury (projections from 2006/07 onwards).

In 1998 the UK government issued its *Code for Fiscal Stability*, which established its objectives for fiscal policy and the rules under which it would operate. The Treasury set these out in the *Budget 2004* statement as follows:

The Government's fiscal policy objectives are:
➤ over the medium term, to ensure sound public finances and that spending and taxation impact fairly within and between generations; and

➤ over the short term, to support monetary policy and, in particular, to allow the automatic stabilisers to help smooth the path of the economy

This highlights two major concerns of the government that represent a change in practice. First, there is a concern for the long-run effects of policy on spending and borrowing. It has come to be recognised that sustainable economic growth has to take into account the needs of future generations. The government therefore has taken the view that its current spending should be met out of current revenues, and that only investment for the future should be met through borrowing.

The second important commitment is to use fiscal policy as a *support* to monetary policy. In other words, monetary policy is seen as the most important way of influencing the macroeconomy, and, although the automatic stabilisers are allowed to cut in, there is no intention of using discretionary policy. This clear statement is intended to increase the credibility of government policy by indicating its refusal to take action that could destabilise the macroeconomy.

This suggests that fiscal policy has two kinds of effect. In the first place, the automatic stabilisers help to regulate the economy over the cycle by allowing aggregate demand to be affected by changes in the government budget deficit during the cycle.

The second one is a supply-side effect. By improving the credibility of government policy, and by ensuring that the macroeconomy is not destabilised by inappropriate interventions, it is hoped that the private sector will have more confidence in the future state of the economy. Such confidence may then affect the amount of investment that firms will be prepared to undertake. This would shift aggregate supply in the long run.

Summary

➤ Fiscal policy is concerned with the decisions made by government about its expenditure, taxation and borrowing.

➤ As government expenditure is an autonomous component of aggregate demand, an increase in expenditure will shift the *AD* curve to the right.

➤ If *AD* intersects *AS* in the vertical segment of *AS*, the effect of the increase in aggregate demand is felt only in prices.

➤ However, if the initial equilibrium is below the full employment level, the shift in *AD* will lead to an increase in both equilibrium real output and the overall price level.

➤ In fact, it is net spending that it is important, so government decisions on taxation are also significant.

➤ The government budget deficit (surplus) is the difference between government expenditure and revenue.

➤ The budget deficit varies automatically through the business cycle because of the action of the automatic stabilisers.

➤ If the government runs a budget deficit, it may need to undertake net borrowing, which over time affects the net debt position.

Monetary policy

Monetary policy is the approach currently favoured by the UK government to stabilise the macroeconomy. It entails the use of monetary variables such as the money supply and interest rates to influence aggregate demand.

The prime instrument of monetary policy in recent years has been the interest rate. Through the interest rate, monetary policy affects aggregate demand. At higher interest rates, firms undertake less investment expenditure and households undertake less consumption expenditure. This is partly because when the interest rate is relatively high, the cost of borrowing becomes high and people are discouraged from borrowing for investment or consumption purposes. There are reinforcing effects that operate through the exchange rate if UK interest rates are high relative to elsewhere in the world. If the exchange rate rises because of high interest rates, this will reduce the competitiveness of UK goods.

Key term

monetary policy: the decisions made by government regarding monetary variables such as the money supply or the interest rate

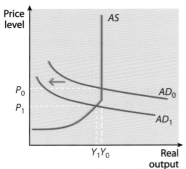

Figure 17.4 *The use of monetary policy*

Suppose the government believes that the economy is close to full employment and is in danger of overheating. Overheating could push prices up without any resulting benefit in terms of higher real output. An increase in the interest rate will lead to a fall in aggregate demand, thereby relieving the pressure on prices. This is illustrated in Figure 17.4, where the initial position has aggregate demand relatively high at AD_0, real output at the full employment level Y_0 and the overall price level at P_0. The increase in interest rates shifts aggregate demand to the left, to AD_1. Real output falls slightly to Y_1 and the equilibrium price level falls to P_1.

Monetary policy in the UK

One of the first steps taken by Tony Blair's government after it was first elected in 1997 was to devolve the responsibility for monetary policy to the Bank of England, which was given the task of achieving the government's stated inflation target, initially set at 2.5% for RPIX inflation. As noted in Chapter 10, the target was amended in 2004, when it became 2% per annum as measured by the CPI.

According to this arrangement, the **Monetary Policy Committee** (MPC) of the Bank of England sets interest rates in such a way as to keep inflation within 1 percentage point (either way) of the 2% target for CPI inflation. If it fails to achieve this, the Bank has to write an open letter to the chancellor of the exchequer to explain why the target has not been met. Such a letter became necessary for the first time in March 2007, when CPI inflation touched 3.1%.

Key term

Monetary Policy Committee: body within the Bank of England responsible for the conduct of monetary policy

A meeting of the Monetary Policy Committee of the Bank of England

Key terms

bank rate: the interest rate that is set by the Monetary Policy Committee of the Bank of England in order to influence inflation

transmission mechanism of monetary policy: the process by which a change in the bank rate affects inflation

Operationally, the MPC sets the interest rate which it pays on commercial bank reserves. This is known as the **bank rate**. The commercial banks tend to use this rate as their own base rate, from which they calculate the rates of interest that they charge to their borrowers. Thus, if the MPC changes the bank rate, the commercial banks soon adjust the rates they charge to borrowers. These will vary according to the riskiness of the loans; thus credit cards are charged at a higher rate than mortgages, but all the rates are geared to the base rate set by the commercial banks, and hence indirectly to the bank rate set by the Bank of England.

Figure 17.5 summarises the **transmission mechanism of monetary policy**. The Bank of England sets the bank rate, which affects both market rates of interest and the exchange rate. These in turn influence other asset prices and expectations about the future, and the degree of confidence among economic agents. These factors then affect both domestic and net external demand, and hence aggregate demand. An increase (decrease) in aggregate demand puts upward (downward)

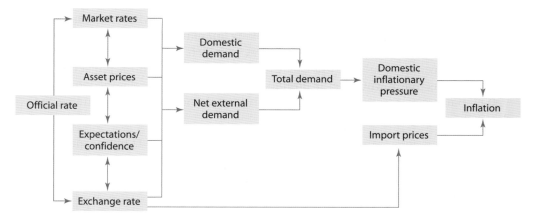

Figure 17.5 *The transmission mechanism of monetary policy*

Note: For simplicity, this figure does not show all interactions between variables, but these can be important.

Source: Bank of England.

pressure on prices, thus affecting the amount of domestic inflationary pressure, while at the same time changes in the exchange rate have an effect on import prices, which also affect inflation. As you can see. that there is a long and complicated chain of linkages that enables a change in monetary policy to affect inflation.

Figure 17.6 shows the target rates for RPIX up to December 2003 and for the CPI thereafter, together with the outcomes. The bank rate is also shown. As you can see, inflation has remained within the 1% band throughout the period, apart from in March 2007. The association between the bank rate and movements in the inflation rate does not seem very close. This is partly because the relationship between them is obscured to some extent by other influences; it also reflects the fact that the MPC takes into account a wide range of factors when deciding whether to change the bank rate or to leave it as it was in the previous month.

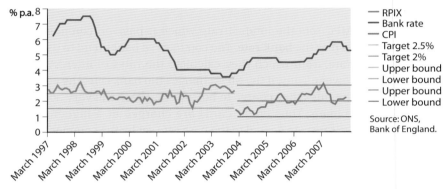

Figure 17.6 *Interest rates and the inflation target, March 1997–January 2008*

For example, at the August 2007 meeting the MPC discussed financial markets developments, the international economy, money, credit, demand and output, and costs and prices. In other words, the inflation target is considered within the broad context of developments in various aspects of the economy, and all of these factors were discussed in some detail before taking a decision on what the bank rate should be. In the event, the MPC at this meeting unanimously decided to maintain the bank rate at its existing level of 5.75%, to which it had been raised in the previous meeting in July. At this point in time, the MPC's central projection for inflation was that it would settle around the 2% target during the second half of 2007, but it also recognised there was substantial uncertainty surrounding the projections.

Similar discussions take place every month, and in the interests of transparency, the minutes of the regular MPC meetings are published on the internet — you can see them at **www.bankofengland.co.uk/mpc**. This means that you can readily check recent developments in the economy.

By influencing the level of aggregate demand, the MPC can affect the rate of inflation so as to achieve the target, although the effects of a change in the bank rate are not likely to take immediate effect. One reason for giving the Bank of England such independence is that it increases the credibility of the policy. If firms and households realise that the government is serious about controlling inflation, they will have more confidence in its actions, and will be better able to form expectations about the future path the economy will take. In particular, firms will be encouraged to undertake more investment, and this will have a supply-side effect, shifting the aggregate supply curve to the right in the long run.

Exercise 17.2

Visit the Bank of England website and check whether the MPC chose to change the interest rate at their most recent meeting. Take a look at the minutes of the meeting to see the factors that were considered in taking this decision.

Summary

➤ Monetary policy is concerned with the decisions made by government on monetary variables such as money supply and the interest rate.

➤ A change in the interest rate influences the level of aggregate demand through the investment expenditure of firms, the consumption behaviour of households and (indirectly) net exports.

➤ Since 1997, the Bank of England has been given independent responsibility to set interest rates in order to meet the government's inflation target.

➤ The Monetary Policy Committee (MPC) of the Bank sets the bank rate, which is then used as a base rate by the commercial banks and other financial institutions.

➤ Giving independence to the Bank of England in this way increases the credibility of monetary policy.

➤ If this encourages investment, there may be a long-run impact on aggregate supply.

Policies affecting aggregate supply

Demand-side policies have been aimed primarily at stabilising the macroeconomy in the relatively short run, but with the intention of affecting aggregate supply in the long run, by influencing firms' and households' confidence in the future path of the economy. However, there are also a number of policies that can be used to influence the aggregate supply curve directly.

Chapter 14 indicated that the position of the aggregate supply curve depends primarily on the quantity of factor inputs available in the economy, and on the efficiency of those factors. **Supply-side policies** thus focus on affecting these determinants of aggregate supply in order to shift the *AS* curve to the right.

Investment is one key to this in the long run, and this chapter has already shown how demand-side policies that stabilise the macroeconomy in the short run may also have long-run effects on aggregate supply by encouraging investment.

 Key **term**

supply-side policies: range of measures intended to have a direct impact on aggregate supply — and specifically the potential capacity output of the economy

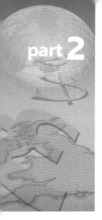
Education and training

Investment is also needed in human capital, and one form that this can take is education and training. An important supply-side policy therefore takes the form of encouraging workers (and potential workers) to undertake education and training to improve their productivity.

This takes place partly through education in schools and colleges in preparation for work. It is important, therefore, that the curriculum is designed to provide key skills that will be useful in the workplace. However, this does not mean that all education has to be geared directly to providing skills; problem-solving and analytical skills, for example, can be developed through the study of a wide range of disciplines.

Adult education is also important. When the structure of the economy is changing, retraining must be made available to enable workers to move easily between sectors and occupations. This is crucial if structural unemployment is not to become a major problem. For any society — whether industrialised or less developed and needing to reduce its dependence on agriculture — education and skills are necessary to enable workers to switch into new activities in response to structural changes in the economy.

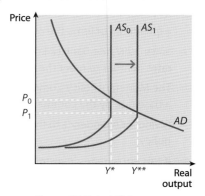

Figure 17.7 shows how such a policy can affect the aggregate supply curve, moving it from AS_0 to AS_1. This move enables an increase in the potential output capacity of the economy, and it need not be inflationary. Indeed, in the figure the overall price level falls from P_0 to P_1 following the shift in aggregate supply, with real output increasing from Y^* to Y^{**}.

Figure 17.7 *A shift in aggregate supply*

Flexibility of markets

The rationale for including retraining as a supply-side policy rests partly on the argument that this provides for greater flexibility in labour markets, enabling workers to switch between economic activities to improve the overall workings of the economy.

There are other ways of improving market flexibility. One is to limit the power of the trade unions, whose actions can sometimes lead to inflexibility in the labour market, either through resistance to new working practices that could improve productivity or by pushing up wages so that the level of employment is reduced.

Indeed, maintaining the flexibility of markets is one way in which the macroeconomic stability promoted by disciplined fiscal and monetary policy can improve aggregate supply. Macroeconomic stability enables price signals to work more effectively, as producers are better able to observe changes in relative prices. This can promote allocative efficiency.

Unemployment benefits

An important influence on labour supply, particularly for low-income workers, is the level of unemployment benefit. If unemployment benefit is provided at too high a level, it may inhibit labour force participation, in that some workers may opt to live on unemployment benefit rather than take up low-skilled (and low-paid) employment. In such a situation, a reduction in unemployment benefit may induce an increase in labour supply, which again will move the aggregate supply curve to the right.

Investment in human capital can increase productivity

However, such a policy needs to be balanced against the need to provide protection for those who are unable to find employment. It is also important that unemployment benefit is not reduced to such a level that workers are unwilling to leave their jobs to search for better ones, as this may inhibit the flexibility of the labour market.

Promotion of competition

An recurrent theme in many policy statements from governments and international organisations like the World Bank and IMF has been the importance of promoting competition. There are several reasons why this might be important in influencing aggregate supply. One possibility is that a monopoly firm in a market may be able to use its market power to maximise profits by restricting output and raising price. If such a firm is forced to confront competition from other firms, it may have to temper its use of that market power, and reduce price in order to sell more output and protect its market share. The intensity of competition may also affect firms' willingness to improve productivity. It is possible that in some markets the lack of competition will produce complacency, depriving firms of the incentive to operate at maximum efficiency. This was especially true in the UK for the formerly nationalised industries such as electricity and gas supply, which were widely believed to have operated with widespread productive inefficiency.

Policies that promote competition may thus lead to improvements in both allocative and productive efficiency. This was one of the motivations behind the privatisation drive that began in the 1980s under Margaret Thatcher. However, it should be noted that there is not wholesale agreement on whether privatisation has invariably led to improvements in efficiency in industries such as the railways or water supply.

Incentive effects

Similarly, there are dangers in making the taxation system too progressive. Most people accept that income tax should be progressive — that is, that those on rela-

tively high incomes should pay a higher rate of tax than those on low incomes — as a way of redistributing income within society and preventing inequality from becoming extreme. However, there may come a point at which marginal tax rates are so high that a large proportion of additional income is taxed away, reducing incentives for individuals to supply additional effort or labour. This could also have an effect on aggregate supply. Again, however, it is important to balance these incentive effects against the distortion caused by having too much inequality in society.

Exercise 17.3

For each of the following policies, identify whether it is an example of fiscal, monetary or supply-side policy. Discuss how each policy affects either aggregate demand or aggregate supply (or both), and examine its effects on equilibrium real output and the overall price level:

a an increase in government expenditure
b a decrease in the rate of unemployment benefit
c a fall in the rate of interest
d legislation limiting the power of trade unions
e encouragement for more students to attend university
f provision of retraining in the form of adult education
g a reduction in the highest rate of income tax
h measures to break up a concentrated market
i an increase in the bank rate

Summary

➤ Policies to shift the aggregate supply curve may be used to encourage economic growth.

➤ Education and training can be viewed as a form of investment in human capital, which is designed to improve the productivity of workers.

➤ Measures to improve the flexibility of labour and product markets may lead to an overall improvement in productivity and thus may affect aggregate supply.

➤ Promoting competition can also improve the effectiveness of markets in the economy.

➤ Incentive effects are an important influence on aggregate supply. For example, if unemployment benefits are set too high, this may discourage labour force participation. An over-progressive income taxation structure can also have damaging incentive effects.

Chapter 18

Macroeconomic policy: priorities and conflicts

Having explored the objectives of macroeconomic policy and the sorts of policies that might be used to achieve those objectives, it is now important to examine the need for coordinating the policies when they are put into operation. In some cases, it will be seen that a policy introduced to meet one policy objective may endanger one of the other objectives. In this case, policy-makers need to understand the potential conflicts. If those conflicts cannot be fully resolved, it then becomes necessary to set priorities in order to end up with a coherent overall policy stance.

Learning outcomes

After studying this chapter, you should:
➤ be familiar with the possible conflicts that may arise between the main macroeconomic policy objectives, including fiscal, monetary, exchange rate and supply-side policies
➤ understand that the use of one macroeconomic policy may outweigh the impact of another
➤ appreciate that some policies may have different effects in the long run than in the short run
➤ understand and be able to evaluate the relative importance of policy objectives and the need to set priorities between them

Macroeconomic policy instruments

The government has three main types of policy instrument with which to attempt to meet its macroeconomic objectives. These were introduced in Chapter 17:

1 *Fiscal policy:* the term 'fiscal policy' covers a range of policy measures that affect government expenditures and revenues through the decisions made by the government on its expenditure, taxation and borrowing. Fiscal policy is used to influence the level and structure of aggregate demand in an economy. As this

chapter unfolds, you will see that the effectiveness of fiscal policy depends crucially on the whole policy environment in which it is utilised, and on the interrelationship between the three types of policies.

2 *Monetary policy*: this entails the use of monetary variables such as money supply and interest rates to influence aggregate demand. Remember that under a fixed exchange rate system monetary policy becomes wholly impotent, as it has to be devoted to maintaining the exchange rate. So here again, the effectiveness of monetary policy will depend on the policy environment in which it is used.

3 *Supply-side policies*: such policies comprise a range of measures intended to have a direct impact on aggregate supply — specifically, on the potential capacity output of the economy. These measures are often microeconomic in character and are designed to increase output and hence economic growth.

Aggregate supply revisited

To analyse policy options, return to the model of aggregate supply and aggregate demand (*AS/AD*). Notice that it is important to be aware of a debate that developed over the shape of the aggregate supply curve: this is important because it has implications for the conduct and effectiveness of policy options.

During the 1970s, an influential school of macroeconomists, which became known as the **Monetarist School**, argued that the economy would always converge on an equilibrium level of output that they referred to as the **natural rate of output**. Associated with this long-run equilibrium was a **natural rate of unemployment**. If this were the case, then the long-run relationship between aggregate supply and the price level would be vertical, as shown in Figure 18.1. Here Y^* is the natural rate of output, i.e. the full-employment level of aggregate output. In other words, a change in the overall price level does not affect aggregate output, because the economy always readjusts rapidly back to full employment.

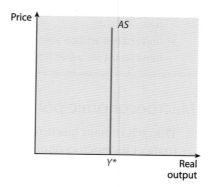

Figure 18.1 *Aggregate supply in the long run (the 'Monetarist' view)*

An opposing school of thought (often known as the **Keynesian School**) held that the macroeconomy was not sufficiently flexible to enable continuous full employment. They argued that the economy could settle at an equilibrium position below full employment, at least in the medium term. In particular, inflexibilities in labour markets would prevent adjustment. For example, if firms had pessimistic expectations about aggregate demand, and thus reduced their supply of output, this would lead to lower incomes because of the workers being laid off. This would then mean that aggregate demand was indeed deficient, so firms' pessimism was self-fulfilling.

These sorts of argument led to a belief that there would be a range of output over which aggregate supply would be upward sloping. Figure 18.2 illustrates such an aggregate supply curve, and will be familiar from earlier discussions. In this diagram Y^* still represents full employment; however, when the economy is operating below this level of output, aggregate supply is somewhat sensitive to the price level, becoming steeper as full employment is approached.

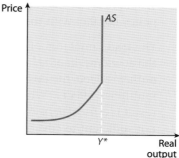

Figure 18.2 *Aggregate supply in the long run (the 'Keynesian' view)*

The policy implications of the Monetarist AS curve are strong. If the economy always converges rapidly on the full-employment level of output, no manipulation of aggregate demand can have any effect except on the price level. This is readily seen in Figure 18.3, where, regardless of the position of the aggregate demand curve, the level of real output remains at Y^*. If aggregate demand is low at AD_0, then the price level is also relatively low, at P_0. An increase in aggregate demand to AD_1 raises the price level to P_1 but leaves real output at Y^*. In such a world, only supply-side policy (which affects the position of the aggregate supply curve) has any effect on real output.

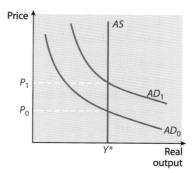

Figure 18.3 *Demand-side policy with a vertical AS curve*

Summary

➤ Governments pursue a range of policy objectives, including low inflation and low unemployment, a favourable balance of payments position, economic growth, maintenance of a good environment, income redistribution and the correction of market failure.

➤ In order to pursue these objectives, governments have recourse to fiscal, monetary and supply-side policies.

➤ In using the *AD/AS* model to analyse policy options, it is useful to distinguish between Monetarist and Keynesian views about the shape of aggregate supply.

➤ Monetarist economists have argued that the economy always converges rapidly on equilibrium at the natural rate of output, implying that policies affecting aggregate demand have an impact only on prices, leaving real output unaffected. Aggregate supply in this world is vertical.

➤ The Keynesian view is that the economy may settle in an equilibrium that is below full employment, and that there is a range over which aggregate supply slopes upwards.

Fiscal policy

What is the role of fiscal policy in a modern economy? And to what extent will fiscal policy conflict with the operation of monetary and supply-side policies?

The traditional aim of fiscal policy was to affect the level of aggregate demand in the economy. In other words, the overall balance between government receipts and outlays affects the position of the aggregate demand curve, which is reinforced by multiplier effects. When government outlays exceed government receipts, the result is a *fiscal deficit.* This occurs when the revenues raised through taxation are not sufficient to cover the government's various types of expenditure.

Figure 18.3 shows that shifting the aggregate demand curve affects only the overall price level in the economy when the aggregate supply curve is vertical — and the Monetarist School of thought argued that it would always be vertical. Hence a key issue for a government considering the use of fiscal policy is knowing whether there is spare capacity in the economy, because otherwise an expansion in aggregate demand from increased government spending will push up prices but leave real output unchanged.

Looking more closely at what is happening, you can see that there are some forces at work that are acting to weaken the multiplier effect of an increase in government expenditure. One way in which this happens is through interest rates. If the government finances its deficit through borrowing, a side-effect is to put upward pressure on interest rates, which then may cause private-sector spending — by households on consumption and by firms on investment — to decline, as the cost of borrowing has been increased. This process is known as the **crowding out** of private-sector activity by the public sector. It limits the extent to which a government budget deficit can shift the aggregate demand curve, especially if the public-sector activity is less productive than the private-sector activity that it replaces.

>
> **Key term**
>
> **crowding out:** a process by which an increase in government expenditure crowds out private-sector activity by raising the cost of borrowing

Fiscal policy and monetary policy

The fact that fiscal policy may have implications for the interest rate suggests that there may be circumstances in which fiscal and monetary policy may come into conflict, given that interest rates are a key part of the transmission of monetary policy. This means that a way must be found of coordinating fiscal and monetary policy. This is naturally difficult to do, given the way that the Bank of England is intended to act independently of the government in conducting monetary policy in order to meet the inflation target.

Fiscal policy and supply-side policies

The operation of fiscal policy may also interact with supply-side policies. Indeed, there may be some aspects of fiscal policy that will have supply-side effects. For example, suppose the government increases expenditure on education and training. The short-run effect is on aggregate demand. In Figure 18.4, the initial effect of the increase in aggregate demand is to shift the AD curve from AD_0 to AD_1. As the economy started at full-employment equilibrium, the only effect of this is to push up the overall price level from P_0 to

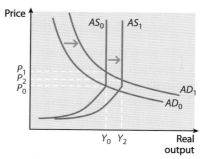

Figure 18.4 *Fiscal policy with long-run supply-side effects*

P_1. However, in the long run, the improved education and training being provided will raise the productivity of workers, and this will have the effect of shifting the position of the aggregate supply curve — perhaps from AS_0 to AS_1. In terms of the overall price level, this falls from P_1 to P_2. In this scenario, fiscal policy of this type has inflationary effects in the short run, but deflationary effects in the longer term, through the impact on aggregate supply.

A similar effect could ensue from an increase in government expenditure on infrastructure. For example, improvements to the transport network could have a short-run effect on the overall price level because of bottlenecks in the economy, but in the long run could reduce the costs faced by firms, and thus induce a shift in aggregate supply.

Automatic and discretionary fiscal policies

It is important to distinguish between automatic and discretionary changes in government expenditure. Some items of government expenditure and receipts vary automatically with the business cycle. They are known as *automatic stabilisers*. For example, if the economy enters a period of recession, government expenditure will rise because of the increased payments of unemployment and other social security benefits, and revenues will fall because fewer people are paying income tax, and because receipts from VAT are falling. This helps to offset the recession without any active intervention from the government.

More important, however, is the question of whether the government can or should make use of discretionary fiscal policy in a deliberate attempt to influence the course of the economy. As already mentioned, the key issue is whether or not the economy has spare capacity, because attempts to stimulate an economy that is already at full employment will merely push up the price level.

Balance between the public and private sectors

Even if the overall size of the budget deficit limits the government's actions in terms of fiscal policy, there are still decisions to be made about the overall balance of activity in the economy. A neutral government budget can be attained either with

high expenditure and high revenues, or with relatively small expenditure and revenues. Such decisions affect the overall size of the public sector relative to the private sector. Over the years, different governments in the UK have taken different decisions on this issue — and different countries throughout the world have certainly adopted different approaches.

In part, such issues are determined through the ballot box. In the run-up to an election, each political party presents its overall plans for taxation and spending, and typically they adopt different positions as to the overall balance. It is then up to those voting to give a mandate to whichever party offers a package that most closely resembles their preferences.

Figure 18.5 shows the time path of government consumption as a share of GDP from 1948 to 2006; it shows fluctuations around a slowly downward trend, suggesting that the public sector has been gradually reducing its share of the economy. Notice that this does not give the full picture, as public-sector investment is not taken into account in these data. There are one or two periods in the figure where the decline seems to have been especially rapid. In the early 1950s this partly reflects the wind-down of government activity in the aftermath of rebuilding following the Second World War. The steep section in the 1980s reflects the privatisation drive of that period, when the government was withdrawing from some parts of the economy.

Figure 18.6 provides an international perspective, showing the share of total government expenditure (both current and capital) by governments in a range of countries. This reveals something of a contrast between on the one hand North America, Australia and Japan, and on the other many European countries, where

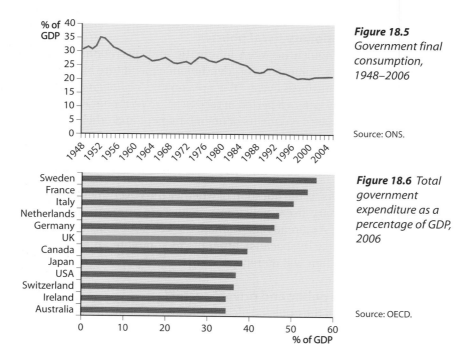

Figure 18.5
Government final consumption, 1948–2006

Source: ONS.

Figure 18.6 *Total government expenditure as a percentage of GDP, 2006*

Source: OECD.

government has been more active in the economy. In part this reflects the greater role that government plays in some countries in providing services such as education and healthcare, whereas in other countries the private sector takes a greater role, often through the insurance market.

Direct and indirect taxes

Fiscal policy, and taxation in particular, has not only been used to establish a balance between the public and private sectors of an economy. In addition, taxation remains an important weapon against some forms of market failure, and it also influences the distribution of income. In this context, the choice between using direct and indirect taxes is important.

Remember that direct taxes are taxes levied on income of various kinds, such as personal income tax. Such taxes are designed to be progressive and so can be effective in redistributing income; for example, a higher income tax rate can be charged to those earning high incomes. In contrast, indirect taxes — taxes on expenditure, such as VAT and excise duties — tend to be regressive. As poorer households tend to spend a higher proportion of their income on items that are subject to excise duties, a greater share of their income is taken up by indirect taxes. Even VAT can be regressive if higher-income households save a greater proportion of their incomes.

When Margaret Thatcher came to power in 1979, one of her first actions was to introduce a switch away from direct taxation towards indirect taxes. VAT was increased, and the rate of personal income tax was reduced. In support of this move, it was pointed out that if an income tax scheme becomes too progressive it can provide a disincentive towards effort. If people feel that a high proportion of their income is being taken in tax, their incentives to provide work effort are weak. Indeed, a switch from direct to indirect taxation might be regarded as a sort of supply-side policy intended to influence the position of aggregate supply.

When she became prime minister, Margaret Thatcher moved quickly to switch the emphasis from direct to indirect taxation

Indirect taxes can be targeted at specific instances of market failure; hence the high excise duties on such goods as tobacco (seen as a demerit good), and petrol (seen as damaging to the environment because of the externality of greenhouse gas emissions).

Sustainability of fiscal policy

Another important issue that came to the fore during the 1990s concerned the sustainability of fiscal policy. This is wrapped up with the notion that current taxpayers should have to fund only expenditure that benefits their own generation, and that the taxpayers of the future should make their own decisions, and not have to pay for past government expenditure that has been incurred for the benefit of earlier generations.

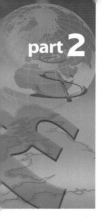

In this context, what is significant is the overall balance between receipts and outlays through time. If outlays were always larger than receipts, the spending programme could be sustained only through government borrowing, thereby shifting the burden of funding the deficit to future generations. This could also be a problem if it made it more difficult for the private sector to obtain funds for investment, or if it added to the national debt. The chancellor of the exchequer is committed to following a **Golden Rule of fiscal policy**, which states that, on average over the economic cycle, the government should borrow only to invest and not to fund current expenditure. This is intended to help achieve equity between present and future generations.

> **Key term**
>
> **Golden Rule of fiscal policy:** rule stating that over the economic cycle net government borrowing will be for investment only, and not for current spending

Figure 18.7 shows total public-sector receipts and outlays since 1986. Outlays here include investment, but you can see how the two series tend to move in opposite directions over the cycle. To some extent this is to be expected, because of the operation of the automatic stabilisers.

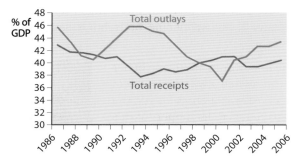

Figure 18.7 *UK public-sector receipts and outlays, 1986–2006*

Source: OECD.

If receipts and outlays more or less balance over the economic cycle, the economy is not in a position whereby the current generation is forcing future generations to pay for its consumption. However, as the economy does go through a business cycle, it is not practical to impose this rule at every part of the cycle, so the Golden Rule is to apply over the economic cycle as a whole. There is also a commitment to keep public-sector net debt below 40% of GDP — again, on average over the economic cycle.

Summary

➤ Fiscal policy concerns the use of government expenditure and taxation to influence aggregate demand in the economy.

➤ If the economy is in a state in which the aggregate demand curve cuts the vertical segment of aggregate supply, demand-side policy affects only the overall price level, and not real output.

➤ If the government funds its expenditure by borrowing, higher interest rates may crowd out private-sector activity.

➤ The stance of the government budget varies with the business cycle, as a result of the operation of automatic stabilisers.

> The overall balance between private and public sectors varies through time and across countries.

> Direct taxes help to redistribute income between groups in society, but if too progressive they may dampen incentives to provide effort.

> The Golden Rule for fiscal policy is that the government should aim to borrow only for investment, and not for current expenditure (averaged over the economic cycle).

> There is also a commitment to keep the national debt below 40% of GDP.

Exercise 18.1

Discuss the extent to which the major British political parties adopt differing stances towards establishing a balance between the private and public sectors, i.e. the extent to which each is 'high tax/high public spending' or 'low tax/low public spending'. Analyse the economic arguments favouring each of the approaches.

Monetary policy

Monetary policy has become the prime instrument of government macroeconomic policy, with the interest rate acting as the key control variable. Monetary policy involves the manipulation of monetary variables in order to influence aggregate demand in the economy.

It is important at the outset to realise that it is not possible to control money supply and interest rates simultaneously and independently. Firms and households choose to hold some money. They may do this in order to undertake transactions, or as a precaution against the possible need to undertake transactions at short notice. In other words there is a *demand for money*. However, in choosing to hold money they incur an opportunity cost, in the sense that they forgo the possibility of earning interest by purchasing some form of financial asset.

This means that the interest rate can be regarded as the opportunity cost of holding money; put another way, it is the price of holding money. At high rates of interest, people can be expected to choose to hold less money, as the opportunity cost of holding money is high. *MD* in Figure 18.8 represents such a money demand curve. It is downward sloping.

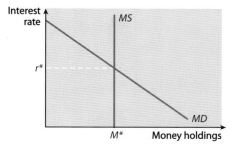

Figure 18.8 *The demand for money*

Suppose the government wants to set the money supply (*MS*) at *M** in Figure 18.8. This can be achieved in two ways. If the government controls the supply of money at *M**, then equilibrium will be achieved only if the interest rate is allowed to adjust to *r**. An alternative way of reaching the same point is to set the interest rate at *r** and then allow the money supply to adjust to *M**. The government can do one or the other – but it cannot set money supply at *M** and hold the interest rate at any value *other than r** without causing disequilibrium.

A problem with attempting to control the money supply directly is that the complexity of the modern financial system makes it quite difficult to pin down a precise definition or measurement of money. For this and other reasons, the chosen instrument of monetary policy is the interest rate. By setting the interest rate, monetary policy affects aggregate demand through the so-called *monetary transmission mechanism*, which was explained in Chapter 17.

Monetary policy and the exchange rate

At a higher interest rate, firms undertake less investment expenditure and house-holds undertake less consumption expenditure. Furthermore, if UK interest rates are high relative to elsewhere in the world, they will attract overseas investors, increasing the demand for pounds. This will tend to lead to an appreciation in the exchange rate — which in turn will reduce the competitiveness of British goods and services, reducing the foreign demand for UK exports and encouraging UK residents to reduce their demand for domestic goods and buy imports instead. All these factors lower the level of aggregate demand, shifting the *AD* curve to the left. Such a policy stance may be needed in order to maintain control of inflation. A reduction in interest rates would of course have the reverse effect. However, notice that the interaction of the money supply, interest rates and the exchange rate makes policy design a complicated business.

Under a fixed exchange rate regime monetary policy is powerless to influence the real economy, as it must be devoted to maintaining the exchange rate. Under a floating exchange rate system monetary policy is freed from this role, but even so it must be used in such a way that the current account deficit of the balance of

Responsibility for monetary policy is delegated to the Bank of England

payments does not become unsustainable in the long run. In other words, the use of interest rates to target inflation has implications for the magnitude of the current and financial accounts of the balance of payments.

Monetary policy and the supply side

As was pointed out in Chapter 17, an important aspect of monetary policy since 1997 has been the delegation of responsibility for it to the Bank of England's Monetary Policy Committee (MPC). The rationale for this is based on the observation that the effectiveness of monetary policy depends quite heavily on people's expectations. It operates much more effectively if people believe it is going to work, because then they will amend their behaviour more quickly, speeding up the process of adjustment to equilibrium. By delegating responsibility for monetary policy to the Bank of England, the credibility of policy is enhanced and it thereby becomes more effective, and the government cannot be

tempted to buy election success by increasing spending financed through inflationary printing of money.

In creating a stable macroeconomic environment, the ultimate aim of monetary policy is not simply to keep inflation low, but to improve the confidence of decision-makers, and thereby encourage firms to invest in order to generate an increase in production capacity – which will stimulate economic growth and create an opportunity to improve living standards. In other words, the hope is to stimulate investment and thus enable an increase in the productive capacity of the economy by shifting the *AS* curve. The problem is that high interest rates may be needed at times in order to achieve the inflation target – and high interest rates will tend to discourage investment.

Exercise 18.2

Use *AS/AD* to analyse the effect of an expansionary monetary policy on the equilibrium level of real output and the overall price level. Undertake this exercise with a Monetarist vertical aggregate supply curve and with a Keynesian aggregate supply curve in which aggregate demand creates an equilibrium that is below full employment. Discuss the differences in your results.

Supply-side policies

Supply-side policies are directed at influencing the position of the aggregate supply curve. In Figure 18.9, Y^* represents full-employment output before the policy, with the equilibrium overall price level at P_0. Supply-side policies that lead to an increase in the economy's productive capacity shift equilibrium output to Y^{**} and the overall price level to P_1.

Notice that the effect on real output is achieved from supply-side policies whether the equilibrium is in the vertical segment of the *AS* curve (or with a Monetarist *AS* curve) or in the upward-sloping segment of a Keynesian *AS* curve, as you can see in Figure 18.10, where the shift in aggregate supply raises equilibrium real output from Y_0 to Y_1.

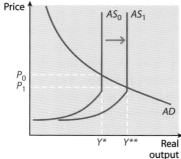

Figure 18.9 *A shift in aggregate supply (with a Monetarist* AS *curve)*

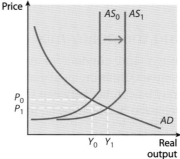

Figure 18.10 *A shift in aggregate supply (with a Keynesian* AS *curve)*

Such policies include measures like encouraging education and training, improving the flexibility with which markets operate and promoting competition. Notice that it is quite difficult to quantify the effects of these supply-side policies. In the case of education and training, some of the effects of increased spending become evident only after very long time lags. In the case of competition policy, again, it is not easy to identify the effects on productive capacity. It is particularly difficult to isolate the impact of these policies when so much else in the economy is changing through time. Nonetheless, these policies do have the effect of stimulating economic growth without inflationary pressure.

Relative merits

In the context of the aggregate demand/aggregate supply model, it is clear that demand- and supply-side policies are aimed at achieving rather different objectives.

The primary rationale for monetary and fiscal policies is to stabilise the macroeconomy. In this, fiscal policy has come to take on a subsidiary role, supporting monetary policy. This was not always the case, and there have been periods in which fiscal policy has been used much more actively to try to stimulate the economy. There are still some countries in which such policies are very much the vogue: for example, it has been suggested that much of Latin America's problem with high inflation has stemmed from fiscal indiscipline, although not all Latin American economists accept this argument. The fact that fiscal policy has not always been well implemented does not mean that such policies cannot be valuable tools — but it does warn against misuse.

In the UK, the use of monetary policy with the support of fiscal policy seems to be working reasonably effectively in the early twenty-first century. Furthermore, it seems to be operating in such a way as to complement the supply-side policies. When a stable macroeconomic environment is created, microeconomic markets are able to operate effectively and investment is encouraged, thereby leading to a boost in aggregate supply.

Supply-side policies aim to influence aggregate supply directly, either raising the supply of factor inputs or improving productivity and efficiency.

Designing the policy mix

The design and conduct of economic policy may be seen as an elaborate balancing act. Differing policy objectives need to be prioritised, as in many cases there may be conflict between them. Choices have to be made about the balance to be achieved between fiscal, monetary and supply-side policies.

The consensus view in the early part of the twenty-first century is that fiscal policy should be used to achieve the desired balance between the public and private sectors. Monetary policy should be devoted to meeting the inflation target in order to create a stable macroeconomic environment; this will then encourage growth and enable improvements in the standard of living. Supply-side policies are perhaps the most important, as these contribute to raising efficiency and increasing the productive capacity of the economy.

The keynote in policy design lies in enabling markets to operate as effectively as possible.

Summary

➤ Monetary policy entails the manipulation of monetary variables in order to influence aggregate demand in the economy.

➤ The prime instrument of monetary policy is the interest rate.

➤ People hold money in order to undertake transactions (among other reasons), and the interest rate can be regarded as the opportunity cost of holding money.

➤ The monetary authorities can control either the money supply or interest rates, but not both independently.

➤ In the UK, monetary policy is conducted by the Bank of England, which has had independent responsibility for meeting the inflation target since 1997.

➤ It is hoped that, by keeping inflation low, firms will be confident about the future, will invest more, and thereby increase the productive capacity of the economy. However, in the short run, high interest rates imposed to reduce inflation may discourage investment.

➤ Supply-side policies are aimed at influencing the position of the aggregate supply curve.

➤ Demand-side and supply-side policies have different objectives. Demand-side policies such as fiscal and monetary policy are aimed primarily at stabilising the economy. Supply-side policies are geared more towards promoting economic growth.

➤ However, effective stabilisation of the economy may also have long-term effects on aggregate supply.

Index

Page numbers in **bold** refer to **key term definitions**.

A

absolute poverty **165**
aggregate demand 169–77
  aggregate demand curve
    176, 177, 184
  components 169–75
  economic growth 190, 191
  macroeconomic equilibrium
    181, 182–83, 184
  macroeconomic policy 197–98,
    214–17, 219–22, 227–31, 235–36
aggregate supply 178–84
  aggregate supply curve 178–81
  economic growth 185, 186, 190, 191
  macroeconomic equilibrium 181–84
  macroeconomic policy 197–98, 215,
    219, 223–24, 228–31, 237–38
agricultural markets
  59–60, 66, 114–16, 123–25
Akerlof, George 111
allocative efficiency
  53, 55–56, 82, 224, 225
asymmetric information **110**, 111
automatic stabilisers 136, **217**, 219, 231
average propensity to consume **171**
average total cost **54**

B

balance of payments
  economic growth 192, 195
  macroeconomic policy
    203–05, 206, 212, 215, 217, 236
  measuring economic performance
    143, 144–47

Bank of England
  139, 145, 220–22, 230, 236
bank rate **221**, 222
biodiversity 92, 193, 194
buffer stock schemes **115**, 116
business cycle **135**, 136, 234

C

capital 5, 71, 173, 180, 188–90
capital account 144, 145
capital goods 9, 10
capitalism **57**
capital productivity **188**
cartels **38**, **61**
centrally planned economy **4**, 5
ceteris paribus
  18, 19–20, 34–35, 44, 64, 130
circular flow of income, expenditure
  and output
    161, **162**, 163, 166–68, 216
claimant count of unemployment
  141, 142, 143
Coase, Ronald 101
commodity markets
  60–62, 86, 114–16, 118
Common Agricultural Policy (CAP)
  123–25
comparative static analysis
  44, 45–47, 74, 182
competitive markets **34**
complements **23**, 24, 32, 37
consumer goods 9, 10
consumer price index (CPI)
  131, **137**, 138–39, 200, 220, 222

Edexcel AS Economics

consumer surplus **49**, 122

consumption

    aggregate demand
        169, **170**, 171–72, 176

    aggregate supply 180

    consumption and investment 9–10

    economic growth 189

    monetary policy 220

consumption externalities
    86, 87–90, 94, 107

consumption function **172**

coordination problem 4–5, 47–48

cost efficiency **54**, 125

cost-push inflation **197**

cross-price elasticity of demand (*XED*)
    31, 32

crowding out **230**

current account 144–46, 192, 204–06,
    212, 215, 217, 236

D

deciles **155**, 156

demand **17**, 18–32

    comparative static analysis 44–47

    demand and consumer incomes
        21–22

    demand and consumer preferences
        24–25

    demand curve **19**

    demand and price of other goods
        23–24

    demand and the price of a good
        18–21

    elasticity of demand
        25–32, 66, 72, 114, 123

    individual and market demand 18

    labour market 68–72, 74–76, 78, 81

    law of demand 19

    market equilibrium 43, 48

    market failure 103–04, 109

    price mechanism in action 59–67

    snob effects 20–21

demand-deficient unemployment **201**

demand for money 235

demand-pull inflation 197

demand-side policies 216–23

demerit goods 108, **109**, 110, 122, 233

depreciation **188**

derived demand 64, 68, **69**, 70, 72

developed and developing countries
    148–60

    economic growth 153–54, 190

    GDP and standard of living 148–53

    less-developed countries 154–55

    other indicators of development
        155–59

discount **96**, 98

disposable income **170**, 171, 172

division of labour **11**, 12

E

economic growth 185–95

    costs of economic growth 192–95

    defining economic growth
        10, **185**, 186–87

    developed and developing countries
        153–54, 159

    importance of economic growth
        191–92

    macroeconomic policy
        199, 205–08, 210–13, 215, 237, 238

    measuring economic performance
        129, 132–34, 135

    sources of economic growth 187–91

economic performance

    measuring economic performance
        128–47

        alternative measurements of
            inflation 137–39

        balance of payments 143–47

        business cycle 135–36

        economic growth 132–34

        economic performance 128–29

        importance of data 129–30

        index numbers 131–32

        inflation 136–37

        inflation in the UK and world
            139–41

real and nominal measurements
130–31

unemployment 141–43

economics 2–16

consumption and investment 9–10

coordination problem 4–5

economic growth 10

factors of production 5–7

markets 13–14

microeconomics and macro-
economics 14–15

models and assumptions 7–8

money and exchange 14

positive and normative statements
15–16

production possibility frontier 8–9

specialisation 11–13

the fundamental economic problem
2–4

total output in an economy 11

economies of scale 54

education

developed and developing countries
152, 158, 159

economic growth 190

macroeconomic policy 207, 224, 238

market failure and externalities
94, 107–08, 111

efficiency 53–56, 82, 125, 188, 224–25

elasticity of demand
25, 26–32, 66–67, 109, 114, 123

elasticity of demand for labour
70–72, 81, 82

elasticity of supply
39–41, 75–76, 175, 182

environment

developed and developing countries
152

economic growth 192, 193, 194

macroeconomic policy
206, 208, 210–12, 233

market failure and externalities
91–92, 94, 97–98

excess burden of sales tax 122

exchange rate

aggregate demand 174

developed and developing countries
150–51

macroeconomic policy
203, 220, 222, 236

measuring economic performance
140, **146**

price mechanism in action 63–64

expenditure 162, 163, 167, 170, 174

exports

aggregate demand 169, 170, 174, 176

income, wealth and the circular flow
167

macroeconomic policy
204, 205, 217, 236

measuring economic performance
144, 145

external costs 87

externalities *see* market failure and
externalities

F

factors of production
5, 6–7, 35, 54–55, 113, 187–88

firms **33**, 51–52, 68

fiscal policy
216, 217–19, 227–28, 230–35, 238

fixed exchange rate system
140, 144, 203, 212, 236

free market economy **47**, 56–58

free-rider problem
103, 104, 105, 114, 118

frictional unemployment **201**

Friedman, Milton 171

full employment

aggregate supply 182

economic growth 186, 192

macroeconomic policy 200–203, 206,
209, 215–16, 220, 228–29

G

GDP *see* gross domestic product

GDP per capita **149**

Giffen goods 22
Gini index **157**, 158
global warming 91, 99–100, 206, 211
Golden Rule of fiscal policy **234**
government budget deficit/surplus **217**
government expenditure
    167, 169–70, 173–75, 182, 216, 232
government failure **118**, 119–25
    minimum wage 119–20
    overview 118–19
    price instability and CAP 123–25
    prohibition 122–23
    rent controls 120
    sales tax 120–22
    subsidies and efficiency 125
government intervention
    costs of intervention 126
    income, wealth and the circular flow
        166
    labour market 77–80
    macroeconomic policy 204, 207
    market failure
        correcting market failure 117–18
        demerit goods 109–10
        labour immobility 113–14
        merit goods 106
        public goods 105
gross domestic product (GDP)
    aggregate demand 169, 170
    developed and developing countries
        148–53, 154, 158, 159
    economic growth 186, 187, 189, 192
    income, wealth and the circular flow
        161, 162
    macroeconomic policy 204, 205, 232
    measuring economic performance
        133, 134, 135, 136
    total output in an economy **11**
gross national income (GNI) 149, 151

H
healthcare 93–94, 110, 152, 159, 190
housing market 62–63, 120, 164
human capital **190**, 191, 192, 224

Human Development Index (HDI)
    158, 159
hyperinflation 199

I
ILO (International Labour Organisation)
    unemployment rate **142**, 143
imports
    aggregate demand 169, 170, 174, 176
    economic growth 195
    income, wealth and the circular flow
        167
    macroeconomic policy
        204, 205, 212, 217, 222, 236
    measuring economic performance
        144, 145
incidence of a tax **66**
income
    aggregate demand 170–72, 174, 176
    balance of payments 144, 145
    demand 18, 21–22
    developed and developing countries
        149, 150, 151
    economic growth 191
    income, wealth and the circular flow
        161–62, **163**, 164–68
income distribution
    155–58, 165, 192, 195
income elasticity of demand (*YED*)
    31, 32
income tax 217, 225–26, 233
index numbers **131**, 132
indirect taxes **65**, 65–67, **120**, 121, 233
inferior goods **21**, 22, 31
inflation
    aggregate demand 171, 173, 174
    economic growth 187, 192
    macroeconomic policy
        197–200, 206, 208–11, 214–15, 220,
        222–23, 236–38
    measuring economic performance
        129, 136, **137**, 138–41, 145
information failure 85, 110–12, 118
injections **166**, 167–68, 174, 175, 216

interest rates
  aggregate demand
    171, 172, 173, 176
  balance of payments 145, 204
  housing market 62
  macroeconomic policy
    198, 204, 220, 230, 235–37
internalising an externality **96**, 97, 118
International Labour Organisation (ILO)
  142, 143
International Monetary Fund (IMF)
  129, 130, 225
investment
  aggregate demand
    170, **172**, 173–74, 176
  aggregate supply 180
  consumption and investment 9–10
  economic growth **188**, 189, 190, 191
  income, wealth and the circular flow
    162, 167
  macroeconomic policy
    199, 206, 220, 223, 224, 237
invisible hand **57**
involuntary unemployment **202**

J
Jobseeker's Allowance (JSA)
  141, 143, 206

K
Keynesian school **228**, 229, 237
Keynes, John Maynard 170–71, 174
Kuznets hypothesis 157–58

L
labour immobility 85–86, 112–14, 118
labour market 68–83
  demand for labour 68–72
  effects of government intervention
    77–80
  effects of migration 76–77
  explaining wage differentials 75–76
  labour market equilibrium 74–75
  labour supply 72–74

  price mechanism in action 65
  trade unions 80–83
labour productivity **188**
labour supply
  aggregate supply curve 179
  comparative static analysis 46
  economic growth 190
  factors of production 5
  labour market 76–77, 78, 80–82
  minimum wage 119–20
  specialisation 12
law of demand **19**
less-developed countries (LDCs)
  154–55, 192, 193
longer-run aggregate supply curve (*AS*)
  183, 184, 215
Lorenz curve **156**, 157
luxury goods 29, **31**

M
macroeconomic equilibrium
  181, 182–83, 200, 203
macroeconomic policy instruments
  214–26
  demand-side policies 216–23
  macroeconomic policy objectives
    revisited 214–15
  supply-side policies 223–26
macroeconomic policy objectives
  196–213
  balance of payments 203–05
  concern for the environment 206
  conflicts between policy objectives
    208–13
  economic growth 205–06
  full employment 200–203
  income redistribution 206–08
  price stability 197–200
  targets of policy 196–97
macroeconomic policy: priorities and
  conflicts 227–39
  aggregate supply revisited 228–30
  designing the policy mix 238–39
  fiscal policy 230–35

macroeconomic policy instruments 227–28

monetary policy 235–37

relative merits 238

supply-side policies 237–38

macroeconomics 14, **15**, **129**

marginal analysis **3**

marginal benefit 55, 56, 98

see also marginal private benefit; marginal social benefit

marginal cost **51**, 55–56, 90, 97–98

see also marginal private cost; marginal social cost

marginal private benefit (*MPB*) 88, 90, 93, 94, 107, 109

marginal private cost (*MPC*) 87–90, 92–94, 97

marginal propensity to consume (*MPC*) **171**, 172

marginal propensity to withdraw (*MPW*) 175

marginal social benefit (*MSB*)

causes of market failure 84, 85

demerit goods 109

market equilibrium and price **49**

market failure and externalities 87–88, 90, 92–93, 97–98

merit goods 107

public goods 103–04

marginal social cost (*MSC*) 84–88, 90, 93, 97, 104, 107

market economy **4**, 5, 56–58

market equilibrium and price 42, **43**, 44–58

aspects of efficiency 52–56

comparative static analysis 44–47

entry and exit of firms 51–52

labour market 74–75

market equilibrium 43–44

price and resource allocation 47–48

price as signals and incentives 50–51

working of a market economy 56–58

market failure

causes of market failure 84, **85**

government intervention and government failure 117–18, 126

other forms of market failure 102–16

demerit goods 108–10

information failure 110–12

labour immobility 112–14

merit goods 106–08

public goods 102–06

unstable commodity markets 114–16

market failure and externalities 84–101

causes of market failure 84–85

dealing with externalities 96–100

economic growth 190, 194

externalities **85**, 86–91

externalities and education 94

externalities and health 93–94

externalities and the environment 91–92

externalities and transport 92–93

global warming 99–100

government intervention and government failure 117–18, 119

instability in commodity markets 86

labour immobility 85–86

macroeconomic policy 206, 233

pollution 97–99

property rights **101**

social cost-benefit analysis 94–96

markets **13**, 14

merit goods **106**, 107–08, 190

microeconomics 14, **15**

minimum wage **77**, 78–79, 119–20, 202

mixed economy **4**

models **7**, 8

Modigliani, Ando 171

Monetarist School **228**, 229, 230, 237

monetary policy 140, 219, **220**, 221–23, 228, 230–31, 235–38

Monetary Policy Committee (MPC) **220**, 221, 222, 236

monetary transmission mechanism
221, 236
money 14, 130–31
money stock **198**, 215
multiplier effect **174**, 175, 182, 216, 230

N
National Minimum Wage (NMW)
77, 78, 79, 119–20
natural rate of output 228
natural rate of unemployment 228
net investment 188
net present value 96
NIMBY (not in my back yard) syndrome
100
nominal values 130, **131**, 145
non-excludability 103, 104, 105, 118
non-renewable resources 6, 193, 195
non-rivalry 103, 104, 105, 118
normal goods 21, 22, 31
normative statements 15, 16, 89

O
Office of National Statistics (ONS)
129, 130, 145, 162
oil 6, 38, 61–62, 140, 183, 193, 197, 212
OPEC (Organisation of Petroleum
Exporting Countries) 61, 62
opportunity cost 3, 4, 8–10, 12–13,
56–57, 73, 173, 235
output gap 187

P
Pareto optimum 54
Phillips curve 209, 210
pollution 91, 97–101, 118–19, 192, 194,
206, 212
positive statements 15, 16, 89
poverty 2–3, 78, 164–66, 191–92, 194,
207, 212
preferences 18, 24–25, 45, 48–50
price
demand 18–21, 23–24
market equilibrium 47–51
price mechanism in action 59–67

price stability
123–25, 197–200, 214–15
price elasticity of demand (*PED*)
25, 26–30, 66, 72, 114, 123
price elasticity of supply (*PES*) 39, 41
private costs 87
private goods 102, 103
producer surplus 50, **51**, 122
production externalities 86, 87–91
production possibility frontier (*PPF*)
aspects of efficiency 53, 54, 56
consumption and investment 10
definition **8**, 9
economic growth
133, 185, 186, 190, 206
specialisation 13
total output in an economy 11
productive efficiency 53, 54–55, 225
productivity 188, 189, 225
prohibition 122, 123
public goods 85, 102, **103**, 105–06, 118
public sector net debt 218, 234
purchasing power parity (PPP)
151, 158

Q
quintiles 155, 156

R
real income effect 20, 22, 73
real values 130, **131**
recession 135, 136, 173, 174, 217, 231
relative poverty 165
renewable resources 6, 195, 212
retail price index (RPI) 137, 138, 139
RPIX 137, 138, 139, 200, 220, 222

S
Samuelson, Paul 6, 7, 57
savings 162, 165, 167, 171, 174
scarcity 2, 3, 47, 52
shadow price 95
short-run aggregate supply curve (*SAS*)
179, 180, 181
Smith, Adam 11, 57

snob effects 20–21

social cost-benefit analysis 94, **95**, 96

specialisation 11–13

stagflation **210**

standard of living 148–53, 191, 212, 238

structural unemployment
113, 195, **201**, 224

subsidies 36, 65, **66**, 67, 109, 114, 125

substitutes **23**, 29, 32, 36, 45

substitution effect 20, 22, 73

supply 33–41
  comparative static analysis 44–47
  firms 33–34
  labour market 72–78, 80–82
  market equilibrium 43, 48
  market failure 103–04, 114, 115
  price elasticity of supply 39, 41
  price mechanism in action 59–67
  short run and long run 40
  supply curve
    34, 179–81, 183–84, 215
  supply shocks 183–84, 202
  what influences supply? 34–38

supply-side policies
223, 224–26, 228, 231, 236–38

sustainable development
6, **193**, 194, 206, 210–12

T

taxes
  aggregate demand 174
  demerit goods 109
  government failure 119, 120–22
  income, wealth and the circular flow
    166, 167
  indirect taxes and subsidies 65–67
  labour market 77
  macroeconomic policy
    199, 206, 207, 217, 225–26, 233
  market failure and externalities
    97, 98
  production costs and technology 36

technical efficiency **54**

Thatcher, Margaret 225, 233

total factor productivity **188**

trade unions **80**, 81–83, 202, 224

transmission mechanism of monetary
policy **221**, 236

U

unemployment
  aggregate demand 173
  consumption and investment 10
  economic growth 187
  labour immobility 113, 114
  labour market 77, 78, 79, 82
  macroeconomic policy
    201–04, 208–10, 211, 217, 225
  measuring economic performance
    129, 136, 141–43
  minimum wage 119, 120

United Nations Development
Programme (UNDP) 154, 158, 165

unit elasticity 27, 28, 39

V

value added tax (VAT)
65, 120, 121, 217, 233

Veblen, Thorstein 21

voluntary unemployment **202**

W

wage rate 69–74, 75–79, 82, 119–20,
201–02, 209–10

wealth **163**, 164, 171

withdrawals
166, 167–68, 174, 175, 216

World Bank 129, 149, 194, 225